The Political Economy of Human Rights

The Political Economy of Human Rights

Prof. D. Chenna Reddy

MANGLAM PUBLICATIONS
DELHI-110053 (INDIA)

Published by :
MANGLAM PUBLICATIONS
L-21/1, Street No. 5, Shivaji Marg, Near Kali Mandir,
J.P. Nagar, Kartar Nagar, West Ghonda, Delhi-110053
Phone : 011-22945677, (M.) 9968367559, 9868572512
E-mail: manglam.books2007@rediffmail.com
manglam.publications2007@rediffmail.com

The Political Economy of Human Rights

First Edition 2009

ISBN 978-93-80013-10-7

PRINTED IN INDIA

Published by Ravindra Kumar Yadav for Manglam Publications, Delhi-110053 Laser Typesetting at M.K Computers, Delhi- 53, Printed at Sachin Printers, Moujpur Delhi- 53

Preface

The origin of this book arose from a growing personal concern with the quality of assessment of evidence in public debates. The modus operandi of journalism means that it is necessary to simplify evidence of 'experts' who conduct a detailed analysis of statistical data. The exigencies of daily deadlines mean that the reporting of experts' interpretation of the evidence is sometimes incorrect. However, the alleged experts have fewer excuses, and there is a need to ground their analysis in peer review. This monograph attempts to do this by providing readers with the capacity to critically engage with the evidence presented in public forums.

The volume of quality data in Indigenous affairs has grown exponentially in recent years. Unfortunately, our capacity to analyse it has not increased at the same rate. The main issue is that there is not the number of suitably qualified social scientists focusing on Indigenous issues in Australia to analyse all the data. Another issue is that the sheer volume of data allows some researchers to search for statistics that suit their ideological predisposition. Needless to say, this sort of approach violates fundamental principles that most social scientists hold dear. It should be made clear that advocates on all sides of the debate have used this strategy to look for either a statistic or an expert whose conclusions are consistent with their own.

The diversity of opinions of authors will be obvious to all those who persevere in reading through the entire book. I hope readers will find their perseverance rewarded because the contrasting approaches of the various chapters suggest some research directions for the area concerned to Political Economy of Human Rights.

— *Author*

Contents

1

Introduction

Blackwell's Dictionary of Sociology lists "political economy" as "a concept referring to the independent workings and interests of political and economic systems, especially in complex industrial societies. So strong is this connection, that it is virtually impossible to understand the workings of one without taking into account its relation to the other."

The entry goes on to say that political economy is "most closely associated with Karl Marx," and that it "draws attention to how the state actively supports the economic system": "In the process, it both protects and promotes the interests of those who dominate and benefit most from it. In return, the state depends on the economic system for its resources. The fact that leaders move freely between corporate and political realms is but one reflection of the fundamental relationship between these two critical spheres of power" (2000).

If political economy has to do with the political dimensions to the production, consumption, and distribution of resources, then the political economy of human rights is the political and economic dimensions to how human rights activism is produced, consumed and distributed. We can think of the resulting "products" as different kinds of activism: various organizations and strategies aimed at different populations, abuses or deprivations. Each of these "products" also entails a particular set of consequences for making claims on the state, as well as for improving or protecting different conceptions of rights for different populations. Since in international law the state is the primary duty bearer in the provision and enforcement of human rights, human rights activism and initiatives typically take the form of claims making against the state. Although there are instances in which such activity can be achieved with minimal resources and organization, sustained public pressure and claimsmaking on states generally require organizational resources that themselves require funding.

What follows is evidence that funding sources, their preferences and their agendas, play a central role in the political economy of human rights in and around Israel/Palestine. These donors do not, however, *determine* the field of human rights activism; rather, they shape that field in fundamental ways. They act in relation to complex web of other actors in the field. These actors are involved in a struggle over, among other things, the very definition of human rights and what significance the different definitions carry. The discussion that follows thus moves beyond the conventional understanding of human rights as a relationship between individuals and the state. It also has a rather different take on political economy than that found in recent calls to consider transnational corporations (TNC's) as critical actors in the study of human rights. My concern is not whether the presence of TNC's is closely correlated with the enjoyment of human rights or whether TNC's themselves are more commonly violators of human rights. The focus here is on the political economic *field* of human rights.

Put briefly, we take the field of human rights activism in (and on) Israel/Palestine to include, minimally: international, national and religious-based human rights NGOs, the media (including key journalists with ties to movement activists), cause lawyers, grassroots activists and groups, human rights courses and programs at universities, international organizations (especially the UN and its human rights bodies like the UNHCHR, the Human Rights Commission, and the Committees on Civil and Political and Social, Economic and Cultural Rights), state officials, treaties and agreements (such as economic agreements with human rights provisions). The field of human rights activism, of course, overlaps with, and exists in dynamic (and to some degree mutually determining, albeit often asymmetrical) tension with, a number of other fields (the field of activism more broadly defined; the economic field; the field of state power; and so on). That said we will not describe here in detail the workings of the field of human rights advocacy on Israel/Palestine. While each of these actors clearly play a role in the field of human rights activism, we narrow the focus here to the role of funders, labor, and political-economic agreements, and their impact on human rights advocacy. Further, it is clear that the human rights initiatives that these have engendered have not yet achieved complete "success" in the sense of full enjoyment of rights for the most vulnerable—in this case, the Palestinians. Notwithstanding the importance of the rather thorny question of what constitutes human rights success, the focus here is more on the "consequences" or "outcomes" than their evaluation. I leave consideration of the former to another occasion.

Jim Ferguson begins his book on development in Lesotho by listing an impressive number of international organizations and statistics about the (quite considerable) amount of official aid given annually (1994). Regarding the impact of this aid, he remarks: "Its dispersal has given rise to a substantial 'development' industry in Lesotho, employing expatriate consultants and 'experts' by the hundreds, and churning out plans, programs, and most of all, paper, at an astonishing rate" (ibid: 8). In spite of the industry's efforts, says Ferguson, the characteristic result of development projects in Lesotho, and indeed everywhere, is "failure."

The consensus in the literature on human rights seems to be rather similar: human rights have no teeth. Human rights are an aspiration to which nearly everyone now agrees, but the reality on the ground is different, and, indeed, shockingly bad. Paralleling the development literature, however, the divide in the literature on human rights is less about how successful human rights advocacy is, but rather over whether human rights are "good" (e.g. the right direction for societies to take) or "bad" (e.g. part of the problem: global capitalism). The question for those who believe human rights to be a good thing is how best to make human rights advocacy more effective or "successful."

I want to move beyond this question of success/failure, not because I think the question unimportant, but because I think it can very easily inhibit analysis. Particularly in a complex case such as Israel/Palestine, it is all too easy to prematurely consider the sum of human rights activism to be generally "failure." Instead, following Ferguson's lead, I want to direct our attention here to the consequences of one, very important dimension to human rights activism, what I describe here as the political economy of human rights. The field of human rights activism, and its political economy, like the apparatus of "development" in Ferguson's analysis, is, in the end, a mechanism that does something.

Very little research exists on the consequences of social movements. Most attention has focused on the origin and direction of social movements rather than on their actual effects. Yet if we are to treat here consequences, the question arises as to what sort of consequences should be examined, for there are many. Social movements could be treated for their impact on movement actors themselves, on the state, on parliamentary or extra-parliamentary politics, or on the social environment. And there are, of course, intended as well as unintended consequences. Perhaps the most salient consequence of human rights funding has been the creation of a human rights movement in Israel/Palestine, and this is the subject of this paper's first section.

Notwithstanding research pointing to funding as the most commonly cited obstacle to "success" in international human rights NGO activities, very little research has been conducted on the funding of human rights, much less on the funding of human rights in Israel. What exists has been more concerned with philanthropy in general or the role of elite actors than the role of capital in human rights, whether in Israel or elsewhere. Part of a study of the Israeli peace movement devoted itself to the impact of funding. Yet besides focusing on peace rather than human rights, this study limited its scope to the *organizational* impact on particular peace groups—on issues like professionalization, salaried staff, and the (perceived) need to continue to exist. It did not attempt to find the records of funders themselves. Nor are funders an object of study in their own right.

Much of the funding, ideas, and even labor involved in human rights in Israel come from abroad, especially from Europe and North America, particularly from key donors like Ford, the EU and the New Israel Fund (NIF). Tracing the flow of capital and labor into the human rights NGOs is essential for gaining an accurate picture of the dynamics of power behind the human rights movement in Israel and Palestine. Not only are donors a primary "constituency" of human rights NGOs, certain donors will be more or less concerned about undermining the Israeli state, or, alternatively, contributing to a Palestinian one. Examination of this constituency is particularly critical not least because of the potential contradiction between the people that rights-oriented NGOs are supposed to represent and the donors that fund the group's activities. Funders' agendas may influence the direction of their human rights funding. For example, Jewish, especially Zionist Jewish funders in the North America, have had an interest in promoting an image of Israel as a democratic state. Besides shifting attention away from Israel's colonial character, this preference leads Jewish funding away from support of Palestinian rights in the Occupied Territories.

We will discuss the role of two of the largest donors, the New Israel Fund and the EU. We choose these donors not only for the amount of funds they contribute to human rights projects in Israel, but also because they represent two of the most important donors in the main regions providing human rights support to Israel, North America and Europe. I focus my attention on two particular projects, each major human rights initiatives in its own right, and each indicative of the influence of the main sources of human rights funding in Israel/Palestine: the New Israel Fund's Law Fellows Program and the Euro-Mediterranean Partnership and its associated Meda-Democracy Program.

The New Israel Fund's Law Fellows program is perhaps the single most successful human rights initiative in the history of human rights activism in Israel. I describe it in these terms because it has, directly and indirectly, (in its own words) created a "cadre" of civil rights lawyers in Israel. The second example is the EU's Meda-Democracy program and its human rights budget line. This program has provided large sums in support of Israeli and Palestinian NGOS since the early 1990s. The Meda-Democracy program is an offshoot of the EU-Mediterranean Partnership, a potentially watershed agreement, apparently economic in intent but with many human rights provisions. To illustrate the impact of the Mediterranean Partnership, particularly the separate EU-Israel partnership, I discuss how advocacy groups have been pressuring the EU to attend to its human rights commitments as laid out in the Partnership.

One aim of this paper is to show how funding has been a crucial condition of possibility for the emergence of a human rights movement in Israel. But the emergence of this movement (and its impressive number of organizations and donor funds) has not simply translated to the widespread enjoyment of human rights in the region, particularly by those most vulnerable to violations in the first place. For instance, despite the evident success of the New Israel Fund's Law Fellows Program in its own terms, this success is qualified by the NIF policy not to fund across the Green Line. This is not to say that none of its programs have impact across the Green Line, but that it is consequently limited in its potential for improving the enjoyment of Palestinian rights in the West Bank and Gaza. Similarly, two key readings of the effect of the EU initiative are possible: (1) the human rights emphasized in the partnership agreement are civil and political ones consonant with and, indeed, bound up with, the broader neoliberal restructuring of the Israeli state and society. These changes and the rights emphasized may come at the expense of social and economic rights; (2) the agreement, whatever its actual intent, opens up a new space for human rights activism, and the Davis project is an example of such activism.

MONEY AND THE BIRTH OF HUMAN RIGHTS ACTIVISM IN ISRAEL

It is no exaggeration to say that funding was a key element in the formation of a human rights "industry" in Israel beginning in the late 1980s. Funding levels for human rights groups in Israel/Palestine have increased dramatically since the outbreak of the first Intifada, and especially since the beginning of the Oslo peace process. Several Israeli Human Rights organizations now have annual operating budgets over one million dollars.

In the mid-1970s in Israel, none of the most important human rights organizations in Israel were yet founded. There were no courses in human rights in Israeli universities; the law schools barely offered a course in civil rights (cf. Laskier 2002). By 1978, there was effectively one civil rights organization, the Association for Civil Rights in Israel (ACRI), and it did not yet have a full-time staffperson. There were two lawyers in the entire country actively working in the field of civil rights and liberties (ibid). Today there are literally thousands of social justice organizations in Israel, many of them specializing in human and civil rights. The New Israel Fund alone supports hundreds of social justice organizations, both financially and administratively (through its consulting wing, Shatil). Palestinian-Israeli NGOs ("PINGOs") have similarly expanded exponentially in number. (Until 1981, when formal registration of NGOs began in Israel, there were approximately 40 PINGOs; by 1998 there were roughly 1000 registered PINGOs [Payes 2002]). The world at large has seen parallel developments. (About one half of all international human rights NGOs were formed after 1979 [Smith *et al*, 1998: 386]).

In 1985, the Association for Civil Rights in Israel's (ACRI) total operating budget was $15,000; by 1988 it was $175,000. The total budget of the key philanthropy supporting social justice NGOs in Israel, New Israel Fund (NIF), was only $1 million in 1985. (Neither Hamoked nor B'Tselem yet existed in that year.) In contrast, NIF currently gives over $500,000 a year to ACRI alone. In the words of one NIF staff person, "In our first full year of operations [1979], 80 donors contributed $80,000; in 1999, 20 years later, 21,000 donors contributed $23.4 million." At the time of writing, at least three of the more prominent human rights organizations in Israel have annual operating budgets over 1 million dollars: ACRI with 1.5 million; B'Tselem with 1 million; Hamoked with 1 million. (By comparison, major international human rights organizations experienced a similar expansion of operating budgets in the same period, though Amnesty International's began earlier.)

The New Israel Fund together with the Ford foundation provided the seed funding for ACRI, B'Tselem, Hamoked, and Kav la'oved. The EU, the NIF and Ford seeded Adalah, the most influential organization advocating for the rights of the Palestinian minority in Israel.

ACRI was the only significant Israeli rights organization until the late 1980s. It was the first Israeli civil rights organization with a permanent staff, and this was in large measure due to increased funding levels. When the organization hired its first full time lawyer in the mid 1980s, this move marked a profound change in how the organization perceived and ordered itself. It began, for instance, to pursue precedent cases. Today there are 8 salaried lawyers working for the organization, and it routinely brings cases to the Israeli High Court.

While funding is certainly largely responsible for the increase in staff in particular organizations, as well as the increase in at least the expense of their activities, it is nevertheless not the only factor in the rise in number of human rights groups and activists (e.g. the rise of the human rights *movement*). Part of the reason for increased funding levels is clearly tied to increased international attention on (and therefore interest in) the Israeli/Palestinian conflict (cf. Hermann *et al* 1998: 96). This interest and attention also spurred Israelis to form a number of grassroots activist groups in the first Intifada (and the same is true of the second Intifada). As has been often observed, the first Intifada was the first Israeli war to be covered continuously on live international news (e.g. Ezrahi 1997).

While these factors—the Intifada itself as well as associated international and local media attention—were certainly key contributors to the emergence of an Israeli human rights movement, it is also the case that the warlike situation predisposed many Israelis to view this movement as anti-Israel. Indeed, since properly speaking, the human rights movement in Israel is above all concerned with the rights of Palestinians, it is viewed as effectively treasonous—as supporting the rights of the enemy.

The fact that local human rights groups are primarily dependent on foreign sources for their budgets adds to the popular perception that these organizations are working *against* the interests of Israelis or the Israeli state—a perception which seems to be confirmed by the fact that most of these NGOs indeed have foreign ties, and presumably also foreign sympathies. As a result, the views of human rights groups are generally not seen to be representative of the Israeli mainstream. What is not considered in this thinking is the reason for the rights groups' dependence on foreign funds. Until recently, *Israeli* contributions to such groups were not legally tax deductible (unlike in the US or Europe). It was in large part as a result of the efforts of Shatil that this law was changed in 1999. This change in law for voluntary organizations (*amutot*) could considerable impact the philanthropic scene in Israel, as wealthy Israeli elites may increasingly give donations to non-profits as a tax write-off. At the same time, no great shift in human rights funding sources has yet occurred.

There are, of course, other reasons for this dependence on foreign aid. For instance Israel in general has long been dependent on foreign aid (cf Khalidi; Gidron *et al*); moreover, the Israeli military, as is well known, is heavily subsidized by the United States.

The question arises as to why *these* sources of funding are not generally thought to be reflective of foreign sympathies—at least by Israelis. (Most Palestinians, and many other observers, feel differently of course.) It is worth bearing in mind that Ford and certain governmental consulates have become increasingly involved in funding human rights worldwide. And this sort of reaction—i.e. assuming international funding and organizations to be contrary to local interests—is not unusual. Egypt and Palestine are telling examples.

Finally, while foreign funding is without doubt a major force in supporting the human rights movement, it does nevertheless fluctuate. According to Hermann *et al*, funding patterns are susceptible to: changes in government; funder perceptions of particular NGOs, whether ideological or otherwise; and the types of donors providing funds (1998). For instance, while some funders are more interested in funding at a time when so-called extra parliamentary activity is more likely to be consonant with the policies of the reigning government (ibid), other funders are more interested in supporting groups in opposition to the ruling government. (The Ford Foundation, for instance, has often been aligned with funding programs and organizations that run contrary to the status quo in their respective locations.

The foundation's influence has at times been so substantial that one observer claimed that Ford was largely responsible for creating the women's movement in the US—largely through massive and strategic sponsorship of women's studies programs, conferences, and advocacy groups).

STOPPING AT THE GREEN LINE: FORD, NIF, SHATIL AND THE DEVELOPMENT OF A CADRE OF CIVIL RIGHTS LAWYERS IN ISRAEL

In this section we first describe the main character and relevance of three philanthropic organizations: the Ford Foundation, The New Israel Fund, and Shatil. We then turn to the description and evaluation of the Law Fellows Program, focusing both on its impact on civil and political rights in Israel and on Palestinian rights in the Occupied Territories.

During the Cold War in the United States the foreign policy establishment, the CIA, the State Department, and the key philanthropic organizations (Ford, Rockefeller, Carnegie) were unified in the fight against Communism (Dezalay and Garth, 2002). Particularly since its break from the American foreign policy establishment in the 1960s, the Ford Foundation has been one of the most influential social justice organizations, supporting human rights worldwide. For instance, it funded human rights efforts in Chile, supporting an organization that was later to become a model for human rights organizations everywhere, the Vicariate.

The Ford Foundation recently announced a grant of $20 million to be given to the New Israel Fund (NIF). In the world of US corporate giving, where universities have fundraising drives of several hundred million dollars, this may not seem like an especially remarkable sum, but in the world of human rights activism in Israel, it is considerable. This grant alone is equal to the total contributions of the EU to both human rights and democratization in Israel for the last five years. Prior to this announcement, Ford was already the largest supporter of the NIF, which itself is the largest single donor for social justice initiatives in Israel, including for human and civil rights initiatives. In the NIF's own description,

> ...almost every decision in the field of civil rights law, human rights law, the environment and religious pluralism [in Israel, of course] was either brought by a NIF grantee or litigated by a NIF Law Fellow... (1999: 2)

Other than from Ford, most NIF money comes from wealthy Jewish Americans and a variety of European foundations. NIF's funded activities remain exclusively within the 1967 borders, the

Green Line. This is a reflection of the organization's mandate as well as its constituency— Jewish American donors tend to be interested in promoting "Israel" in part by making it more socially or ethically respectable (in short, more "democratic").

In NIF's own terms, the Association for Civil Rights in Israel (ACRI) is its "flagship" grantee and the country's "premier human rights organization." It is well-known in human rights circles, however, that ACRI is one of the more "moderate" rights organizations and maintains strong ties to the state. ACRI's activities have traditionally been focused almost exclusively within the Green Line.

The three organizations listed in the section of the NIF Annual Report (1999) entitled "Human Rights in the Occupied Territories" are the following: B'Tselem, Rabbis for Human Rights (RHR), and the Israeli Coalition Against House Demolitions (ICAHD). It is arguably the case that these organizations are most often on the front lines of human rights activism in the name of Palestinian rights, and yet the latter two (and to a lesser degree, B'Tselem) receive rather meager funds when compared to ACRI. The significance is clear: the most important front-line Israeli human rights organizations working in the Occupied Territories do not get the majority of their funds from NIF.

In its early years, the New Israel Fund would have nothing to do with *peace* issues and organizations, because they were considered too politically radical at the time. It was afraid of losing tax-exempt status in the US. It did not want to fund over the Green Line, because it was afraid of alienating potential donors. As a former NIF director explained to me:

NIF really tried its best to look *loving* of Israel. Again, the word Zionist comes to mind. A pro-Jewish state. I think to this day, there are only Jewish members of the board. There's only one [non-Jew] I can think of, and they didn't know at first. Her father was a very well-known Jew. The annual report is designed to look loving of Israel. An image of an Ethiopian child waving an Israeli flag. At the same time, to me if we can correct some of the problems—we're there to support Israelis who want to correct some of the problems. We were very intent on looking *kosher* to Jewish society. Still, we constantly made mistakes, like serving ham. This was primarily for donors. To get big money, you had to look solid; you had to look liberal rather than progressive or radical. We were all of us on the staff to the left of the funders, as is often the case. I remember crafting our proposals for the Jew who prays and who wants to feel good about Israel...(Swirsky 2001). The New Israel Fund agenda appears quite clearly here. This agenda is reflected in the sorts of activities the organization actually supports. The Ford Foundation, by contrast, has a rather different agenda. Unlike the New Israel Fund, Ford is not in any significant way "nationalist." Granted, it funds Palestinian NGOs that are themselves arguably nationalist, or at least involved in state-building, but Ford's concern is social justice. In the latter case, social justice is translated to mean a national home for the Palestinians. But as we have seen, Ford—in addition to providing direct financial support to more "radical" Israeli human rights NGOs—also funds the New Israel Fund.

Shatil

NIF established Shatil in 1982 as a sort of consulting wing providing direct support to social justice organizations in Israel in the form of advice and training. The word *shatil* means "seeding," and the organization's consulting activities are oriented towards just that: programs like assisting new activist groups in writing grant proposals for the NIF and other foundations; helping to build coalitions between various advocacy groups working on similar issues, and so on. To give a sense of Shatil's involvement in human rights activities, I cite the following statistics from Shatil's programming plans for 1999:

(1) to provide at least 75 organizations with "direct technical assistance and capacity building support" (as compared to 60 in 1998 and 68 in 1999);

(2) assisting at least 5 national or local coalitions dedicated to specific human rights issues;

(3) to place at least 70 volunteers in 50 human rights organizations (as compared to 65 volunteers and 45 organizations in 1999). Since 1992, Shatil has placed more than 900 volunteers from abroad with more than 300 different social change organizations in Israel.

In its report detailing activities from July 1999 to June 2000, it seems that Shatil came close to meeting or exceeded all of these goals (support for more than 70 human rights NGOs and more than 5 coalitions) and significantly exceeded goal #3 by placing 87 volunteers in more than 50 human rights organizations. The projections for the coming year reflect an upward trend in exerting effort to assist human rights organizations and coalitions. In total, Shatil has been responsible for bringing more than 1000 volunteers into 300 social justice organizations in Israel.

By its own account, Shatil's impact has been diverse and substantial. Much of this impact is summarized in Shatil's brochures in terms of legislative and judicial "landmark decisions" (Shatil 2001a, 2001b):

(1) Successfully effecting the passage (in 1991) of landmark legislation outlawing sex discrimination (on the basis of sexual orientation) by employers;

(2) Due in part to Shatil's coalition-building efforts, passing a Public Housing Law in 1998 (allowing public housing residents the opportunity to purchase their dwellings at a significant discount);

(3) Property tax reform legislation passed by the Knesset in 1999 eliminating taxes on non-cultivated land, the imposition of which had disproportionately affected Arab citizens as they tend to live on larger tracts of such lands;

(4) Other Shatil-led coalitions played a key role in getting a Free Compulsory Education Law passed in the Knesset in 1999;

(5) After many years of campaigning, Shatil managed to effect the passage of a Freedom of Information Law in 1998, the first such comprehensive law of its kind in Israel. The law allows the public to demand information from local and national agencies.

Notwithstanding these impressive achievements, we might view with skepticism any self-report about achievements in the human rights world (or any sphere of influence for that matter). For instance, Shatil takes credit in its PR materials for having helped to "stabilize" The Israeli Coalition Against House

Demolition's (ICAHD) "administrative structure and establish a presence within the Israeli media." This claim should be moderated by the fact that ICAHD director Jeff Halper is exceptionally media savvy and has alone, and with the support of his many allies, exerted considerable effort in attracting both national and international attention to ICAHD's campaign.

Moreover, and more importantly, none of the achievements listed effect human rights across the Green Line, which raises the question of what precisely human rights *are*. In this case, they decidedly are not Palestinian human rights in the Occupied Territories. This tendency not to support human rights activities across the Green Line carries more weight for our discussion of the consequences of the human rights movement. Palestinian human rights are arguably the most crucial human rights issue in the Israeli-Palestinian conflict, and one of the most important donors to human rights in Israel, the New Israel Fund, tends not to support activism centered on these rights. Money and support for that comes from elsewhere, from the Ford Foundation and from the EU and European Consulates.

Law Fellows Program

According to the narrative of the New Israel Fund, Herman Schwartz, a Professor at the Washington College of Law (American University, Washingon DC), traveled to Israel in 1983 and saw that only two lawyers were working in civil liberties at the time. Moreover, there was effectively no litigation under way in the areas of civil liberties and civil rights. Schwartz believed that this situation resulted from two main factors: a lack of training and finances to encourage lawyers to conduct public interest work and the cultural and historical tenor of the country (cf. Laskier 2002). Schwartz decided to create a program which would help to foster a civil rights/civil liberties bar in Israel, including a cadre of trained lawyers working in the field both in full-time positions and through pro-bono work.

Since no adequate training facility existed in Israel at the time, Schwartz planned to bring a series of fellows to the Washington College of Law to get an LLM and work in the field of civil rights in the US (typically for the ACLU), and then again for a year on their return to Israel (often for ACRI, the Association for Civil Rights in Israel). Washington College of Law agreed to provide tuition waivers to the fellows and NIF provided seed funds, including the funds for the second year civil rights internship in Israel. NIF selects two fellows per year, of whom at least one is always a woman, and in more recent years, at least one is Arab.

The impact of these fellows has been remarkable, to say the least. They have taken countless cases to the Supreme Court, founded many organizations, and attracted innumerable journalists to write about their cases. They have not only formed the core of a civil rights bar in Israel that was virtually non-existent twenty years ago, their activities have had a ripple effect throughout Israeli society, and indeed, when we consider the impression made by a few key High Court cases abroad, all over the world.

Now twenty years after its founding, the list of graduates of the NIF/WCU Law Fellows program reads like a "who's who" in the civil and human rights community in Israel. As of 2002, a total of 36 fellows have now come out of the program, and it is clear that these people have had a profound impact on the legal (and political) community in Israel. Most of these people work in civil rights, at least by taking pro-bono cases; many have founded influential organizations and/or sit on the boards of others, often as chairs of boards; many work full-time as public interest lawyers; many are in academia, and have started human and civil rights courses, programs, and legal clinics. A brief look at the fellows' activities reveals the following: the first fellow, Joshua Schoffman, helped form and later headed the legal department for ACRI; he is now the Deputy Attorney General for the State of Israel. Neta Ziv, co-founded both the Women's Legal Defense Center and B'Zchut (an organization focused on the rights of the disabled); she now runs the (quite activist) legal clinic at Tel Aviv University. Dan Yakir currently heads the legal department for ACRI and has worked in the field of AIDS activism. Another fellow, Moshe HaCohen, was instrumental in forming a Public Defender program in Israel modeled after the US system; he is currently the public defender in Jerusalem. Tawfiq Jabareen founded the Association of Forty for Recognition of Arab Villages; Gidon Bromberg founded Eco-peace; and Hassan Jabareen founded Adalah, the ACRI equivalent for the Arab minority in Israel. Muhamed Dahle is Chair of Adalah's Board of Directors. This is only a partial list. Hammutal Guri, the current NIF coordinator of the Fellows Program, summarizes the impact of the program:

We're happy to say that we have achieved a cadre of civil rights lawyers, because these people have impacted not only the organizations where they work, but, if in the academy, for example, Neta Ziv has established 2 or 3 new law clinics at TAU, so these people make an impact whether they are in academia or in NGOs, writing articles, or appearing in the media (as some frequently do).

...and now this "cadre" includes many other people who didn't go through the program but who are part of the network of civil rights lawyers. In terms of the direction [of the program], we try to choose people so that in the future they'll help the preferred goals of NIF and the NGOs. It's another resource that we give the NGOs, if they get a lawyer for a year paid by the NIF, then it's a real resource, and often these people don't leave after a year, they stay on...

Again, we should bear in mind that this is a self report by the key NIF staff person responsible for the Fellows Program. A contrasting view was heatedly reported to me by one Israeli activist: the Fellows Program, and in fact the Israeli human rights movement in general, was elitist. In his view, both tend to overlook Israel's "own" (e.g. Jewish) poor and oppressed. Moreover, while it is quite clear that the NIF Fellows and their protégées, assistants, and colleagues are some of the most important, influential and active in the Israeli human rights scene, it does not appear to be the case that Palestinian human rights in the Occupied Territories are now markedly more respected. There are, of course, many possible explanations for the latter fact. The one worth underlining here is the NIF policy not to fund organizations across the Green Line. Recall that Fellows have to work for an *Israeli* social justice organization following their legal training in the US. The great majority of the organizations chosen focus their efforts within the Green Line. Even the Palestinian Fellows are Palestinian *Israelis*, and therefore tend to be mostly interested in working for the rights of the Palestinian minority in Israel.

THE EU AND THE EURO-MEDITERRANEAN PARTNERSHIP AGREEMENT

"There is no rationale to at least my government's funding of projects... The principal reason for that is simply fiscal years." (Anon. European consulate head, 2000).

While the rationale of governmental funding may appear to be obtuse, there is a logic nonetheless, even if that logic is to find the most efficient way to move funds in the direction of fundable projects within what the donor government considers to be the acceptable blocks of time or funding periods (in this case, fiscal years). Even this logic is not as straightforward as it might at first seem. For instance, the mandate might be restricted only to developing countries and yet a particular consulate is located within a country where human rights problems are rife but that its government nevertheless classifies as "developed."

For the EU, the object of funding must be a "developing country." The "developing country" is a category developed for a bureaucracy with a world-wide reach, and it engenders particular effects: a) because they consider Israel to be developed, neither the EU nor most European Consulates generally fund Israel or Israeli human rights organizations (but they do fund Palestinian ones); b) in order to meet the definition of "developing" and thereby be eligible for funds, local Israeli NGOs attempt to meet these funding criteria by emphasizing their work with, or for, Palestinians (and funding is often obtained in this manner); c) as a result of a), actual partnerships are formed between Palestinian and Israeli NGOs; d) many NGOs take the attitude, 'we need funding; make us fit the priorities.' The other clear effect is that since "Palestine" and "Palestinians" are more obviously "developing," and for this and other reasons, the PA and Palestinian NGOs (human rights and otherwise) receive far more EU and other European funding than Israeli human rights NGOs do.

THE EURO-MED AGREEMENT

Despite its many explicit facets, according to the interpretation of several scholarly commentators, the thrust of the EuroMed agreement is largely economic. It is centered on free trade provisions and is motivated by self-interested concerns for Europe to "develop" the Mediterranean region in an attempt to mitigate the perceived threat of migration and related security concerns. It may be hoped that the Mediterranean region will benefit economically and "advance" politically (e.g. "develop") in the process, but this does not appear to be Europe's primary aim. Indeed, it may be, as one author has suggested, that the agreement's human rights and democracy provisions were included primarily as "formalities" (Joffé 1997: 20). When pressure concerning these issues is applied, it is done outside of the formal agreements (ibid). Thus, in this view, NGOs are "far more likely" to bring about change, particularly human rights NGOs (ibid). What goes unmentioned here, however, is that such human rights NGOs are funded by the EU under the Meda Democracy budget line. They make possible the sorts of activities that may in fact bring real change in these domains.

But I want to turn now to the content of the agreement itself. Two key points will should become clear in this discussion: (1) the agreement makes "human rights" a priority, but a specific understanding of human rights is implied; (2) these human rights, along with "the rule of law" more broadly, are seen to be critical for attracting investment and thus creating "prosperity."

The Barcelona Declaration (the final document of the Euro-Med agreement) outlines three main areas of work: security; economic; social and cultural. The first section of the agreement outlines the political and security dimensions of the partnership. The stated aim is to establish "a common area of peace and stability," which would be a "common asset" that all signatories agree to promote "by all means at their disposal." What this specifically means turns out to depend on, at least rhetorically, on "essential principles of international law", in particular those of the UN Charter and the UDHR. Moreover, the words "human rights" are repeated three times in the first 16 lines of text. Besides human rights, "fundamental freedoms" are mentioned twice and various other rights are enumerated in these same first 16 lines. The concern for human rights suggested at least by the very frequent mention of the term is striking for an agreement largely considered to be economic in character.

Beyond the frequent mention of rights language at the outset, it is worth describing some of the bullet points outlining the partnership to get a sense of the underlying logic. The first point declares to act "in accordance with the United Nations Charter and the Universal Declaration of Human Rights." The second calls for the development of the rule of law and democracy while at the same time claiming to recognize the right to self-determination in choosing and "freely" developing " a state's own political, socio-cultural, economic and judicial system." The third bullet calls for "respect for human rights and fundamental freedoms" as well as guarantees "the effective legitimate exercise of such rights and freedoms" and then goes on to list examples, including freedom of expression, association, conscience and religion, as well as non-discrimination "on grounds of race, nationality, language, religion or sex." The fourth bullet calls for dialogue and information exchange on matters of human rights and fundamental freedoms as well as racism and xenophobia; the fifth calls for respect for diversity and pluralism and signals the importance of human rights education, as well as "fundamental freedoms."

The next major section of the Agreement concerns the Economic and Financial Partnership: "Creating an Area of Shared Prosperity." The major components of this partnership dimension concern free trade, economic cooperation, and a "substantial increase" in financial assistance to partnership member states by the EU. The free trade component principally involves the creation of a free trade "area." This will involve, notably, "the pursuit and the development of policies *based on the principles of market economy*" (182). The second component of the economic and financial partnership, economic cooperation, is noteworthy for its emphasis on creating "an environment conducive to investment." Most telling here is what is thought in fact to be conducive to investment, conceptually linked by the framers of the agreement to the first dimension of the partnership: respect for human rights, democracy, and the rule of law, and generally, the principles of international law. Thus "human rights" are thought to be conducive to investment, but what *kind* of human rights? Indeed, it is quite clear that the sort of human rights implied in the agreement are civil and political, not social and economic. (The fact that the agreement is meant in part to "develop" the Mediterranean region does not contradict this fact. It is often the case that economic transitions and "social security" provisions, especially ones given constitutional status, are seen as mutually contradictory [Rittich 2000]).

Moreover, the impact of human rights activism on the ground depends a great deal on the conception of human rights at hand. A conception of human rights centered on the liberal individual, in particular individual property rights and freedom of contract, might well contribute both to the new neoliberal ethos in Israel and to the increasing economic and social inequality that characterize the country in the era of liberalization. The Basic Laws of 1992, a set of legal rights often thought of as the "Constitutional Revolution" in Israel, make up the legal foundation for the new economic order (Hirschl 2000). [[The next couple of paragraphs are still being worked out]].

According to Hirschl, in the Israeli High Court's interpretation of the Basic Laws, "...the right to private property is awarded a supreme constitutional status and the constitutionally protected rights to 'human dignity and freedom' and 'freedom of occupation' are exclusively understood...as a bundle of 'negative' rights" (190). (Negative rights are commonly equated with civil and political rights, while social and economic rights are generally understood to be positive rights (e.g. requiring positive action or resources).) According to Hirschl, activist attempts to challenge this non-interventionist, anti-statist view of the Basic Rights have been unsuccessful (but not entirely, I would suggest, as we will see below) (201).

Hirschl's argument about Israel fits with many scholarly commentators' prediction of very limited "success" for the Meda initiative overall although the meaning of "success" varies for each of the many commentators. Joffé, for example, predicts that the initiative will largely benefit certain sectors of Europe and a small minority of the Med region, thus exacerbating economic and cultural divisions within particular Med regions (1997: 27). In this way, the Euro-Med partnership parallels other agreements that turn largely on the notion of "free trade": they increase an already growing class and culture divide. In this line of argument, those who are already more powerful stand to gain more easily in a situation of free trade (cf. Falk 2000). Hirschl's view explains in part how this has happened in Israel. The next two sections focus on how, notwithstanding the fact of increased socioeconomic inequality in Israel, individuals and activists can, and do, make very different use of these agreements than their framers may have intended.

Funded Projects under the MEDA Program

Between 1996 and 1999, the MEDA Democracy Program (MDP) had funded 148 "operations" for a total of E22.85 million. The EU consulate in Tel Aviv increased its grantmaking to human rights initiatives in Israel considerably under the direction of the head of mission in charge in the mid-1990s. In 1994 "there were maybe two or three projects funded annually, and those were run by people who were savvy about how to get to Brussels" (Meir 2000). By 1998, there were seven funded human right projects under the MEDA budget line and many more were funded in 1996 and 1997. This increase in funded programs was in part achieved by the efforts of the head of mission and his staff in interpreting the arcane rules of EU funding to include human rights for Palestinians in Israel. (Recall that Israel, unlike Palestine, is not a "developing" nation and is therefore not eligible for EU aid for human rights.)

As for what these and other similar projects have actually done, the MEDA program has its own take. According to the 1999 Annual Report for the MEDA program, "The main findings of the evaluation indicate that...Projects were mostly well designed, linked well with other programmes and were efficient and relevant to need. Training and education projects targeted a limited number of beneficiaries but had high impact on them, whereas *human rights and democracy awareness programmes targeted larger numbers but yielded lower beneficiary impact*." (MEDA Programme, 1999: 60).

Invoking the Euromed Agreement for Human Rights Compliance: Uri Davis and the Restoration of Palestinian Property

Uri Davis, a seasoned Israeli human rights activist and anthropologist, has started a new organization, Al Beit (Association for the Defense of Human Rights in Israel), which, in its attempt to restore expropriated land and property to 1948 Palestinian refugees specifically draws on the EuroMed agreement as a means of pressuring Israel. According to Davis, the Euro-Mediterranean Agreement of June 1, 2000, (which established an association between EU states and Israel), opens up a possibility for 1948 Palestinian refugees (both internal and external) to repossess property titles, under Israel's own, and notorious in human rights circles, Absentee Property Law of 1950. Davis submitted a grant proposal to the EU People-to-People Programme (Budget Line B7-4100) in January of 2001.

The grant proposal as a whole is concerned with the Euro-Med Agreement and its impact on Israel's commitment to human rights, specifically concerning Palestinian refugees and internally displaced (of 1948), and Europe's role in holding Israel accountable through the reciprocal agreement. For Davis, the Euro-Med Agreement contains two key articles, numbers two and four. Article Two states that relations between the EU and Israel will be based on respect for human rights and democracy; these principles guide "their internal and international policy and constitut[e] an essential element of this Agreement." Article Four outlines the common goals of peace, security, and democracy. Moreover, as Davis puts it, "Israel, *on account of its high level of economic development*, should enjoy special status in its relationship with the EU..." (7). As Davis points out, the Agreement institutes for the first time a formal political dialogue between Israel and the EU: "It commits Israel and the EU to a common vision of society based on the same value of democracy, respect for human rights and the principles of market economics."

Davis argues in the proposal that the right to property is an inalienable right as outlined in the Declaration of the Rights of Man (1789). (E.g. "No one shall be arbitrarily deprived of his property.") In connection, Israel's Absentee Property Law of 1950 plays a key role in Davis's text. Davis argues that the Absentee Property Law of 1950 alienates "*ALL* 1948 Palestinian refugees from their TITLES to their property inside Israel—an act which represents a fundamental and gross violation of all rights of ALL Palestine refugees and their descendents".

According to Davis—and this is a bold claim—refugees have the right to repossession and/or restoration of the *titles* to their properties (13, emphasis in original). This "does not entail the evacuation of a single Jewish family from their homes" (ibid). But it does entitle the refugees property assessments done by the UN and private firms. This is a counter to the typical Israeli dismissal of the "right" to return: *Where will all the Jews go? They'd just kick them out? I can't support another exile.*

How much of this EU-I Agreement Davis emphasized merely because it was a grant application to the EU is difficult to assess. The question remains as to why should the EU (not to mention other potential Palestinian supporters) push for *this* deserved right as opposed to the many others which have, and continue to be, violated. Nevertheless, the main point worth underlining here is that activists like Davis will focus on what *they* think is important, regardless of the original intent of such agreements.

Before turning to the concluding section, it bears mention that besides Davis, several other activist groups have invoked the Euro-Med Partnership both for broken human rights provisions and as a means of political pressure. Three of the more prominent instances are Amnesty International , The Euro-Mediterranean Human Rights Network, and the World Council of Churches:

(1) In a recent press release, Amnesty International urged the EU to press Israel to comply with the terms of the Association Agreement, and in particular, to "address human rights violations." To bring its point home, AI quoted Article 2 of the Agreement, which stresses that "respect for human rights...constitutes an essential element of this Agreement.

(2) A recent press release put out by the Euro-Mediterranean Human Rights Network (EMHRN) calls for a suspension of the Association Agreement with Israel.

(3) The World Council of Churches, and particularly APRODEV, its European counterpart, has put forward a number of similar statements calling for a suspension of the bilateral agreement with Israel until the latter fulfills its human rights obligations under international law (2002, 2003).

This is essentially what interested Uri Davis about the agreement: it could be invoked to pressure the Israeli State on human rights issues. In this instance, the EMHRN describes the founding principles of the agreement as "re-affirming respect for human rights as the basis of all international relations" and that therefore the Mediterranean states should insist that Israel immediately withdraw from the Occupied Territories. The main point in invoking Davis and these last examples is to illustrate that this sort of claimsmaking can [begin to] transform what was meant to be merely a promotional regime into something with more "teeth"—which is to say, more enforceable. This need not be what the signatories of the agreement originally intended. The very act of claimsmaking could itself become an enforcement mechanism. Regimes meant initially to be "promotional" can become, through claimsmaking and other NGO and grassroots activities, customary or enforceable law (cf. Steiner and Alston; Thomas 1999). I do not mean to suggest that the latter has yet occurred, but there are early indications of a trend in this direction.

Beyond Helskinki?

The history of human rights activism has seen agreements before whose intent was economic but nevertheless contained human rights provisions potentially impacting interstate relations. Whether or not the states involved actually expected much—or indeed *any*—change in human rights on the ground matters little if NGOs and activists take these agreements *as if* the states involved meant what they said (cf. Thomas 1999). This is indeed what appears to have happened following the Helsinki accords. These accords are justifiably seen as sort of a watershed for the international human rights movement, after which the USSR began, against its will, to bring itself more in line with the human rights provisions of the accords. In the case of Helsinki, this was not a unidirectional process, and we need not expect it to be so in the case of the Euromed. Nevertheless, a possibility has been opened. As with Helsinki, the Euro-Med Agreement may enable patterns and tactics of rights claims unforeseen by its drafters.

Conclusion

There are different effects money might have on human rights: give rise to a human rights industry; make that industry dependent on continued funds (much as it is already dependent on continued rights violations); and so on. If these effects have in fact occurred, there may also be some truth to the suspicion that the human rights movement, indirectly anyway, has also contributed to the perpetuation of the Israeli occupation (e.g. Kretzmer, 2002). Consider that many human rights groups shy away from overtly "political" activities, such as protesting the occupation *per se* or explicitly advocating full Israeli withdrawal from the West Bank and Gaza. Rather, they attack one or more "evils" of the Occupation: administrative detention, torture, closures, encirclement, collective punishments, etc. The human rights movement may therefore have contributed to a more "humane" occupation, and therefore, to delaying its end by making it seem less pernicious in the meantime. The counter to this, of course, is that human rights groups have, rather, routinely challenged the complacent notion that the occupation has been generally benign, particularly to Palestinians. And if movement efforts at Palestinian human rights protection have largely failed, we can hardly conclude that the human rights movement made the occupation so benign that it would therefore be more likely perpetuated.

Finally, a note on "failure": whatever one's views on its value (inherent or otherwise), human rights activism does not fail to carry effects; even if it is in the moment "ineffective" in terms of its stated goals, it has not "failed." The aftermath of confrontations and other human rights actions have long-term reverberations. In this sense, "no uprising fails":

> Although, from the front line of the struggle, it would seem that the assessment of practical effectiveness must of needs be all or none, the historical record raises more equivocal questions about the nature of socio-cultural determination... *More than this, if we confine our historical scrutiny to the zero-sum heroics of revolution successfully achieved, we discount the vast proportion of human social action which is played out, perforce, on a more humble scale.* (Comaroff 1985: 261-2, citing Ileto, my emphasis)

Thus, even if we accept the argument—presented by many human rights directors with whom I spoke—that money does not generally influence the direction of their activities, it is very probable that the availability of funds in types of projects in fact, in part at least, "created" those projects by encouraging groups to go where the money is. (Thus there is much work on Israeli-Palestinian dialogue and not so much work on protecting the rights of accused terrorists).

The last 15 years have seen an extraordinary development of international military interventionism in the name of human rights. The 1990s were a decade of humanitarian interventions whose declared objectives included putting an end to large-scale violations of rights and bringing to justice the perpetrators of abuses. The early 2000s have been marked by two major military campaigns led by the United States – in Afghanistan and Iraq – which started as wars to combat international terrorism and destroy weapons of mass destruction respectively, but quickly incorporated an extensive human rights rhetoric that identified promotion of individual freedom and rights as one of their key objectives. The aim of this study is to provide a political economy approach to the phenomenon of international human-rights enforcement that has developed in the post-Cold War period. This seeks to do the following:

1. To outline the concept of human-rights enforcement;
2. To specify what this study identifies as problematic about it;
3. To identify the shortcomings of the existing literature on the subject;
4. To delineate the key elements of a political economy approach adopted in this study; and
5. To sketch out the structure of the book.

2

Human-rights Enforcement in the Post-Cold War Years

The 1990s witnessed a range of international military operations justified as interventions to stop massive violations of individual human rights, particularly the right to life and the right not to be tortured. The operations with such objectives are usually referred to as 'humanitarian interventions' and there is a general agreement among experts that in the 1990s the following instances of international use of force constituted acts of humanitarian intervention: the UN-authorized actions in Northern Iraq, carried out mainly by the US, Britain and France; Bosnia-Herzegovina, by a multinational UN contingent, UNPRO- FOR; Somalia, by the US-led UNITAF force and later by the UNOSOM II contingent; East Timor, mainly by Australian forces; and Sierra Leone where a series of military operations was undertaken by the Economic Community of West African States (ECOWAS), Britain and UN troops. In addition to these, there was also a case of humanitarian intervention in Kosovo, which was undertaken by the North Atlantic Treaty Organization (NATO) without UN endorsement.

Each of these operations constituted a step towards a progressive international recognition of large-scale human-rights violations as crimes warranting some form of international coercive action. The Kosovo case was a culmination of this process and had three major outcomes: first, in addition to human-rights protection the Kosovo operation included a new objective that previous interventions did not have, namely the goal of punishment – the capture and prosecution of the key perpetrators of atrocities;

second, it set a precedent for an international military action unauthorized by the Security Council and carried out outside the UN framework; third, it led to an emergence of what some analysts referred to as the 'Clinton doctrine' (for example, Krauthammer, 1999; Klare, 1999; Daalder, 1999; Brown, 2000), or a commitment, first expressed by the former US President during the Kosovo operation, to use force in the future to stop massive human-rights abuses anywhere in the world, even without a UN authorization if necessary.

The legal, political, normative and technical precedents set by a 'decade of humanitarian intervention' in a way prepared the ground for the War on Terror of the early 2000s, particularly for the use of human-rights protection as one of the proclaimed objectives of the wars in Afghanistan and Iraq. It has been noted by some critics of these military campaigns, as we will see below, that human rights were invoked by the coalition leaders when no weapons of mass destruction were found in Iraq and when it was necessary to justify and legitimize the war on alternative grounds. However, even before this the rhetoric of human rights was used in presenting the case for military intervention in both cases. Thus, in outlining the objectives of the imminent war in Afghanistan, US President George W. Bush stated that it was a war to 'defend international human rights' and to punish 'enemies of freedom' who 'do not respect or value individual human rights' (Bush, 2001a).

The same argument was made by the former Italian Prime Minister Silvio Berlusconi who asserted that the coalition waged the war against the Taliban in order to 'guarantee respect for human rights.' The British Prime Minister Tony Blair also made a series of statements concerning abuses of rights practised by the Taliban in his presentation of the case for war (Blair, 2001). George Bush and Tony Blair were joined by their spouses – Laura Bush and Cherie Blair – who made several speeches on women's-rights abuses in Afghanistan. Laura Bush, for example, told Americans in a radio address in November 2001 that 'the brutal oppression of women is a central goal of the terrorists' and that 'civilized people throughout the world' should unite and fight 'the brutality against women and children in Afghanistan.' This argument was further elaborated in the US Department of State's Report on the Taliban's War against Women, released shortly after Laura Bush's radio address.

The same is true in relation to the preparations for the war against Iraq. For instance, speaking at the UN General Assembly before the invasion, George Bush explicitly mentioned human-rights abuses in his critique of the Iraqi regime: 'Iraq continues to commit extremely grave violations of human rights, and the regime's repression is all-pervasive. Tens of thousands of political opponents and ordinary citizens have been subjected to arbitrary arrest and imprisonment, summary execution, and torture and all of these horrors are concealed from the world by the apparatus of a totalitarian state' (Bush, 2002a).

Tony Blair, speaking on 10 September 2002, similarly referred to the denial of individual freedoms in Iraq as a justification for a military intervention: 'We want the Iraqi people to be free to live fulfilling lives without the oppression and terror of Saddam' (Foreign and Commonwealth Office, 2002, p. 3), an argument that was later reiterated by British Foreign Secretary Jack Straw, who stated that 'the abuses of the Iraqi regime extend far beyond its pursuit of weapons of mass destruction in violation of its international obligations' and include 'torture, rape and other horrific human-rights abuses' (Daily Mail, 2002, p. 2). In other words, despite significant differences between pre- and post-September 11 contexts, and the fact that the War on Terror began in response to an attack on the United States, we can nevertheless observe an unquestionable continuity between the humanitarianism of the 1990s and the wars against the Taliban and Saddam Hussein's Iraq in the new century. On the one hand, one of the outcomes of the 'decade of humanitarian intervention' was an increased acceptance by the international community of legitimacy of the use of force to protect human rights and to bring to justice the perpetrators of massive human-rights violations.

On the other hand, the 1990s set important precedents for the use of force outside the UN framework, particularly by the United States. The Taliban in Afghanistan and Saddam's regime in Iraq had perpetrated significant violations of individual rights and, given the legacy of interventions of the 1990s, it was consistent to identify these violations as sufficient reason for intervention. Whether this was done out of a pragmatic plan to give legitimacy to an otherwise legally dubious campaign, as its critics assert, or from a real concern for the victims of human-rights violations in these countries, is of secondary importance to the analysis in this book. What will be highlighted is the fact that we are dealing with a phenomenon that has been developing over the past 15 years or so since the end of the Cold War, a phenomenon that will be referred to here as 'human-rights enforcement' and which constitutes the focus of this study. It will be suggested that the concept of 'human-rights enforcement' enables us to deal with what the War on Terror and the humanitarian interventions of the 1990s have in common, that is, the use of force against perpetrators of human-rights violations; at the same time it will not ignore their differences nor collapse the significant distinctions between them. What this book seeks to offer is a historical and holistic analysis of the post-Cold War practice of human-rights enforcement. What explains the development of this phenomenon? What are its implications for the late-modern world? What actors and social forces benefit from its development? These are questions that will be dealt with throughout the book.

What is problematic about human-rights enforcement? As will be seen in the next section, humanitarian interventions of the 1990s and the War on Terror of the early 2000s have stimulated a large amount of academic and non-academic writing. What this body of literature identifies as problematic about these phenomena usually relates to their legality in respect of existing norms and procedures for the use of international force, or their selectivity, which has led many scholars to question the real motives and intentions of the interveners.

The present study has been motivated by different concerns and what it sees as problematic about post-Cold War human rights enforcement has so far escaped the attention of experts. The starting point for the analysis is the fact that the late-modern world is characterized by a development of a global form of capitalism whose functioning results in massive inequality and large-scale human suffering from poverty and poverty-related problems. Although these phenomena are in themselves not qualitatively new, inequality and poverty have sharply increased in the last 15 to 20 years marked by a general shift towards neoliberal economic reforms; today they have reached dramatic levels. For example, one of the latest in a series of gruesome reports on 'human development' regularly published by the United Nations Development Programme (UNDP) – which equally regularly fails to lead to any comprehensive action to force change – states that 1.1 billion people currently live on less than $1 a day, more than 1 billion people lack access to safe water, another 2.6 billion do not have adequate sanitation, and almost 2 million children die each year for want of clean water and basic hygiene, and 1.4 million more die from diseases that could be prevented by vaccination (UNDP, 2004).

At the same time, amidst this human misery there has developed a global moral discourse at the core of which lies the idea of the promotion and protection of individual human rights, support for democratic and transparent state institutions and, more recently, encouragement of socially responsible business practice. Since the end of the Cold War, which has been largely perceived as a victory of freedom over tyranny, there has been a commitment expressed by a multiplicity of different state and non-state actors to further combat oppressive and authoritarian regimes, to spread democratic values and institutions, and to promote individual rights. These rights are primarily political and civil rights, such as the right to freedom of thought and expression, the right not to be tortured, the right to be free from arbitrary detention, the right to equality before law and the right to vote. The practice of human-rights enforcement has therefore developed as an integral part of this moral discourse and has played an important role in its further development by increasingly subjecting the rule of state sovereignty to scrutiny in terms of their respect for human rights.

We are therefore dealing with two phenomena whose time-frames coincide – the ascendance of global capitalism in its neoliberal form with hundreds of millions of people being condemned to abject poverty, on the one hand, and a development of a global moral discourse which identifies individuals and their political and civil emancipation as its key objective. A crucial question that arises in this respect is whether these two phenomena are causally related or not. Does this economic order require such a moral discourse to help sustain an unjust set of social relations? If the answer to this question is negative, then we may assume that there is nothing problematic about human-rights enforcement in this respect, and that it is a noble and commendable practice that saves at least some individuals from horrible fates. If the answer is positive, however, then the use of force to protect human rights becomes rather problematic. A closer examination of this question reveals that there are at least two indications that point to an existence of a possible causal relation between global capitalism and the catastrophic outcomes of its functioning on the one hand, and human rights protection, promotion and enforcement on the other.

First, a general global moral discourse of human rights and democracy, and the practice of human-rights enforcement in particular, are permeated by notions of freedom, equality and justice which are defined in exclusively formal terms, that is, in terms of respect for individual negative rights. It advances as absolute a conception of freedom and justice which is, in fact, partial – confined only to the political and civil rights of individuals – and which seems to underprivilege and objectify explanations of human suffering from massive economic inequality and poverty. This is not to say that it renders poverty and misery invisible – no moral discourse would ever be able to achieve this given their scale and scope – but it relegates them to the realm of the economy, which in turn, is naturalized as a sphere that has its own laws and mechanisms; this sphere comes under nobody's control and its understanding is the prerogative of economists who can help us make sense of its functioning and develop better economic policies – and nothing more than that. In other words, this moral discourse makes an implicit distinction between political crimes, whose perpetrators are identifiable and ought to be punished, and economic problems that have no such identifiable architects and which cannot be seen as crimes. Rather they are viewed as unfortunate outcomes of objective processes and laws – the 'invisible hand' of classical or liberal economic theory inspired by Adam Smith and Hegel – and which may be corrected or ameliorated only to a limited extent (for example, by means of economic aid to the states affected).

The values and ideals of individual rights may therefore be said to result in the privileging of the human suffering from political causes over that which is brought about by the functioning of the capitalist economy; they also naturalize and objectify the capitalist economy, which is, in fact, a specific historical product of human activity and has nothing natural about it.

Second, a global moral discourse which involves a continuous reiteration of a commitment by different states and non-state actors to fight tyranny and oppression and to promote individual rights and liberties, and a wide range of policies adopted to this end – including the use of force in some cases – seems to provide the emerging global order with a significant degree of moral legitimacy. This legitimacy appears to have two dimensions: retrospective and contemporary. In the case of the former, its roots go back to the Cold War period when superpower rivalry was constructed in the West as a struggle of good against evil, of freedom against tyranny and of individual rights against repressive state institutions.

The West, led by the United States, finally prevailed and with this prevailed such an interpretation of the Cold War. The disappearance of socialist/communist dictatorships was equated with a victory of a free and just order, and because the Western system was built on a capitalist mode of production, the collapse of the USSR and its allies was also equated with the supremacy and inevitability of capitalism. In short, capitalism emerged from the Cold War as a system said to guarantee individual freedom and which is seen as the most efficient and the only viable way of organizing production. The global moral discourse, which today has at its core the idea of individual negative rights, provides the existing order with a retrospective legitimacy in comparison to an alternative which not only failed economically, but was also marked by political repression and massive violations of human rights. This makes a radical critique of capitalism much more difficult today for its alternative ended up suppressing and flagrantly violating individual freedom in the service of collective goals.

As regards the contemporary dimension of moral legitimacy, it lies in continuous condemnation of instances of human suffering caused by political factors and an adoption of policies, including military intervention, that provide the developing order with very strong moral appeal. It is an order in which torture, mass murder, war crimes and genocide are increasingly less tolerated, and where the perpetrators are more and more often brought to justice. What could be better illustrations of such a commitment than the removal from power and the prosecution of the likes of Slobodan Milosevic and Saddam Hussein or the establishment of tribunals for war crimes in the former Yugoslavia and for acts of genocide in Rwanda? In short, the global moral discourse in general, and a practice of human rights enforcement in particular, seems to contribute to a construction of a more righteous and just emerging global order, particularly in the light of massive poverty and human misery that currently affect hundreds of millions of people.

Together, these observations reveal a perplexing and irrational contradiction that seems to mark post-Cold War human-rights enforcement: actors coming to the rescue of people threatened with imminent slaughter appear to be unintentionally contributing to a reproduction of a system that subjects an incomparably larger number of people to suffering and death from poverty, hunger and disease. That such a causal role can be played by human-rights enforcement clearly requires a careful investigation and an analysis of a relationship between global capitalism and the use of force to protect human rights. So far such an analysis has not been provided by the existing literature on humanitarian intervention and the War on Terror. A review of available studies reveals that not only do they not attempt to examine the relationship between global capitalism and human-rights enforcement but they also frustrate any such attempt to do so by continuously constructing them as two separate phenomena; and by treating human-rights enforcement as an exclusively legal/political phenomenon with no relationship to the economy or the system of production.

The Existing Literature

The majority of available works on the humanitarian interventions of the 1990s tend to be policy-oriented and 'problem-solving', that is, they focus on ways of improving intervention techniques, post-intervention policies and aim to learn lessons from the past cases. Those approaches that go beyond such technical-instrumental questions usually focus on issues of the conformity of interventions with international law, the national interests of states involved in military operations, or the ethical dilemmas posed by interventions. The same is true of the literature on the War on Terror, which is also dominated by policy-oriented works, particularly with respect to policies of post-war reconstruction and state- building in Afghanistan and Iraq, as well as the multiplicity of legal studies and those concerned with US national interests or US 'imperial' ambitions.

The role of human rights in the War on Terror is curiously neglected except in terms of the impact of anti-terrorist legislation on human rights, or abuses of rights of suspected terrorists captured by the coalition forces, or with respect to the employment of human rights as a cover for real interests of the US and its allies (which are widely described in terms of getting hold of Middle Eastern oil reserves). Overall, the body of literature on post-Cold War enforcement of human rights suffers from two major shortcomings: it is, for the most part, reductionist and ahistoric. The reductionism of the existing analyses has two dimensions: methodological and ontological. In the former case, most of the available analyses suffer from a problem often referred to in social theory as 'methodological individualism'; this belief, whose roots are found in the writings of Max Weber, posits that social phenomena can be explained by examining the intentions, properties and capabilities of individual actors. In this view, a social whole is nothing but a sum of constitutive units whose behaviour is governed and determined by their motivations, interests and powers.

What is problematic about this approach to social reality is that it completely ignores causal roles played by structures and totally disregards what is known as an 'agent/structure dilemma; or a problem 'of finding a way of accounting for human experience which recognizes simultaneously and in equal measure that history and society are made by constant and more or less purposeful individual action, and that individual action, however purposeful, is made by history and society' (Abrams, 1982, p. xiii). The agent/structure relationship involves reciprocal causality: structures govern agents' behaviour, usually by setting limits on options available to them and to what they perceive as normal or acceptable, whereas agents, through their conscious and purposeful activity, reproduce – for the most part unintentionally and unconsciously – the structures within which they operate. For example, the structure of a capitalist society compels individuals who do not possess capital or land and have no alternative sources of income to enter into a wage-labour relation with those who possess the means of production. Those individuals who succeed in finding a job and securing paid employment do not intend to reproduce the capitalist structure of production – their intention is simply to get a source of income – but their actions, nevertheless, produce such a consequence; that is, they reproduce the wage-labour relation that is central to capitalist production.

As Bhaskar puts it: people, in their conscious activity, for the most part unconsciously reproduce . . . the structures governing their substantive activities of production. Thus people do not marry to reproduce the nuclear family or work to sustain the capitalist economy. Yet it is nevertheless the unintended consequence and (inexorable result) of, as it is also a necessary condition for, their activity. The literature on post-Cold War human-rights enforcement is predominantly 'methodologically individualist' as it reduces this phenomenon to a mere foreign policy tool of individual states and it always sees the outcomes of each particular operation in terms of the deliberate and conscious plans, intentions or interests of the actors involved. An impression that one gets from reading, for example, Realist accounts of humanitarian interventions or critics of the War on Terror made by the likes of Noam Chomsky (for example, Chomsky, 1999a) is that the US and Britain simply invented human rights to deceive everybody and achieve their national interests or to implement their imperial projects.

It is nothing short of amazing how such authors ignore what structures must be in place for states to be able to act in the name of human rights, or for a dominant conception of freedom to be defined in terms of negative individual liberties, or for terrorists to be designated as enemies of freedom and human rights. The fact that the US-led intervention in Haiti in 1994 was followed by an imposition on Haiti of a policy of free trade with the US and a set of other neoliberal reforms as a precondition for financial aid immediately leads the likes of Chomsky to conclude that humanitarian intervention is nothing but a means for the US to extend its neoliberal empire. No questions are asked as to why neoliberal reforms have come to constitute a kind of a 'matrix' or a set of hegemonic standards with reference to which some actors may discipline others, or why human rights are becoming a globally accepted criterion for the evaluation of state governments and for the coercion of those who do not conform to this standard.

The fact that today agents who may exercise power over other agents with reference to the established norms and structures are substitutable is totally overlooked by these commentators. Thus, in some cases it may be the United States disciplining another state by using these standards, in others it may be the World Bank or the IMF or other global institutions, yet in others it could be multinational corporations. Furthermore, there are cases when actors discipline themselves in a rather Foucauldian manner in order to conform to the existing standard of normality, even without prior coercion, for a range of reasons (for example, to gain a better investment rating or to stand better chances of obtaining foreign aid in the case of poor states, or to conform to the emerging norm of social responsibility in the case of corporations adopting codes of good business).

No do existing analyses allow for a possibility of there being unintended consequences of enforcement actions. For instance, to continue with the earlier example, had the intervention in Haiti not been followed by neoliberal reforms, no questions about humanitarian intervention and neoliberalism would have been asked, as they were not asked with respect to Somalia or Kosovo because there was not such an identifiable empirical outcome. The aim of this study, as mentioned above, is to investigate a relationship between post-Cold War human-rights enforcement and global capitalism in its neoliberal variety even when no empirical connection is available; that is, it is to enquire about unintended consequences that the development of the phenomenon of human-rights enforcement in the post-Cold War period might have had with respect to the structure of a global capitalist economy as a whole and not just to the individual states that have experienced interventions.

This leads to the second element of reductionism – the ontological. The existing literature on human rights enforcement treats it as a purely political, legal, military or technical phenomenon in complete isolation from the economy, except occasionally when, as in the case of Haiti mentioned above, there are some observable indications of such a relationship. No study of humanitarian intervention or the War on Terror, as we will see in the next chapter, has ever attempted to inquire into a potential relationship between human-rights enforcement and global capitalism. The reason for this lies in the traditional separation of polity and economy that characterizes social science; they are treated as discrete and only sporadically or conjuncturally connected realms. The roots of this separation go back to the development of capitalism and the emergence of the notion of the 'self-regulating market', the central mechanism responsible for allocation of resources and distribution of goods and services in a capitalist society.

This set in motion a transformation of the study of political economy as a single field into the two separate disciplines of politics and economics. This separation first appears in the writings of Adam Smith whose work, as Winch observes, stands 'as an important landmark in a more complex and troubled version of the history of liberal individualism, one in which "economy" and "society" are replacing "polity.' The following passage where Smith discusses Thomas Hobbes' assertion that 'wealth is power' illustrates this well: Wealth, as Mr. Hobbes says, is power. But the person who either acquires, or succeeds to a great fortune, does not necessarily acquire or succeed to any political power, either civil or military. His fortune may, perhaps, afford him the means of acquiring both, but the mere possession of that fortune does not necessarily convey to him either. The power which that possession immediately and directly conveys to him is the power of purchasing; a certain command over all the labour, or over all the produce of labour which is then in the market (Smith, 2000, p. 34).

What is crucial in this statement is that by political power

Smith refers to a position of influence within the state apparatus, in the realm of the public political sphere. He clearly fails to acknowledge that the power to possess capital and the related power to extract surplus from the labour of others are in themselves political and had always been seen as such, as his citation of Hobbes illustrates. Smith's view, as well as the current dominant view of politics and economics as discrete spheres, is explained by the difference between capitalist and pre-capitalist forms of surplus extraction. The latter had been characterized by political means of personal or juridical dependence, while in capitalism the function of surplus extraction is performed by economic means – through a wage-labour relation – and political coercion is no longer necessary to obtain surplus.

This, however, does not mean, as Smith states, that the power to extract surplus no longer involves political power. There are, in fact, two dimensions of political power involved in the process of extracting surplus by means of wage-labour: on the one hand, it is the power to exercise command and control over employees, to ensure that they perform the required tasks and that their work results in profit which is unequally shared between the employer and the employees; on the other hand, such a method of surplus extraction requires a particular political organization of the society, that is, a state capable of providing the security of private property and necessary legal and institutional forms to ensure a smooth functioning of the economy. The latter observation is informed by Marx's view that the economic structure of society is the real foundation which conditions a legal and political superstructure, and to which specific forms of social consciousness correspond.

This is not say that economic relations determine other social institutions, but only to point out that the latter ultimately take such forms that are compatible with the existing material relations. It cannot, for example, be asserted that the capitalist organization of production necessitates individual rights; however, it can be observed that today justice and freedom are defined in terms of negative individual rights, a notion that is compatible with the operation of capitalism; we cannot understand such a conception without examining the transformation of feudal production relations into capitalist ones and the changes in political, legal and ideational realms that this put in motion. To return to the literature on human-rights enforcement, it takes for granted and reproduces the apparent separation of politics and economics and of the use of force in the name of individual rights from the global capitalist economy. This study seeks to correct this shortcoming and examine the nature of the relationship between the emerging neoliberal order and human-rights enforcement.

The second shortcoming of the existing literature – and one directly related to the problem of reductionism – is its profoundly ahistorical nature. Like historians of antiquity who were unable to master the dialectical complexities of particularity and universality and remained trapped at the level of anecdotal particularism, the existing analyses of the history of humanitarianism are predominantly descriptive, and offer little more than the reporting of individual past events described in terms of the decisions or intentions of the actors involved. No reference to the structural context is made, and no synthesis between historical particularity and historical universality is attempted. For example, legal studies looking for historical precedents of contemporary military humanitarianism see history as a collection of events that took place in the past and simply narrate what happened. The same applies to scholars following an approach to international relations known as the English School, who explicitly define their project as historical but who seldom achieve anything beyond a simple reporting of phenomena.

Thus, with respect to human rights, the English School does nothing to explain them, but only describes the evolution of this norm in the international society of states. But the most problematic manifestation of the ahistoricism of the existing literature is a development in recent years of a multiplicity of studies using medieval just-war theory to analyse the ethical, legal and military aspects of contemporary events. The most popular way to employ just-war theory has been to list its conditions for a war to be regarded as just and describe the manner in which a war is conducted, usually referred to in Latin as jus ad bellum and jus in bello respectively, and then to apply them to the intervention in question. Thus, if just-war conditions are satisfied, the war is just; if not, the war is unjust. The problems of such an approach lie in its treatment of the modern practice of human-rights enforcement as nothing but a continuation of practices whose origins go back to the Middle Ages. This results in a construction of the history of humanitarian wars as a linear evolution from medieval just-war theory through to early modern humanitarianism as an exception to the Peace of Westphalia, through to modern human rights-based humanitarianism as an exception to the UN Charter. Such an interpretation of the history of humanitarianism ignores profound changes that have taken place in social structures and relations of production over centuries.

This problem is inseparable from both methodological and ontological reductionism; they do not allow such analyses to acknowledge differences between seemingly similar actions such as, for example, the use of force by medieval monarchs to protect Christians outside their kingdoms and contemporary instances of humanitarian intervention to enforce human rights, because these differences lie in the causal relations of these practices with their respective social contexts. Thus, the humanitarianism of St Augustine, Thomas Aquinas and other theologians and ecclesiastics was grounded in religion and was part of the feudal ideology which involved interpreting all social relations as God-ordained and therefore unquestionable; this inevitably helped feudal relations to be sustained. Contemporary military interventions, in contrast, take place in the context of global capitalism. The aim of this study is to examine how they contribute to the reproduction of the latter. As will be argued below, contemporary human-rights enforcement, at the core of which lies the idea of individual rights, is a fundamentally different phenomenon from the just-war doctrine based in theology; to see one as evolving from the other is to create a false continuity and ignore differences in the causal powers of these phenomena in relation to their respective social contexts. Having outlined what are seen here as the key deficiencies of the existing analyses, I will now provide a brief summary of a political economy approach.

THE POLITICAL ECONOMY APPROACH

To overcome the deficiencies of the existing works on post-Cold War human-rights enforcement – their reductionist and ahistorical nature – the present study develops a political economy approach which seeks to provide a holistic and historical analysis. It is rooted in Marx's methodology which is in turn based on an assumption that social phenomena do not exist in isolation but constitute a totality or an organic unity. That is to say, it seeks to enable the theorization of any particular part or unit of social reality in relation to a total social whole, an entity that cannot be reduced exclusively to politics, economics, social reproduction and so on, but that constitutes a complex set of dialectical internal relations between these domains. As Arthur observes, knowledge of any phenomenon 'must take the form of a system of related categories rather than a series of discrete investigations.'

Nevertheless, as already mentioned, the key to understanding each particular historical configuration of social totality lies in the material relations which constitute the foundation of any society. For Marx, to ensure the process of social reproduction, any society must first and foremost produce the means of subsistence; the way that material production and distribution are structured constitutes the society's 'essence' which influences other social institutions and relations, and is in turn influenced by them. To repeat, this does not mean that the economy determines everything else; it only means that production relations set ultimate limits on other social institutions. It also means that changes in economic relations will eventually lead to corresponding transformations in political, legal and other social domains. As Marx puts it, 'the changes in the economic foundation lead sooner or later to the transformation of the whole immense superstructure.'

Marx's method allows us to correct both forms of reductionism – methodological and ontological – that characterize existing studies of human-rights enforcement. Concerning the former, individual agents and their actions can be examined in relation to a set of social structures within which they interact, for 'society does not consist of individuals, but expresses the sum of interrelations, the relations within which these individuals stand.' Concerning the latter, legal, political or ideational phenomena cannot be understood without an ultimate examination of their relationship with the existing economic structures. Overall, Marx's method resolves the agent/structure problem as follows: first, agents' behaviour is influenced and shaped by a complex set of different relations which together constitute an organic unity or totality; and secondly, social totality, in turn, cannot be properly explained or understood without reference to the existing relations of production. As Marx famously puts it, 'men make their own history, but they do not make it as they please; they do not make it under self- selected circumstances, but under circumstances existing already, given and transmitted from the past.' And these already existing circumstances are based on the 'economic structure of society', which is 'the real foundation on which arises a legal and political superstructure and to which correspond definite forms of social consciousness.'

However, to argue that structures influence the behaviour of agents, while the latter reproduce the structures, does not completely resolve the agent/structure problem; the question arises as to why agents reproduce structures which are based on unequal and exploitative relations. A crucial concept in this respect is 'ideology'. The notion of ideology in Marx's writings has had different interpretations. In this study I follow Larrain (1983), Maclean (1988a), Allman (2001) and a number of other analysts who interpret the concept of ideology in Marx's writings, particularly in The German Ideology, as a critical concept, or what Larrain refers to as ideology in the 'negative sense'. In this view, ideology designates ideas which express or interpret social reality inadequately or incompletely, or which distort or misrepresent it. What is important to stress here is that this 'distorted form of knowledge' is not reducible to the deliberate project of a class. Ideological ideas are 'encouraged to a great extent' by a social reality which is 'inverted', that is, which appears different from what it really is. As Allman argues, ideology refers to ideas which are 'only the partial truth, or fragments of something that we cannot fully comprehend unless we can grasp it in its entirety. In this way they distort the truth and thus prevent us from fully comprehending a situation – in other words, they 'tend to frame our thinking within certain horizons or parameters.'

In short, ideology in the negative sense refers to ideas which misrepresent existing relations of power and exploitation, but which do so not because of an intentional project by some dominant social force, but because reality so presents itself that it encourages such views on the part of both the dominant and the subordinate. However, although ideological ideas may be shared by all classes, ideology serves the interests of the dominant class because the role it plays in the negation or concealment of contradictions inevitably contributes to the reproduction of those contradictions. For example, as will be seen later, in feudal society both lords and peasants or serfs shared a view that society and their respective social roles were God- ordained, had a divine purpose and, therefore, could not be questioned. Religion was an ideology which helped sustain feudal relations of personal dependence and undoubtedly benefited the feudal lords, but it was not reducible to their deliberate project or 'conspiracy', because both the serfs and the feudal lords interpreted reality in such a way. The concept of ideology will be of central importance to the following analysis of post-Cold War human-rights enforcement because it avoids reducing consequences to the conscious plans of agents and permits a structural analysis of their behaviour.

In relation to the ahistoricism of the literature, Marx's method of 'historical materialism' enables us to not only describe and report what happened in the past, but also to explain it. Historical materialism is a structural analysis applied to past events: these events are located within their historical social context – a historical social totality – with the primary focus being placed on material relations. Such an approach avoids the 'anecdotal particularism' of existing studies which, as has been said, reduce history to a reporting of past events seen purely in terms of the intentions or decisions of agents. It equally avoids the opposite extreme, that is, a historiography that explains everything in terms of universality; this was the method of many medieval historians who saw everything as an outcome of divine providence. Marx's method approaches history as a constant interplay of universality and particularity and strives to create a synthesis of agents and structures.

In this study the history of modern humanitarianism – which goes back to the medieval doctrine of just war – will be examined in terms of its relations of reciprocal causality with social structures in different historical epochs. It will be seen that contemporary instances of human-rights enforcement are fundamentally different, in terms of their causal roles, with respect to the late-modern global political economy (GPE), from the medieval tradition of just war, its place in the ideology of feudal society, and the way it contributed to the latter's reproduction. This will demonstrate how problematic are the existing accounts of the history of human-rights enforcement which construct it as a linear evolution or continuous development from medieval times to the present.

Before proceeding to a summary of arguments that will be developed in this study by using a political economy approach, one more methodological issue vital to the analysis needs to be addressed. It is the relationship between theory and practice, between substantive events and the way they are studied, between instances of humanitarian enforcement and the academic literature on the subject. It is usually assumed in social sciences that theory and practice are two categorically separate realms. Such a view results from the dominance of a positivist epistemology; this is based on a belief that to be scientific, social inquiry must adopt the methods of impartial observation and description of the physico-chemical sciences. What this assumes is that it is not only possible but also imperative for social scientists to separate themselves from social reality and study the latter in an objective (meaning value-free) manner.

However, in the natural sciences subjects are distinct from objects, which is not the case in social inquiry; in this human beings study themselves. Treating society as equivalent to nature externalizes it, or as Bauman argues, it takes society as 'unproblematic nature-like society' which it turns into a 'second nature'. This, in turn, has very serious implications for practice. By declaring that to be scientific social analysis must be value-free, and by treating practice as categorically separate from theory, such an approach plays two causal roles: on the one hand, by taking the existing society as its starting point, as given, it inevitably contributes to its reproduction, and to sustaining the status quo, which in turn serves the interests of those who benefit from it; on the other hand, it limits possibilities of radical change by dismissing as 'normative' and unscientific those approaches that reject the theory/practice dichotomy. To borrow Cox's famous dictum, 'theory is always for someone or some purpose' the academic literature on human-rights enforcement generally takes for granted the appearance of its separation from global capitalism and thereby reproduces it. As a result, it contributes to a development of a global moral discourse which privileges human suffering from political causes over human suffering brought about by the functioning of the global economy. It therefore plays a role in the relegation of poverty and poverty-related problems to the domain of a 'self-regulating market', thereby objectifying and naturalizing the capitalist economy. Marx's methodology is rooted in a denial of a categorical separation of theory and practice and treats theory as part of practice – as part of the substantive phenomenon that it seeks to analyse. It also explicitly develops a theory of praxis, that is, a theory which is from the beginning transformative, and that seeks to understand society in order to change it.

Overall, Marx's methodology can be described as holistic and historical. The idea of social totality enables us to locate events that we want to analyse within a larger social structure and examine them in terms of a constant interplay of agents and their social contexts, of particularity and universality. The notion of social totality rejects the reduction of phenomena to exclusively legal, political, economic or moral realms, and instead seeks to comprehend them through the organic unity of these domains. Particular attention is paid to the economy, to the way the process of production and distribution is

organized and the manner in which it dialectically relates with other social institutions and forms. Applied to history, such a methodology goes beyond a mere description or reporting of events, but explains them with references to historical social structures, again paying key attention to the material relations that prevail in the historical epoch in question. It also overcomes the theory/practice dichotomy by seeking to analyse not only substantive events and practices, but also how they have been studied by others and the implications of that study for the events and practices concerned.

3

Political Economy in Developed Countries

Economic theory, usually, feels more comfortable dealing with needs rather than with rights. Within economic analysis satisfying needs implies the use of concepts like cost, benefit, and price, the matter being, here, capability, in other words purchasing power. With rights the matter is quite different; it is about qualification, about the reasons why one should qualify to enjoy rights and the consequences of the use of such criteria. Whilst dealing with needs, economics can take shelter in a positivist approach, dealing with rights pushes it to risk normative stands. When dealing with rights economics can basically take one of two, or three, approaches. Some take rights as an integral part of normative economics, and in this view exercising rights is just another manifestation of making a social choice. Those that define both the ends and the means of economic development in terms of human rights are amongst this group. The second option is to take rights as a constraint within which social choice is made. This rights-as-constraints view has been developed, for instance, into the so-called game form formulation of individual rights, where focus is on the analysis of social situations where rights are given. We could also add a third approach of the interaction of economics and rights, where economics can be seen as a constraint on rights. Indeed, in order to enjoy many rights, out of a wide palette, availability of means, economic means, is frequently a necessary condition.

This article will adopt the first approach mixed with the third, where deepening human rights is in itself a social choice. It is because the drafters of the Universal Declaration on Human Rights thought that availability of means was important that positive rights were to be proclaimed in this Declaration, and economic rights detailed later on. Although it has not been the object of a discussion such as its relevance would suggest, the right to work takes a prominent place amongst economic rights. In this discussion we will briefly describe the historical process that led to the proclamation of the right to work, present some the arguments within political economy that intend to legitimize it, discuss the possibility of the existence of competition amongst human rights, debate on the responsibility of securing the right to work and finally analyse its policy implications. The general purpose of studying the right to work, here, is to argue that although it may be possible for a consumer centred economy to thrive despite the exclusion of a large part of its members from the production of social utility; this will not be acceptable for a people centred economy.

THE RIGHT TO WORK

It is in the French Constitution of 1793 that the existence of such thing as a human right to work, that is to say the right of an individual to a freely chosen job allowing a dignified existence, is explicitly recognized. Half a century later the discussions that accompanied the drafting of the French Constitution of 1848 are probably amongst the best documented debates on this matter, displaying passionate speeches of both the defenders and the detractors of the existence of a constitutional right to work. Before that, rather than a human right, work would most probably be considered as an outrage. Indeed, for the ancient Greeks as well as for the Romans, labour, even paid labour, was considered unfreedom, and therefore the idea of ensuring every individual the access to a paying job would seem senseless in the least. In the middle-ages and until the industrial revolution this association of work and deprivation of freedom is not as explicit but the depreciating character of work persists. In the fifteenth century to be enrolled in public works was a punishment and in the seventeenth century, in order to oblige some of the poor people to work, the state was forced to intern them in concentration factories.

During a very large period of time, it seems, therefore, that society needed people to work more than people claimed society for a job.

Although there are several references to the right to work from 1848 on, it was not until 1948 that, in the surge of the discussion about universal human rights by the recently created United Nations Organization, the right to work got explicit general recognition as a human right. In article 23 of the Universal Declaration of Human Rights (UDHR) it is proclaimed that:

- Everyone has the right to work, to free choice of employment, to just and favourable conditions of work and to protection against unemployment.
- Everyone who works has the right to just and favourable remuneration ensuring himself and his family an existence worthy of human dignity, and supplemented if necessary by other means of social protection.

This proclamation clearly states not only that people have the right to a job but also to a decent job, and therefore that ensuring the right to work and favouring any kind of job does not have the same meaning. Furthermore, people have the right to protection against unemployment, which should be understood as a set of mechanisms protecting an individual from becoming unemployed and not only from the consequences of being unemployed, that is to say that not only he should have the right to a monetary compensation for being out of a job, for example, but also that he is entitled to some kind of job security. Despite the legal weight that the Universal Declaration has assumed over the years it did not impose binding obligations on the governments of the signatory states. In order to afford individual countries to assume such obligations concerning human rights, two international treaties, the International Covenant on Civil and Political Rights (ICCPR) and the International Covenant on Economic, Social and Cultural Rights (ICESCR) were approved by the General Assembly of the United Nations in December 1966 after a discussion that lasted almost two decades. In 1976 both covenants came into force when they received the required minimum of thirty five ratifications.

Concerning the right to work the ICESCR proclaims the following:

Article 6

1. The States Parties to the present Covenant recognize the right to work, which includes the right of everyone to the opportunity to gain his living by work which he freely chooses or accepts, and will take appropriate steps to safeguard this right.
2. The steps to be taken by a State Party to the present Covenant to achieve the full realization of this right shall include technical and vocational guidance and training programmes, policies and techniques to achieve steady economic, social and cultural development and full and productive employment under conditions safeguarding fundamental political and economic freedoms to the individual.

Article 7

The State Parties to the present Covenant recognize the right to everyone to the enjoyment of just and favourable conditions of work which ensure, in particular:

(a) Remuneration which provides all workers, as a minimum, with:

(b) A decent living for themselves and their families in accordance with the provisions of the present Covenant.

There are two main dimensions to the right to work in both the UDHR and the ICESCR. The first one is quantitative and sustains that the right to work means the existence of sufficient jobs for everyone and not only the right to compete on terms of equality for scarce employment opportunities. It is not incidentally that The United Nations Charter, drafted in 1945, proclaims in article 56 that the United Nations shall promote "Higher standards of living, full employment and conditions of economic and social progress and development". Curiously, by the time the right to work was finally recognized along with the other economic, social and cultural rights, economic theory was in the process of abandoning the Keynesian distaste for involuntary unemployment, inflation becoming now the main threat to the economy, and unemployment some sort of variable manipulable to control inflation.

The second dimension of the right to work is qualitative and regards those criteria that determine whether a particular job qualifies as decent work. These criteria sum up what could also be called the rights of an individual at work and concern wages, working hours, working conditions, the right to join and form unions to protect their interests, and so on. Different policies are usually demanded to secure each of these dimensions, and although trade-offs between them could be expected, ensuring the right to work should not tolerate them. That is why some public action aiming to just creating jobs may not qualify to right to work securing policy if it contributes to erode the rights at work.

As with the former proclamations of the United Nations on human rights there is no schedule imposed on the countries to secure the right to work of their citizens. Indeed the obligations of State Parties regarding economic rights are subject to different interpretations. Some consider that they are only rights in manifesto sense and, therefore, are not justiciable and cannot be treated as individual legal claims, in other words they do not constitute a duty for others. In this sense the right to work can only be treated as a solemn statement of an important policy goal, implying at the most political responsibility only. For some others on the contrary, rights are always justiciable and, therefore, economic rights presuppose a duty for the community even if it is accepted that the realization of these rights could be restrained by the availability of means.

Indeed, the ICESCR states in article 2 that:

Each State Party to the present Covenant undertakes to take steps, individually and through international assistance and co-operation, especially economic and technical, to the maximum of its available resources, with a view to achieving progressively the full realization of the rights recognized in the present Covenant by all appropriate means, including particularly the adoption of legislative measures. This characteristic of economic rights can shed some light over why, since the ICESCR was approved and even in countries that have ratified it, more than just a delusion, employment for all seems to have expired as a goal, but it does not matter much when it comes to the definition of the goal of securing the right to work. The key question, therefore, is not to determine the legal implications for signatory countries as much as to recognize what are the obligations of society, and, thus, of the economy, if it chooses to pursue the enhancement of human rights, and of economic rights in particular.

THE GROUNDS OF THE RIGHT TO WORK

For those members of the international community that have signed and ratified the proclamations described above the process through which they were approved confers the right to work plenty enough legitimacy. But given the highly political nature of the process that led to their adoption (see Harvey, 2002) it should not come as a surprise that, especially among economists, economic rights are considered just a legal ornament. Indeed, because many economists take work as a commodity and, therefore, as a variable submitted to the supposedly natural law of supply and demand, they tend to be suspicious of political processes, and often take them as illegitimate interferences with the economic realm. Therefore, it may be useful to search for different sources of legitimacy for human rights, and economic rights in particular, other than political and philosophical, if one intends to make economics take economic rights seriously. The starting point of this argumentation is the universal acceptance of the right to live, not only in terms of the legal protection from being murdered, but also in terms of the access to the goods necessary to support life, and the perception that we are living in a merchant society, in other words a society where the great majority of these goods are obtained through purchasing.

In a primitive society where there were no property rights and no division of labour, to have the right to live, that is to say to have access to the means necessary to support life, would mean the same as to have the right to hunt, to fish or to gather. Once social division of labour made its appearance, and therefore, the subsistence mode of production was substituted by the first merchant mode of production, the access to the means necessary to support life implies earning an income. In this situation it is of the utmost importance that one has access to means of production, namely land. History followed its course and the means of production were progressively subjected to private appropriation and accumulation in the hands of a few, leaving the great majority of the population with no other alternative to obtain an income than to sell their work force. In its 1891 encyclical Rerum Novarum, Pope Leo XIII's reflects this position in a claim for a right to work:

The Preservation of life is the bounden duty of each and all, and to fail therein is a crime. It follows that each one has a right to procure what is required in order to live; and the poor can procure it in no other way than by work and wages.

Along with the recognition of the right to work as an interpretation of the right to live in an economy dominated by the capitalist mode of production, this citation also reflects the general view of the Catholic Church as far as the role of work is concerned. Work has always been glorified in the Christian tradition regardless of the Catholic versus Protestant fracture, partly because work fitted perfectly in the church's philosophy of submission regarding the poor, the humble attitude of the worker symbolizing the appropriate attitude for the servant of God.

Thus, in so far as work in the capitalist mode of production has become the main means of acquiring an income, to recognize the right to live is equivalent to recognize the right to work. The right to work is nothing but the metamorphosis of the primitive rights of hunting, fishing and gathering resulting from the advent of capitalism, the fatal and necessary consequence of property. In this view the right to work is sustained, not on some kind of absolute and universal legitimacy to which human rights cannot aspire, but on the historical conditions that characterize the capitalist mode of production, and namely the intrinsic inequality before the right to live of the individuals involved in the wage relation.

The wage relation, in theory, confronts two individuals that stand as equals, one expressing supply and the other, demand, in a market where labour is exchanged. In this commercial relation each of the parties is supposed to have the same need for each other in terms of asserting their right to live, each one being free to contract with the other. In reality, more than just a theoretical hypothesis, this is a myth. It is not difficult to understand that, as far as the struggle for life is concerned, one of the parties is strongly disadvantaged. A. Smith, himself, recognizes this fact in the Wealth of Nations. A landlord, a farmer, a master manufacturer, a merchant, though they did not employ a single workman, could generally live a year or two upon the stocks which they have already acquired. Many workman could not subsist a week, few could subsist a month, and scarce any a year without employment. In the long run workman may be as necessary to his master as his master is to him; but the necessity is not so immediate.

In the eighteenth century, in many European countries, the main problem was not so much unemployment as a consequence of a shortness of jobs but much more as the result of corporations that limited the access to a job. Therefore the first claims for a right to work meant a demand for freedom to compete for jobs, and not so much a demand for the availability of jobs for all. Although they differ in substance, it seems to me that some of the arguments set forth are valid to legitimize both conceptions of the right to work. A liberal economist like Turgot, for example, criticising the corporative labour market, says that: We owe to all our subjects the assurance of the full enjoyment of their rights; we owe this protection above all to this class of men who, having no property besides their work and their industry, are all the more in need and in right of a work (...) since it is the only resource they have in order to subsist (in Tanghe, 1989).

The differences in the origins of unemployment cannot hide the fact the problem for the worker is exactly the same, he cannot find a job. That it happens as a consequence of a shortness of jobs or as a consequence of overregulated job markets, is of little importance for him in his quest of subsistence. The socialists in the nineteenth century, for example, will also refer to this argument in order to justify their claim for a right to work, consisting now in the provision of jobs for all. In the discussions of the French constitution of 1848 Louis Blanc would state:

Is it true or not that all men have a right to live from the day they were born? Is it true or not that if a few end up seizing all the instruments of work, getting hold of the power of working, the others will be condemned (...) either to be slaves of the former or to die? (...) Is it fair that, if all men have the right to live from the moment they were born, the power of realizing this right should be concentrated in the hands of a few (...) (in Tanghe, 1989).

On account of the inequality established in the capitalist system between the two contractors in the labour market, freedom to work, in other words freedom to engage in contract, becomes meaningless without a right to work. This right to work stems not only from a natural right to live but also from the historical particularities of economic development, that is to say from the surge and consolidation of the capitalist system. This claim for a right to work makes all the more sense that the wage relation concerns, nowadays, more than three quarters of the active population in advanced countries, and that, to a certain extent, the economic system doesn't seem to aim the production of riches anymore, but plainly the creation of jobs (see Tanghe, 1989, p 223). The speeches of public servants announcing the captivation of large investments is very revealing. They seldom stress the satisfaction of consumers or the creation of wealth that will result from new activities, the emphasis is generally placed on the new jobs that will be supplied.

The next argument to legitimize the right to work can be found in the basic ethics of mainstream economic theory itself. Although one of the central aspects of mainstream positivist economics is the fact that it is supposed to separate the economic phenomena, belonging to the scientific realm, from those belonging to the moral realm, there is an intrinsic moral code underlying every exchange process. This moral code tells us that in order to satisfy human needs one has an obligation to produce some effort, to consent in sacrifice. In a commercial society where human needs are met through the intermediation of money, the counterpart that the economic moral code demands from individuals is a certain amount of work, or any other socially useful activity, except in cases of incapacity caused by obvious misfortune.

Even in the so called primitive societies, the absence of merchant exchange does not imply that one meets his needs without any sort of counterpart. B. Perret reminds, for example, that at the time of giving a child a monthly allowance, every parent knows instinctively that it is dangerous to dissociate money from effort. There is, therefore, an obligation to work and by definition an obligation corresponds to a right. "As well as there is no father without a son, there is no right without an obligation and vice versa" says N. Bobbio. The economic moral code presupposes, therefore, the existence of a right to work, in the same way that if there is a compulsory period of schooling for children of a certain age, none of them can be refused to attend classes. If the argument that you cannot seat any more children in the classroom seems unacceptable to drive back a child, in the same way it would seem unconceivable to refuse a job to someone on the basis of the fact that there are no more jobs available. This right does not concern a particular job, with a particular firm, but a political economy that fails to allow the citizens to contribute to the commonwealth fails fundamentally.

Let me now slightly presume of the reader's patience to explain why I sustain the existence of the moral code described above. Mainstream economics is based on the assumption that every human being naturally responds more or less in the same way when facing decisions in the economic realm; its nature is built upon the utilitarian principle according to which human behaviour is directed to obtaining pleasure and avoiding pain. The construction of this principle didn't result from the systematic observation of human behaviour. It is most probable that it was developed through an effort of introspection which constitutes the closest approach to the scientific method of psychology available in the eighteenth century. Although this conception of man was built upon strong convictions rather than upon rigorous research, these principles are confirmed by modern neurology. A. Damásio says that pain and pleasure are the "handles needed by the body to make the instinctive and the acquired strategies act effectively. He also stresses that pain acts to sound an alarm in order for the human being to be on its guards, urging him to avoid its origin and to correct its consequences, operating as a protection for his survival. Human beings sometimes do it instinctively but they also have the ability to connect one idea to the other and, therefore, to act rationally.

In this manner human beings, when behaving in the economic realm, are supposed to look for the maximum of pleasure involving a minimum of pain. When the intensity of pain equals the pleasure received one has reached the maximum of satisfaction that is possible, as one additional unit of pleasure would have to be obtained through the endurance of a higher amount of pain. It is important to stress that, in economics, pain is always present; there is no such thing as a maximisation problem which does not involve pain. Therefore the search for utility, that is to say pleasure, in an exchange based society, implies for the individual giving up a socially equivalent amount of utility, in other words it implies an endurance of pain. Economic theory considers legitimate, or moral, an exchange of pain with pleasure, but not an exchange involving pleasure only for the same individual. There is a line in the film "What's New Pussycat" that explains this problem better than any handbook in Economics. The character played by Woody Allen is sitting at the terrace of the Closerie des Lilas café in Paris and informs a friend that he has found a job dressing and undressing dancers at the famous night club Crazy Horse Saloon. Very happy for him, the friend asks "how much is it a month?", and Woody Allen replies let's say, "100 dollars a month". His friend looking astonished exclaims "that's not much!", and Woody Allen replies "that's all I can afford!". The moral utility, therefore, can only be obtained through some kind of sacrifice of utility of a different type, that is to say in exchange of a disutility.

Now, in mainstream economic theory, utility is obtained in the consumption sphere. Indeed, our needs and desires are satisfied through the destruction of the utility contained in the commodities we acquire. Logically, disutility should be endured in the opposite sphere, which is to say at work. This principle that considers work as a disutility and, therefore, as a counterpart of an utility, is very clearly stated in Genesis 3.19 when it announces that "you shall eat your bread in the sweat of your face" as much as in the modern accounting systems. The conclusion is that in order to enjoy the utility offered by the consumption of goods and services one is obliged to endure a disutility, which is to work. The moral code of mainstream economic theory presupposes, therefore, an obligation to work, thus recognizing implicitly a right to work.

The last argument in favour of the right to work is based on the social utility of the existence of such a right. There is a general agreement on the fact that unemployment is the cause of social harm in many aspects. Firstly, it is of one the major causes of poverty and it is associated with a wide range of psychological and physical affections which in common contribute to lessen the well being of many. Secondly it is believed to be at the origin of increased criminal activity and other anti-social behaviours. This last argument was also put forward in the nineteenth century in France namely by utopian socialist Charles Fourier. According to him, if the proletarian doesn't manage to sell his work force he has no alternative but starving or engaging in wrongful mendicity; he also said that the first task of politics was to find a new social order that would make proletarians prefer work to idleness and brigandage.

Thus if society is concerned with its sustainability, in other words if it organizes itself in order to last, it should be worried not only about the well-being of its population but also about preventing this well-being from getting affected by anti social behaviours. These behaviours can come not only from isolated individual acts, such as crime, but also from mass movements that can provoke serious disruptions. The rise of fascism in Europe in the pre-second world war and some forms of terrorism certainly found a fertile soil in the social discontentment provoked by mass unemployment. That is also the essence of H. Hude's argument. For him the free liberal society in which we live demands the realization of three conditions, the right to live, that is to say the access to the means necessary to support life, the obligation to work, without which there is a risk of social irresponsibility, and the right to earn its living, in other words the right to work.

Consequently, H. Hude sustains that acting against unemployment is a priority, as the stake is preserving the free society, and he adds that if it's impossible to respect this right to work in a given set of economic rules, then we should enrich this system and change its rules. In this view implementing the right to work is not only a duty for the community but also a necessity. In spite of the fact that the majority of economists will consider the argumentation above of heterodox extraction, I believe I have shown that the right to work also finds legitimacy in the liberal thought. Nevertheless, I consent that liberals most probably would find reasons for criticizing the right to work, and, therefore, I will present the essence of these critics. The first critic regards the fact that too much concern for rights could lead to the pursuit of policies that reduce rather than enhance human welfare, and in the particular case of unemployment, instead of creating jobs would end up boosting unemployment. The argument is based on the perverse effects on welfare of pursuing notions of fairness.

Stating that strict adherence to principles such as the right to work would have a perverse effect on the ability of society in providing everyone with a job could possibly be demonstrated, but it does not question whatsoever the legitimacy of a right to work; only the principles that are supposed to shape a rights-based methodology to implement full employment. The present article is not the place to analyze this perversity argument in depth. Nevertheless, it constitutes an important pillar of what A. O. Hirschman (1991) called the rhetoric of reaction and for this reason calls for a general comment. In relation to the quantitative aspect of the right to work, the debate on employment policies is very vivid and has not reached unanimous conclusions on which are the policies that have contributed to create jobs and which are those that have not.

But with respect to the qualitative aspect of the right to work, the rights at work, the validity of the perversity argument means that legislative measures that, for many years, have been implemented in a great majority of countries in the world should have worsen the working conditions of the population. This argument seems simply preposterous. A. O. Hirschman reminds us that in the nineteenth century the universal suffrage, one of the pillars of modern political rights, was also accused by many of having a perverse effect on democracy. The next essential argument concerns the intolerable intervention of the state in private affairs that would result from the recognition of the right to work. In the debates of the French constitution of 1848, the liberal L. Faucher says that: To proclaim the right to work it's to constitute the state as the purveyor of every existence, the insurer of every fortune and the entrepreneur of all industries. The right to work (...) is a seizure not only of what it is, but also of what might be, it is the community not only of the acquired wealth but also of the means that produce it. The fact that the right to work would be ensured by the state would also mean, for the liberals, the end of the freedom to work, that is of the freedom to choose where and for whom to work, which is contradictory with the right to work itself. It seems that, in the liberal's perspective, the right to work would compete with other rights, and Tocqueville adds that the right to work is also the denial of the right to property, on which he is accompanied by the not so liberal Proudhon. We will come back more thoroughly on this last subject in the next part of this article. The criticism of the right to work does not come only form the liberal side of the political spectrum, some progressive criticism can also be accounted. A progressive critique of the right to work can be found in authors like P. Van Parijs (1995) or G. Standing (2005). For the former ensuring the right to work would mean to give an unjustified privilege to waged labour, discriminating other forms of activity, either self employment or unpaid work. G. Standing criticizes the right to work because of its association with the use of labour to discipline the poor and the obligation to work that it conveys, and adds that Karl Marx himself was scathing about it, dismissing the notion as a bourgeois dogma. He disbelieves that the right to work can guarantee decent jobs, stating that many jobs undermine the right to work not only because, according to him, they involve controls and discipline that are not freely chosen, but also because many jobs in society are degrading and poorly paid. In this way it seems senseless to consider a right to something that not only does not promote the well being of the lower classes, but can also contribute to oppress them. Finally Standing criticizes the right to work on the same grounds as many liberals saying that this right can hardly be implemented as it would probably lock an economy into a rigid and ultimately stagnating mess, and would need a very complex evaluative and judgemental apparatus to impose on governments and employers some obligation to provide jobs.

The unworthy character of work and, as for the liberal critique, the improbable feasibility of a right to work, constitute, for Standing, a major obstacle to considering its legitimacy, then. In defence of the right to work one could reply that while claiming the availability of a job for everyone that wishes to work, one is not implying that everybody should be forced to work and that one wishes to protect the degrading jobs that still remain. In an ideal society people should probably work much less than today, or not work at all, and all the same be able to live in dignity. One of the reasons for the claim for a right to work is that we live in a capitalist society where a job is the major source of income, and therefore regardless of one's wish to live in a different system, it will be through giving a job to everyone that we will entitle the majority of the world's population with a decent life today. I personally believe that democracy should not be exhausted in the universal suffrage, and I also admit that many voting processes may have contributed to dissolve the democratic participation ideal, but should we, then, not protect the right to vote in our quest for a more profound democracy? I do not think so, and, for the same reason, believing that the ideal relation between income and work should be different from the one we have today should not prevent me from defending the right to work.

COMPETING RIGHTS AND THE CAPITAL VERSUS LABOUR CONFLICT

As we have seen above, in the nineteenth century the liberal critique sustained that accepting the right to work meant the denial of the right to property. The existence of a contradiction between the right to work and the right to property could explain not only why the legitimacy of a right to work has been often denied but also why the right to property seems to have been secured more effectively than the right to work. The first stage of the analysis of a possible competition between rights concerns the inquiry on the existence of such a thing as a recognized right to property. Indeed, the Universal Declaration of Human Rights proclaims the following in article 17: 1. Everyone has the right to own property alone as well as in association with others 2. No one shall be arbitrarily deprived of his property The right to work and the right to property are both, therefore, recognized human rights, and as such considered as valuable.

In this regard they should not be considered as competing rights. The 1993 Vienna Declaration on human rights proclaims in article 5 that: All human rights are universal, indivisible and interdependent and interrelated. The international community must treat human rights globally in a fair and equal manner, on the same footing, and with the same emphasis (...). This is not quite the opinion of N. Bobbio. He sustains that there are very few fundamental rights which do not compete with other fundamental rights, that one cannot assert a new right in favour of a group of individuals without suppressing some old right in detriment of another group of individuals. Therefore, according to Bobbio, in order to realize some human rights one is obliged to restrain the realization of other human rights (Bobbio, 1992, p 21). The question one should ask, then, is if work and property constitute a good example of competing rights. In the proclamation of the human right to own property there is no specification on what is supposed to be owned, but when some sustain that there is a conflict between the right to work and the right to own property, it's the property of capital that it is being referred to. Therefore, in discussing the competition between the right to work and the right to property, we are in fact discussing the competition between the right to work and the right to own capital. What is, then, the nature of this alleged competition?

According to the liberals during the discussion of the French constitution of 1848, the state should be responsible for the eventual implementation of the right to work, and on account of the fact that the state doesn't have proper resources, the enforcement of the right to work would have to be done through taxation and inevitably the proprietors would end up paying it. In this view the right to work is considered an amputation of the entrepreneur's income, and Proudhon himself says that, if profit becomes null, proprietors loose their interest in property, and if property is discouraged, property vanishes. The right to work would be an attempt on property, then, because it would diminish its profitability. If one accepts this argument in order to confront the right to work with the right to property one should consider many other attempts on the right to property.

Taxation sustains many activities, such a public works, justice, national defence, and many others; should they also be considered attempts on the right to property? Furthermore, there are many other sources of profit corrosion in corporations, like domestic and international competition, volatile consumers, inflation, should they also be considered attempts on the right to property? In the nineteenth century the reduction of the working hours was attacked by N. Senior on the grounds that profit was obtained during the last hour of the working day and that, therefore, any reduction would end up suppressing profit. More recently, the employers' reaction to paid vacations also brought the argument of diminishing profitability, but economic history showed not only that general profitability did not suffer, with the reduction of the working hours and paid vacations but also that new forms of property were developed in result of increased leisure.

It doesn't seem plausible, thus, to admit that the right to work and the right to property are competing rights. I believe that there is, indeed, a conflict but it does not concern these two human rights. It is true that economic orthodoxy has, somewhat successfully, conveyed the idea that labour rights clash with what has generally been called economic freedom, and that instead of a plain regulatory system, freedom of market has been upgraded to a fundamental right by this same orthodoxy. This approach is very contestable as this would suppose that the economy, or most often the markets, like individuals or the state, would have the right to be considered subjects of the law. Furthermore, this kind of argument was in fact used quite commonly to contest many rights and sometimes even basic human rights as during the Pinochet dictatorship in Chile. There is certainly a conflict; however we believe that it occurs between capital and labour and not so much between the right to work and the right to property. The first aspect of this conflict concerns the contradiction between labour considered as a productive factor and labour taken as end or an asset.

The second aspect of this conflict regards the microeconomic and the macroeconomic role played by unemployment. In the traditional economic system, labour is both a productive factor and an end. It is a productive factor that along with capital participates in the production of value and it is an end in the sense that in compliance to the moral code of economics one has an obligation to work. On the one hand, in order to maximise social utility through consumption, society should aim to supply the largest amount of jobs possible. On the other hand, firms in order to maximise their profit have to focus on minimising the use of productive factors, and, therefore, should aim to supply the smallest amount of jobs possible. There is, therefore, a conflict on what are the worker's and the firm's utilities. The second aspect concerns the role that unemployment has been called to play in order to regulate microeconomic and macroeconomic variables. The microeconomic aspect of this conflict concerns the fact that for firms unemployment is useful to attain certain objectives. For a long time, unemployment, and the spectrum of hunger, has been seen as some sort of menace to workers in order to make them work harder and stay in line. In this respect the more recent model trying to explain unemployment as a result of what has been called efficiency wages is nothing but a modern version of unemployment as an instrument to promote workers' discipline. In this case, involuntary unemployment may appear to be a nuisance for the workers, but for firms it may be considered, on the contrary, as a quite productive device.

Furthermore it appears that according to empirical studies the wage tends to be lower in regions where unemployment rate is high and vice versa, giving unemployment another important role in containing the firm's costs. In a sort of extrapolation of this last role, from the micro level to the macro level, the famous Philips curve argued that there was a long run trade-off between inflation and unemployment. Some economists like M. Friedman and E. Phelps contested that relation and considered that in the long run there seems to be an equilibrium unemployment rate, called Natural Rate of Unemployment (NRU), which persists regardless of the rate of inflation. The more modern version of the NRU takes a slightly different stand, considering the NRU an economic equilibrium that if reached by the economy allows inflation to remain constant, or in other words a rate of unemployment where inflation does not accelerate, this being called Non Accelerating Inflation Rate of Unemployment (NAIRU).

In one version or the other the principle is the same. Unemployment appears to be an instrument in controlling inflation and full employment is no longer a goal. The trade-off between unemployment and inflation embodies, therefore, the conflict between labour and capital. Workers are interested in the lowest rate of unemployment possible and capitalists are, on the contrary, specially interested in the lowest rate of inflation possible. The Philips curve and the natural rate theory of unemployment, in any of its vérsions, becomes, then, a clear theoretical and practical manifestation of the capital versus labour goal conflict, and more precisely the conflict between labour and financial capital, as inflation is supposed to affect primarily financial interests.

In this last example there is no case for talking about competing rights because there is no such thing as a human right to stable prices. It may be a strong preference, revealed eventually by a major part of the population, but it cannot aspire, whatsoever, to the same status as a recognized human right. The competing rights hypothesis can, therefore, be eliminated, leaving us with conflicting interests only. What is at stake, here, is, then, the weight of each of these claims in terms of public policy intervention. Writing about the funding of human rights, N. Bobbio says that the origin of the right to work and the right to property is historically determined by the nature of the power relations that characterized societies in the midst of which these claims were made. In a society where only the proprietors had active citizenship, it seemed obvious that the right to property should be taken as a fundamental right, and in the same way, as industrialization developed and the workers movements made their appearance, it became obvious that the right to work should be considered a fundamental right.

If the fact that, after the great depression of the 1930s, and until the 1980s, priority was given to fighting unemployment could, partly, be the manifestation of a shift in democracy, from a democracy of the proprietors towards a democracy of the workers, the fact that, on the contrary, fighting inflation appears nowadays to be more important in public policy, suggests that the weighs of the scales have been inverted. In the conflict of interests between capital and labour, the former seems therefore, to have recovered the dominant position that it had temporarily lost with Keynesianism. In turn, the fact that economic literature has never talked about such a thing as a Non Accelerating Unemployment Rate of Inflation (NAURI) is also very revealing of which of the conflicting sides as captivated the more interest from economic research.

STATE OR CORPORATE RESPONSIBILITY

If one believes in the right to work, one should also believe that each individual has a credit on society concerning the availability of a job. If there are not enough jobs for everybody, and, therefore, the individual's right to work is not being secured, to whom should he turn? As far as human rights are concerned it is usually considered that society is embodied, here, by the state, and that there is a duty of the state in providing the institutional protection of the citizen's rights even if, in the case of economic rights, it is weighed by a provision of the possibility. This means that there is a positive obligation of the state to do everything within reach to realize fundamental rights, although there is no subjective right of the citizen in this respect.

Therefore, the state is not forcibly legally responsible but can ultimately be politically responsible, in other words the state is accountable before the voters, not before the courts. What are, then, the actual obligations of the state in securing the right to work? This is a crucial question, although not easy to answer. Indeed, according to N. Bobbio the problem about human rights today, and particularly economic and social rights, is not so much about its legitimacy, as it is usually easy to obtain general agreement on its proposition, but about the methods of its enforcement. In this respect a line must be drawn between the quantitative and the qualitative aspects of the right to work. Regarding the qualitative aspect of the right to work, the rights at work, the role of the state is facilitated as they are more easily justiciable. Equality in the access to work, for example, can be enforced through legislative measures and the prevaricators can be taken to court, for not respecting it, the same can happen if a firm is not paying a certain wage when laws determine the existence of minimum wages. It is much more complicated as far as the quantitative aspect of the right to work is concerned.

In this case, should securing the right to work mean the obligation of the state in purveying the amount of jobs equal to the difference between the number of jobs that the economy autonomously requires, at a certain moment in time, and the number of jobs necessary to employ every citizen capable and wishing to work? Should it just mean that the state, being given instruments of policy, should use them in order to promote the supply of sufficient jobs in the economy? Finally, should securing the right to work mean that the state could legally force the firms to create jobs against their will? In Portugal, for instance, in the aftermath of the revolution of April 25th 1974, some large farms in the southern part of the country were obliged to hire workers, based on the perception that according to technical criteria, such as the extent of the arable surface and factor productivity, it was economically possible for the farm to support a larger workforce. Therefore, it can be both legitimate and enforceable to oblige firms to hire extra workers in certain conditions, but it doesn't seem easy to determine the criteria sustaining the state's decision for every economic activity, which takes us to consider that this kind of policy to secure the right to work cannot be generalized. Direct job creation by the state, and various sorts of incentives to job creation by the private sector are the only policies left, then.

Although there is a consensus on the fact that regarding human rights the responsibility for its enforcement is given to the state, some objections can be made. Firstly, at the time where there are growing claims from society that the state should get thinner, the budgetary consequences of the exclusivity of the state in enforcing the right to work are problematic. In 1848, P. J. Proudhon had already alerted for the fact that the enforcement of the right to work by the state only would probably lead to its ruin. Secondly, it may be considered unfair that being unemployment some sort of social nuisance partly provoked by the logic pertaining to the market economy, that it should be at the expense of the state only that the right to work should be enforced. Some interventions, like direct job creation, wage subsidies, tax cuts, and other policies can also be understood as an intolerable externalisation of social costs by the private sector, in other words we would be facing an unfair socialization of prejudice and a privatization of profit as an excuse to fight against the lack of work, this being specially true when the tax burden weighs mainly on labour income. In France, for example, the amount of subsidies distributed to firms in the name of joblessness, has amounted to 24.5 billion euros in 2004, which means that it has been multiplied by 40 since 1973. In France, again, in 2004, some 8,5 million workers have seen their wages complemented by state subsidies, and far from reducing the unemployment rate, this measure has above all allowed firms to be exempted of paying decent wages. The famous Speenhamland edict of 1795, also granted English rural workers a wage complement that was justified by the need to secure the right to live of the poor by the state. This intervention had the same perverse effect seen above. Land owners seized the opportunity to reduce wages making undue profit as these cuts largely compensated the taxes they had to pay in order for the state to finance the grants. In addition the small farmers that did not hire workers also had to pay the tax but, unlike large farmers, could not find a compensation to higher costs on lower wages. Furthermore, very small farmers that used to work on wages for the large farmers to complement their income also had to pay the tax, but could not benefit of the grant because they owned land. Thus, with the Speenhamland edict the bottom of the social scale in rural areas was charged more than the top and collected less benefits. This is a very good example on how the poor frequently end up paying for policies that are supposed to benefit them, and into the bargain contribute to raise the riches' profits.

Finally, how can one dismiss the firm from the responsibility of securing the right to work and at the same time promote what has been called Corporate Social Responsibility (CSR) as a new management paradigm. The introduction of the concept of stakeholders, that is to say individuals and communities affected by corporate decisions, operates a shift in the usual perception of the enforcement of economic rights in general, and the right to work in particular. Considering workers, including the unemployed, as stakeholders, one cannot say, therefore, that firms remain accountable before the shareholders only. Therefore, acknowledging that the majority of jobs are supplied by firms, it doesn't seem proper to keep on sustaining that securing the right to work, or fighting unemployment, does not concern firms somehow. It does not seem fair, thus, that economic rights, should be the exclusive responsibility of the state. One can reach the same conclusion when discussing this same issue through the efficiency point of view. As M. Freeman says, there was a widespread belief that the implementation of economic and social rights requires strong states that not only might be more likely to violate civil and political rights, but also that historically have not done much to secure the right to work either.

Would markets alone do a better job? M. Freeman believes unregulated markets will almost certainly do not. If one agrees with M. Freeman on this and also on the fact that Non Governmental Organizations (NGOs), which could theoretically substitute both the state and the markets, have limited resources and problematic accountability, securing the right to work, nowadays, demands, therefore, not only supporting a state apparatus of a certain dimension, which is contradictory with the liberal claims of a substantial reduction of public intervention, but also a deeper corporate involvement in the process. In the next chapter of this article we will analyze traditional job creating policies by the light of the right to work proclamations and propose a general draft of what should be a right to work securing policy stemming from this view of corporate and state co-responsibility.

ENSURING THE RIGHT TO WORK AND ECONOMIC POLICY

In order to propose policy solutions to secure the right to work one has to determine what is the extent of the damages to the right to work and what are the causes underlying those damages. We have seen that in different texts to secure the right to work means to ensure full employment. As full employment is different from zero unemployment, frictional unemployment having to be accepted because it is not prejudicial to society, quite on the contrary, a figure that apparently could raise some consensus on a definition of full employment is two percent of the active population unemployed. An analysis of historical figures can only but show that, although unemployment rates have fluctuated understandably, they seldom got close enough to the figure of two percent, even during periods of rapid economic expansion. Today, half a decade into the 21st century, the standardised unemployment rate in the countries of the OECD for January of 2006 is 6,3% and in the Euro area this same rate is 8,3% (OECD, 2006).

What strikes the most after reviewing historical figures on unemployment is that despite the fact that unemployment has always been present, society didn't seem to suffer extremely, and the economy apparently continued on its prosperous path. It seems as if men have become superfluous. Economics handbooks usually alert to the inconvenience of unemployment but the fact is that the sanity of the economy does not depend on fully employing all those willing and capable to work. If one adopts a paradigm within which economics should promote and deepen human rights, recognizing the ability of the economy to proceed prosperously, in spite of unemployment, should not mean, however, that one should find it desirable, and therefore comfortably ignore the right to work.

The next step to design right to work securing policies is to determine the causes of unemployment, taking for granted that if one attacks the source of unemployment one can solve the problem. Literature on labour economics displays an immense variety of causes of unemployment. The most often referred to are overregulated labour markets, characterized by rigid wages, weak mobility and excessive job protection legislation, overgenerous social protection schemes for the unemployed, mismatch of supply and demand and feeble economic growth rates. This palette of causes for unemployment most often require microeconomic interventions, devaluating the once all mighty macroeconomic policy inherited from the Keynesian tradition. If securing the right to work means ensuring full employment, than action has to concentrate on creating sufficient jobs to satisfy the jobs for all purpose, in other words on filling a job gap, either by increasing the labour demand, that is to say the number of jobs supplied, or by reducing the labour supply, that is to say by reducing the willingness of individuals to work.

If one consents in leaving the reduction in labour supply slightly in the background, ensuring the right to work means creating more jobs, therefore. Nevertheless, as we have warned in the beginning of this article not all job creation mechanisms qualify for right to work securing policies. What demands should such a policy meet, then? The first requirement is that it must contribute to fill the job gap, the second is that it should not jeopardize other requirements of the right to work, namely the rights at work, the third is that the jobs to be created should be productive and not just occupational and, finally, that the burden of securing the right to work should be equitably distributed among the members of society, in other words that there should be corporate and state co-responsibility.

Let us now review the traditional microeconomic job creating policies under the light of these demands of right to work securing policies, starting by labour market deregulation policies. Please keep in mind that the issue here will not be so much the effectiveness of these policies in creating jobs, as there is no consensus on the empirical findings concerning that subject, but mainly the ability of such policies in meeting the other demands of the right to work. Under the designation of deregulation of the labour market we can find many policies. Amongst the most important of them we can find the reduction of trade union influence, the introduction of wage flexibility, in most cases questioning the existence of minimum wages and the reduction of job protection mechanisms.

Excessive job protection allegedly discourages job creation based on the assumption that creating a job in a relatively warm period of the economy can become a liability as the firm will no be able to suppress it when, on the contrary, the economy cools off. Wage rigidity is considered an obstacle to the adjustment of demand for labour, preventing firms to create jobs at a lower wage than the legal minimum. Trade unions, in turn, are supposed to be responsible for wage rigidity and excessive job protection. Under the light of right to work policies these kind of measures are strikingly menacing of the qualitative aspects of the right to work, and therefore, cannot qualify as right to work securing policies. Wage flexibility is partly responsible for the importance of the working poor phenomenon, which is to say people that despite being employed do not manage to enjoy a decent life standard. This status concerns about 6 to 8% of the workers in the European Union of 15 members, and 10 % in the United States. Job protection softening is responsible for what has been called job precariousness that prevents many workers from enjoying regular working rights and benefits, such as the right to go on strike or to get paid vacations of the ICESCR), and are at the origin of a dangerous dualization of the labour market.

The progressive irrelevancy of the modern work contract is particularly alarming in this sense. Before the existence of a work contract it was the task rather than work that was being paid, which placed the worker in a weaker position in the bargaining process; the work contract, on the contrary, introduced two fundamental elements in a rights at work securing vision; it introduces rights and duties and, thus promotes equality of the intervenient parts in the labour transaction, and it brings true recognition of the entity of the worker and, therefore, the recognition of the worker as the central character in modern society.

At last, reducing trade union influence is clearly contrary to the text of the ICESCR, that specifically recognizes in its article 8 a) the "right to form trade unions and join the trade union of his choice". In conclusion, to create jobs under these circumstances can hardly qualify to right to work securing policies. Attached to labour market deregulation policies one can find very often reforms in the unemployment benefits system as a set of measures supposed to favour employment. It is said that overgenerous benefits, like high replacement ratios and long duration of the benefits, can reduce both the intensity of job search and geographical mobility, and, thus, be a cause of unemployment. Reducing these benefits would, then, stimulate unemployed workers to accept more easily jobs that otherwise they would refuse. The first comment that these policies suggest is that it seems very clear that they do not aim to fill the job gap. These measures tend to push unemployed workers to accept the jobs that are available, but do not to stimulate the availability of more jobs.

The second comment concerns the philosophy underlying these measures. By concentrating the efforts on reducing unemployment benefits what society is telling the unemployed is that, on the one hand they are the main responsible for their situation and that, on the other hand, the only solution to force them to work is by threatening them with misery, a pre-industrial workfare scheme revisited. Now, this is exactly what was aimed to be avoided in the right to work proclamations when stating "the right of everyone to the opportunity to gain his living by work which he freely chooses or accepts". Is someone acting freely when taking a job because his unemployment benefits have been withdrawn? Reducing the labour supply is one very obvious way of filling the job gap; it does not mean more jobs available but less people willing to work.

At first view it does not seem to attempt to the right to work ideal. Distributing subsidies to convince people to withdraw from the job market either temporarily or definitively has many positive aspects. It allows people to concentrate on activities they would not otherwise have been able to do and to which they attach great value, such as bringing up children or taking care of the elderly, for example. One should be cautious of eventual perverse effects that may surge, though. Early retirement incentives may put excessive pressure on eligible workers that nevertheless prefer to stay in the labour market, and contributes to the development of an age stigma. Temporary retirement with the intention of favouring families that have young children, for example, can also be transformed in an instrument of gender discrimination, as it may preferably push women out of the labour market.

One policy that can be very effective in delivering more jobs and has been used throughout history to alleviate poverty and reduce unemployment in many circumstances is the so called state as the employer of last resource, in other words the state being directly responsible for closing the job gap. In spite of the presumable effectiveness of this policy one cannot deduce that it is a right to work securing policy in the sense that it doesn't meet some of the demands that have been considered above. First of all it would place the burden of the right to work exclusively on the state, with all the budgetary and inequity consequences that we have already seen in the previous chapter. The second objection concerns the type of jobs the state would create. If these jobs are created in order to deliver public goods, one should ask why they haven't been supplied before based on the need for these goods, and not just on the need to create jobs.

If these jobs are situated out of the public goods sphere and are supposed to meet the needs of the consumers of private goods, one should question the reasons for not having seen them supplied by private economic agents, and therefore, should also question the nature of an economic system that leaves unsatisfied an important fraction of the populations needs. If these jobs do not correspond to any of the profiles, if they do not add utility, then one should ask why people should ioose any time doing useless work. Let's remind that in the right to work proclamations it is stated that in order to ensure the right to work the States Parties should "achieve steady economic, social and cultural development and full and productive employment", not considering what could be called just occupational jobs. Another set of policies often proposed, although only implemented in a sort of positive discriminative fashion, in alternative or as complements, is the use of wage subsidies and tax cuts to reward each new job created. Once again what seems to be a good idea might not be. On the one hand, there are some doubts concerning the effectiveness of these measures on account of the frequent substitution effects that have been noticed, in other words some firms in order to benefit from those subsidies or tax cuts, hire workers in substitution of other workers previously laid off.

On the other hand, it is another step of social cost externalization by firms, in the sense that they benefit from subsidies or tax cuts for jobs that they had to create anyway, thus receiving an unjustified bonus. Indeed, this set of policies can produce a windfall effect allowing firms to transform social costs into private profits and thus, unduly overcharge the public treasury. I will stay longer on the last of the policies to be scrutinized in this paper, work sharing or better said work time redistribution. The starting point of the proposal for work sharing as a means to fill the job gap and secure the right to work is the observation that for quite some time now it seems that there are not enough jobs available to satisfy everyone's right to work. By saying this I am not putting forward the argument of the lump of labour, in other words the belief that there is only a fixed amount of work to be done and that, therefore, there would be no other way to fill the job gap than by sharing this allegedly fixed amount of work amongst all the work force. This is considered to a fallacy and has been pointed out by many economists.

By this I mean that, despite the fact that there is no fixed amount of work to be done, jobs have, nevertheless, become a scarce asset. The argument that sustains the inexistence of this lump of labour concerns the fact that economic growth can increase the amount of work to be done. The problem about economic growth is that not only there are doubts about the sustainability of growth in the long run, but also that economic growth has not even been a reliable instrument for increasing the amount of work to be done, that is to say for creating new jobs. The fact that in France, between 1970 and 1992, there was a 70% increase in total output and only 6% in employment is a good example of this divorce between growth and jobs.

Redistributing work time by reducing work hours could, then, seem the only instrument available to reduce the job gap. French economist R. Passet (2000, p 249) states that, since the end of the nineteenth century, job creation, in France, is the outcome of working time reduction, not of economic growth. The concept of job sharing needs to be specified in order to avoid some objections due to misunderstandings. Job sharing cannot concern a mechanism within which employed workers come to share their meagre wage with the unemployed through the implementation of involuntary part time jobs, which constitutes a softer version of technical unemployment, that frequently several firms use in order to reduce the global wage burden. Work redistribution has to be understood in terms of a broader redistribution of wealth, and this should concern the whole of society.

The former way of understanding work sharing means that the redistribution of wealth would be done among wages only, and that is contrary to the idea that the burden of right to work securing policies should be equitably distributed. Work sharing experiences that have been implemented within this philosophy resulted mainly in lower wages and job precariousness, not qualifying, though, to right to work securing policies even if the job gap has apparently been reduced. Work sharing that meets the demands for right to work securing policies imply a reduction of working hours without a reduction in wages, which means that income redistribution is not done within wages only but within global income, including income from capital, therefore. In doing so, work sharing meets its major obstacle, which is the capital versus labour conflict around the distribution of income, or in other words the conflict between wages and rents.

As we sustained before, the concept of a Natural Rate of Unemployment in itself was a manifestation of this conflict. In this view the NRU, or the NAIRU, could also be interpreted as the level of unemployment resulting from the status quo on income distribution. Any change in the level of unemployment would suppose changes in the distribution of income, either through the reduction of working hours without the correspondent reduction in wages, or through the acceleration of inflation, both representing an erosion in the real level of rents. It doesn't seem probable that this distribution of income will be accepted without significant transformations in the political and economical systems; therefore, securing the right to work through work sharing within the prevalent system, or at least respecting its essence, will not be easy to implement without some kind of agreement between the state and the corporate sector. If subsidizing wages by the state means an unbearable socialization of costs for the community, reducing the work hours without reducing wages will also be an unbearable burden for the corporate sector. In this sense the much proclaimed Universal Basic Income (see Van Parijs, 1995; Revue du MAUSS, 1996; Standing, 2005; Howard, 2005) can come as a solution; not as a substitute for wages because that would mean nothing more than leaving the work cost unchanged for firms, but as a complement, with the purpose of distributing more equitably the burden of reducing work hours. This aim of equity would also mean that taxation would have to reflect this redistribution principle too, but this issue shall not be treated here as this article is not the best place to discuss equity in taxation.

CONCLUSION

Economic literature is abundant with respect to the role of human rights, many scholars having reached the conclusion that economic development, for example, benefits enormously of the care for human rights. The point of view of this article was, somewhat, inverted, as its purpose was to discuss the importance of Political Economy in the promotion of human rights. Indeed, deepening human rights is not only a political and institutional process that influences the economy but also the outcome of an economic process, not just because there are recognized economic rights but because deepening human rights in general may require transformations within the economic system. In this article I intended to contribute to the approach according to which one defines both the ends and the means of economic development in terms of human rights. The main goal of economics as a science is told to be the search for efficiency in the allocation of resources, but if one really cares about human rights, if one chooses to pursue the goal of human rights, this implies some changes in the economics paradigm. I believe that one should not expect the right to work to be secured through decentralized decisions by the market only, by the arts of some trickle down effect.

Economic rights, unlike rights of freedom, require state intervention but implementing right to work securing policies will be useless without the conscience of the need to secure simultaneously the two main aspects of the right to work; the quantitative and the qualitative. Most of the traditional state instruments that are displayed to create jobs tend to systematically minimize the qualitative aspect of the right to work and miss the point when dealing with the quantitative aspect. Plus, they tend to place the burden of securing the right to work exclusively on the state, which maybe considered unfair. The promotion of human rights has a cost and this charge should be as equitably distributed as possible, as human rights are supposed to benefit all. In the last part of the article I made a strong case for work sharing, as part of a much broader process of income redistribution, in order to secure the right to work. I should add, now, that this shouldn't be seen only as job creating mechanism. It should be taken also, and perhaps mainly, as a means for a deeper transformation in the economic system, a step not only to secure the right to work but to fulfil the dream of catching the inaccessible star, which is liberation from work.

CASE STUDY OF BANGLADESH

Bangladesh is a country of extremely impoverished people and land and other resources are owned by a small percentage of the elite. There is also a great deal of pressure on land due to expanding population. However, the most important lacuna is the lethargy of the ruling elite to create a more equitable system of rights management. It's noted that in 1970 landless people were 19.8%, it reached 68.8% in 2001. Reading this data when considering various schemes to distribute government owned land to the landless poor makes the situation look even worse. Right to property is an issue that involves both economics and law. Economic policies are in the domain of the urbanized educated elite professionals who dominate the resource management structure. Thus economists also serve the policymaking elite that has several laws laid out to transfer property to the poor but has not evolved a system to do so. The professional elite is not pro-poor.

The other half of property rights accessing depend on the legal system that in Bangladesh has been largely birthed by the colonial land reforms policies. It is agreed to be the most repressive land management and revenue collection system ever. Lawyers have a poor reputation as rights facilitators and are seen to be self-seeking and those involved in litigation generally suffer huge financial reverses and often end up as paupers. In fact, people are scared of the legal world and its not seen as sanctuary of the vulnerable. This has had a baneful impact on the wish of people to exercise their property rights.

The government is the largest landowner in Bangladesh and has a scheme to hand over such land to the landless. However, this has achieved limited success because the process has fairly excluded the poor in many cases, made it difficult to retain land if granted to the poor and caused both economic, legal and extra–legal suffering to the claimants. So although a scheme exists, it has not ensured property rights to those entitled, a section of the poor, due to the machinations of the local elite, the legal and the administrative system. Litigation is very expensive and is beyond the capacity of the poor to sustain.

However, poverty alleviation efforts are on to provide livelihood support to the poor and the extreme poor. In several cases, the poor have reached a level of economic well being to buy land. The extreme poor have been given land lease to pursue economic activities after land was bought by development agencies. There is some security in such cases and the rights to cultivation but property rights are still missing because land cost is high and retention of land is also beyond the capacity of the poor.

The situation of the minorities and women are at the bottom. Appropriation of Indigenous People's land on various grounds ranging from security measures to building eco-park is common. As their own laws governing ownership are not formally recognized by the State their land security is very weak.

Hindus have suffered loss over time and the Vested Property Act which allowed people to take possession of Hindu land on the grounds of absenteeism has given appropriation a legal face. Though no longer valid, its application continues, often in violation of law by another law.

In case of women, their legal right to land ownership (not just re inheritance) is governed by personal law that limits their ownership. In general, because of lack of resources, lack of bodily strength, customary practices etc, they are common victims of eviction from land. In case of women, their poverty also excludes them from property ownership especially in "female headed" households which are the poorest of families. Husbands desert them as economic burdens though some husbands' return only if they become economically better.!

Most disputes are settled in the informal legal arena that is village based known as salish. This is more accessible compared to the centrally imposed formal legal system. However, while a network of national elite runs the formal system, the local elite runs the other. In both cases, the poor get no chance of gaining or accessing property rights.

The gap is not within the legal regime but primarily in its application. Facing enormous pressure, power and lack of opportunities, which they are unable to cope with, there have been various form of resistance albeit very limited ones. Political landless organizations have almost disappeared in the last two decades but there are still a few NGOs left working with the landless.

These NGOs and organizations have agitated and won the advantage for the poor in several cases. But the scale of the problem is so high that it means such activities have a limited impact. Since in each case, state agencies had confrontations with the State machinery and almost each decision in favour of the landless was a reluctant one on the part of the State, there is only so much space that exists for agitation unless that is wider in nature and interrogates the nature of the State.

Recommendations

Limited and incremental achievement is possible rather than dramatic progress. There are historical and tradition evidence and practice of granting property rights to the poor and such a notion is well recognized, but its implementation is best with problems. Implementation of existing laws could help as is evident from both Bangladesh and India – West Bengal. However, while in West Bengal, there are trends towards some degree of structural change, the gain in Bangladesh through land transfer is episodic. So administrative reform is essential which will express the interest of the State that it wishes to establish property rights of the poor.

Khas land distribution is a good scheme but it has to be made better. The flaws have been spelt out very elaborately in various reports and it seems the problem is not in the scheme but in its implementation. Unless khas land distribution is considered a genuine opportunity to create property rights for the poor, the biggest opportunity will be lost. While the difficulties in implementing the scheme includes considering changes in the political economy that is unlikely to be realized immediately, there is a definite necessity for adjustments for more practical results. As that has not happened, an independent land distribution commission may have to be set up.

Poverty alleviation and property rights go together and that means that poverty alleviation activities must consider creating property rights as an essential component. The Commission understands that eradication of poverty without land distribution is almost impossible, at least in principle, must be respected because it will provide opportunities for poverty alleviation as well.

Data show that beneficiaries of khas land have seen an improvement in their life, though not without difficulties, and attendtion needs to be focused on the problems faced by the poor in accessing and retaining khas land. There is already some estimate of what is distributable and this realistic assessment must be made public information.

Both land and water bodies as well as common properties should be included along with environmental assessment guidelines so that land transfer doesn't lead to natural damages by (environmental) abuse and misuse of transferred lands. Recognizing that this is a tall order given the role of the elite at various levels, it needs to be pursued at a wider scale.

Only a handful of NGOs are involved in property rights creation of the poor. Not only must legal aid be scaled up, various NGOs should undertake some schemes including social mobilization activities in view of the complexities of the problem. As of today, the principal poverty-alleviation NGOs have not played a leading role in property-rights matters and this needs changing. For example, BRAC should get involved – incrementally one agrees — but right now there is a possibility of chanellling activists NGOs to take the route of even agitation for transfer of property to the actual and real poor. To go to scale, the bigger players need to be involved. NGOs must serve as the alternative that may create the space for rights seeking when the State is a rather a insipid player in the scheme things. Evidence suggests that various social groups is more prepared to play a pro-poor role, rather than the State.

Agitation should be encouraged albeit without resorting to violence. The system is so loaded against the poor and the informal system of law and order so armored against accountability that this would be a meaningful but new form of negotiation. It's possible to organize more effective form of exerting pressure.

Instead of strengthening the formal system at the cost of the informal one, one may look for harmonizing, spreading better forms of legal aid and ensuring large scale projects in conjunction with social mobilization that has proven effective in general poverty alleviation projects.

Special attention needs to be paid to the minorities, Indigenous People and women as their problems have both legal and applied nuances which are not easily and readily discernable. While Hindu property is no longer under the cloud of the VP Act, Hindu land grabbing continues unabated. There is inconsonance between the indigenous systems of land ownership and that of the State. Personal religious laws governing inheritance and sharing must be interpreted in accordance with the principles of fairness and equity that is inherent in all religions. And these must be codified in law.

The changes in gaining property rights will not come about immediately or quickly. One has to set up guidelines to say when the steps will be taken and how they are to be monitored and adjusted. Since the nature and partisanship of the State are skewed in favour of the landed, there is an now an emerging obligation on the part of the State to assert that the constitutional principles of fairness and socio-economic well-being (e.g., provisions of basic necessities of Article 15 of the Constitution) will be realized – or at least attempt to realize these – more vigorously and realistically. The State can not continue to shy away from its responsibilities for the well-being of its citizens, including right and access to property for those who have so far been marginalized and excluded through mechanisms, if not directly supported but then not discouraged, paved by the State.

4

Property Rights of the Poor

PROPERTY, POVERTY AND RIGHTS

There is near universal recognition that poverty has become the most endemic problem of our times. It has certainly resisted attempts of technology to fix it or "development" ideas sourced in western cultures through mediated efforts to end it. They have failed and this failure has now become a crisis. An extremely well off and terribly poor world has crated a dis-balance that not only militates against universally agreed rights of all people to lead a reasonably well socio-economic life that fulfills basic needs. This dis-balance also generates other forms of problems from which the developed world can't also remain free.

Poverty may well have become the greatest generator of socio-political unrest affecting global security. That is why an emergency search for solutions is on. In this framework, granting property rights to the poor and ensuring access to justice through legal systems is an important concern of the Commission on Legal Empowerment of the Poor.1 While discussing the topic in brief, one must remember that the subject issue is being discoursed in the background of hundreds of years of colonial and post-colonial rule where the evidence of pro-poor governance is not high. This paper has been prepared based on the country situation of participating countries in the review.

However, the absence of universality needs to be strongly emphasized as at this stage of late capitalism and extreme underdevelopment living together, the distortions have made generalizations difficult and sometimes dangerous prescriptions.

"Property rights can be defined and distributed in many different ways. Property rights are the legal and social rules under which economic and social behaviour takes place. For each physical or conceptual goods or services, there exist a bundle of rights to the various uses of the item. 5. Prosperity and poverty have become synonymous in Bangladesh, a country whose road to rapid pauperization took place through the British colonial land and revenue collection reform package, a botched attempt to introduce land reforms for ushering in capitalism in agriculture. This system, known as The Permanent Settlement (1793), not only favoured private ownership of land which till then mostly vested in the State, without ensuring if the landlords wished to be productive wealth makers or not. In fact, it was a dismal exercise leading to sub-infudation, absentee landlordism, peasant pauperization and socio-religious militancy and the rise of negative politics at the national level. Whether intended or not, it pauperized the peasantry and generated a series of classes and sub classes that, over time, have come to control most of the institutions and became the principal resistors to pro-poor land reforms.

It's also a fact that the legal system of Bangladesh was dominantly informal and organic when British colonialism took over in 1757, as it was elsewhere. However, with the introduction of the "Permanent Settlement "system, a formal and national system was required since the law though "formal and national" affected the "local and informal" society most. A huge number of litigations arose over property rights of the wealthy and this generated a new class of professionals, the lawyers, whose prime source of income came from land related cases. This tradition is still maintained and lawyers are not looked upon as the friends of the poor. In fact the judicial system inspires more fear than respect. Common social mythology is that a case will drag on, create many complications and ultimately ruin a family in every way.

Thus, land and legal reforms are not connected in the sense of providing relief but as that of suffering due to land related conflict. Gathering legal justice through formal channels of law is rarely considered a fact of life. Thus, law as a source of ruination greatly influences public imagination on property rights of any class. In case of the poor the situation is thought to be worse because they rarely have any property and the most they have are their homestead patch which is under threat of takeover by the powerful ones.

"Despite their centrality to peaceful and sustainable growth, land issues have often been ignored in the Poverty Reduction Strategy process". It has also been inferred that the poor have access to property that lie as dead capital and they can be turned into assets. However, such statements in case of (very) income poor countries like Bangladesh are likely to cause confusion as the total land availability is itself low and the distribution of land through legal reforms is only a part of the solution. While land is desirable for all, the low level of market development has not been contingent on land reform measures only. A host of factors have played parts both in poverty alleviation attempts and growth of the rights movement in recent years. Unlocking the potential of land may follow unlocking livelihood opportunities.

An essential role of land as security or collateral for economic activity is also contestable because of the micro-credit system where loans are not granted on the basis of land or resource collaterals. Formal system with its collateral and often corruption by-passes the poor while the extreme poor have only very recently gained attention.

However, the search for land as an economic and social goal is very much valid and pursued in Bangladesh by all classes. In fact, the complexity of the issue is partly the result of the fact that all classes are in search of land but only a few can acquire it, making land ownership an essential ingredient of class installations. Before the property rights of the poor are secured, its important to ensure that the poor can have access to property, especially land. Most poverty alleviation efforts have tended to circumvent the land ownership issue of the poor because for many it's an impossible venture to pursue as land prices outmatch household resources by many times and access to government owned land is also very limited.

LAND, LAW AND REFORMS

State authorities are not unfamiliar with the existing property and land rights situation. A whole host of laws are in operation to transfer land to the poor through established legal means. The Government of Bangladesh is the largest landowner in the country, It is constitutionally committed to transfer land to the poor and secure their property rights through several initiatives. Thus the legal intention is certainly there which can't be said about the operational side of the same matter. The situation has over time been gradually declining and we note the following pattern in land ownership or its absence.

"According to the government, 57% of the people are landless, poor and live below the poverty level. But NGO sources say that the number of landless is more than 68%." Land ownership pattern over time as cited in the paper is as follows:

Table :

1947- 14.3 %

1970- 19.8%

1975- 32%

1984 –46%

2001- 68.8%

According to Kamal, 10% of absentee landowners own 51% of total cultivable land. Rich and middle farmers own 71% of total land and receive 31% of the institutional credit.

The concentration of land ownership must also be read as an indicator of the governance trend. It's a society where the powerful have a stranglehold on resource distribution with a low level of accountability. The Bangladesh Economic Association in its annual report has provided the following data8 "Total land availability in Bangladesh is 37.4 million acres of which 60% are agri land. One crore 6 million acres (43%) are privately owned. 2.4 million acres are contested in the courts. About 2.5 million land related court cases are on. About 10 million acres of land are used by the government. Identified khas land and water bodies total 5 million acres. 2.1 million acres are under the government control through the Vested property Act. Abandoned property amount to 1 million acres."

"Of the 140 million inhabitants, 91 million (65%) are poor, 45 million (32.1%) are middle class and 4 million (2.9%) are rich."

This says that social relationship with prosperity and poverty must be recognized that is linked to the state policies. Land can certainly be distributed or used more equitably than it's being done now. However, the fact that such a trend has become dominant is significant in terns of understanding the role of the State as a mediator in ensuring rights.

A major sector of concern has been the rise of the extreme poor as a class or sub-class of the poor who exist without any protection or sustainable income. Consuming less than 1850 kcal a day, they have been routinely overlooked even as micro-credit borrowers because they have no income or assets to start up self-employment even. They are unable to resort to other resources to pay back the loan which is scheduled immediately for repayment under the micro credit system. In many ways, they have become socio-economic leftouts.

This population segment has risen to a very high percentage, which has been variously been estimated, from 20 % to 31%. When one third of the national population is unable to participate in any income generating activity, the crisis goes beyond that of property ownership. One is forced to interrogate the nature of the state. The government is yet to undertake any social programmes though the country's largest NGO- BRAC -has undertaken a project titled Challenging the Frontiers of Poverty – Targeting the Ultra Poor that is directly handing over assets to the ultra poor. It has covered 100,000 families from 2002 to 2006. Grameen Bank is also supporting programmes for the destitute section of the population. However, there is no national programme to tackle this issue.

Thus property rights, or more explicitly livelihood support and rights, are being generated through a system of loans or grants to the poor by the NGOs. Obviously, the main delivery is credit. Through this system millions have acquired one form or other of economic rights and this deserves pondering. Direct property and land rights concerns the government handing over khas or their own land to the poor. This is a lengthier and more complex process, which has been later discussed in this paper. It's through this two dominant process that chances of the property rights of the poor have a possibility of emerging.

A lot of the above reads as a stream of consciousness by someone not very well informed on land laws or property rights issues.

LEGAL SITUATION AND PROPERTY

Property rights are fundamental but there is no full agreement about what it should mean and how it should be applied. There are divergences amongst experts who deal with such issues — legal experts, economists and development workers rarely sit together to discuss how to go about the problem. The following quotation will illustrate.

"Law like economics is comprised of technical terms that carry specific meanings. " When economists ignore the meanings of law there is confusion and the resultant analysis may be less coherent."

The problem therefore is multiple dealing not only with the complexity of the lack of property rights but also of coherence amongst those who wish to resolve the problem.

In Bangladesh, the general legal environment is not conducive to the poor and securing of property rights. This position is not a concern of property rights alone. It's an overall situation where law has become a profession that provides opportunity to achieve social power and status rather than provide legal services especially to the poor. This is not an argument against lawyers but a statement concerning the system within which law operates.

While there was a hallowed aura about the higher judiciary, it has over the last few years been significantly damaged due to some contested decisions, both judicial and political. Proximity to political decision making, lobbying for offices, controversial court decisions, insistence on their higher status without a perceived higher moral positioning, etc have contributed to this perception that holds sway now.

The subordinate judiciary has fared worse as they are perceived to be under the executive and which has severely curtailed their independence. The Supreme Court order to separate the two has not been followed by the executive in the last five years citing administrative inadequacy. The legal community is almost totally partisanized into two political groups causing weakened independence. The lawyers, barring a few, don't enjoy public confidence as public servants or upholders of a legal system. In the month of November/ December 2006, lawyers attacked each

landless people of the char filed a case in the Court for getting yearly lease of the land and the Court gave verdict in favor of the landless people. Hence from 1985 onward the 44 families dwelling in the char started cultivating the land by taking yearly lease. In 2005 when the landless farmers appealed for lease, the lease was ceased without any valid reason by the TNO violating the Court verdict. On the other hand the influential elite, by exerting political influence, with the assistance of the local administration and using the police force made plan to plunder the crops of the marginal farmers. On behalf of the TNO it was announced that, "2/3rd of the paddy should be deposited in the office of land administration (from this the local influential elite will receive one portion and the other portion will be received by the local administration together with the lease money)."

In this situation the landless people represented by lawyers and leaders of landless groups met the district administration officer and submitted a written complaint. The DC after reading the papers of the landless members and scrutinizing the evidences gave an oral declaration for reaping the paddy. But next day the DC called the landless leaders and said "the order given by TNO will remain valid". In the mean time the landless people made preparation to reap the crop sown with their sweat and blood. The landless farmers from the neighboring areas also volunteered to help them in cutting the paddy without any payment. Almost 3 hundred landless farmers managed to reap and store the paddy from 36.86 acres of land on 10th December 2005. At night the police, directed by the influential elite, came to take the paddy. But the landless farmers sat united in vigilance to guard the paddy. The police realizing the situation was forced to turn back.

On 11 December 2006 nearly two thousand male/ female landless members barricaded the office of TNO against terrorist attack and police operation. In the face of the demand of landless members the TNO was compelled to inspect the area in person and he declared that after two days decision will be given. In this situation the landless members guarded the paddy unitedly. But even after two days when the TNO did not give any decision the landless members threshed the paddy and distributed it among themselves.

5

Deconcentration International Society for Political Economy

Larger concentrations of economic power increasingly endanger democracy, the constitutional state, as well as the ecological and social foundations of society. How we live – what we eat, how we work, what we learn and recognize, how we communicate, and which air we breathe – is determined more and more by large corporations.

It is said that this new unfreedom is unavoidable. "There is no alternative!" The growing power of worldwide conglomerates is justified today in the same way that; in former times, feudalism and state socialism were. Concentrations of economic power are seen as inevitable.

We are convinced: There are alternatives! The existing structures of economic power can be overcome. Social Science has to make its contribution to this cause, just as the thinkers in the Enlightenment worked against the economic and politicaleconomic interests of their own age.

We founded Deconcentration International to develop a renaissance of "political economy." Deconcentration International works at creating concepts, which prevent and dismantle economic power. We address both the scientific and the general public.

The concentration of economic power is made possible by numerous powersupporting regulations in constitutions and in individual laws. What is created by politics can also be abolished by politics.

DECONCENTRATION INTERNATIONAL ADVOCATES A DIFFERENT ECONOMIC CONSTITUTION

Deconcentration International is an interdisciplinary and international forum for work in the social sciences and for debates in economic and constitutional politics, critical of economic interests. We join the intellectual and political tradition based on human rights. Despite the success in establishing liberal institutions – democracy and constitutional states – the concept of a free society, which dates from the great bourgeois revolutions, has only partially established itself. A corporate-free market economy – the economic system for which the radical-liberals fought – has never been realized, despite brief successes.The original concept of an economic order compatible with human rights is almost completely forgotten. Deconcentration International wants to revive, in the scientific as well as the political public, the tradition of minimizing power. The existing economic system, the oligopolistic market economy, cannot be reconciled with a liberal constitution. We need another economic order.

DECONCENTRATION INTERNATIONAL WORKS FOR CONCEPTS TO MINIMIZE ECONOMIC POWER

Although they come from different work contexts and countries, the members of Deconcentration International share a fundamental perspective: "It is not the misuse of economic power that is to be fought against, but the economic power itself."

How can power minimization be accomplished? In the different areas of law – corporate law, liability law, trademark law, patent law, tax law, and constitutional law – the prevailing legal circumstances have to be changed so that the impetus towards concentration of power can be transformed into a tendency towards deconcentration. For example, the copyright and patent law established by the government makes it possible for Microsoft to monopolize markets. What would happen if the states no longer protected the software monopolies? How would it be, if the principle of "open sources" – with the help of democratic laws and constitutional rules – were extended to large areas of the economy ? What are the chances, and what are the problems? These are the questions asked by Deconcentration International.

Deconcentration International is an open forum: for city planners with ideas to minimize the influence of big investors, for biologists and farmers engaged against biopatents, and for constitutional lawyers who wish to develop constitutional proposals for a corporate-free European democracy. Today the concentration of economic power has became a global problem. At the same time, new chances for dissolving oligopolies are growing. If the legal framework is rearranged towards the minimization of power, the potential of technologies which have been neglected until now (for example, solar technology) can be expanded. What could be achieved if our ecological resources (for example, water and seed) and our infrastructure (for example, Internet and electricity) were withdrawn from the corporations and changed into "common ground" of the globalized economy.

DECONCENTRATION INTERNATIONAL ADVOCATES THE RESPONSIBILITY OF FREE SCIENCE

The constitutions of democratic states are based on the knowledge that human rights and their institutions, such as a free press or an independent judiciary, are incompatible with dictatorship. Deconcentration International works to develop this constitutional thinking . Not only the state can censor, but so too can private enterprise. For example, the Murdoch Corporation turned off the satellite transmission for BBC programs to China, not tolerating any critical reports on the regime in Peking, due to their interest in the enormous Chinese market. What applies to media groups is also true for the world-wide oligopoly of agrarian chemicals, for the financial corporations that are active on a global scale, or for the petroleum, and automobile enterprises which control their markets. The concentration of capital on a scale that was once inconceivable, brings about new types of human rights violations. Lawyers, economists, and other social scientists have to consider the new threats to freedom and the reasons for poverty, analyse them, and develop solutions. New questions have to be asked. Corporations, just like human beings, have their own basic rights and are thus inviolable in their existence. Can this be justified? Is the limited liability of joint-stock companies compatible with a free market economy? Are large corporations unconstitutional, or does the politics of deconcentration conflict with the basic law of property? Since the beginning of the seventies, researchers have repeatedly warned of the "limits of growth. "In 1992 most of the Nobel Prize winners demanded that the destruction of climate, water, ground, forest, and animal and plant species, be stopped. To this day however, the influence of the corporations that profit from the destruction of ecological resources has prevented the democracies from taking necessary measures . For this reason researchers today have to go one step farther. Democracy and the ecological foundations of life can only exist when limits are set to the growth of corporations. Economists, lawyers, political scientists, sociologists, engineers and natural scientists, all have to take positions in public on the reasons for the paralysis of democracy, with its far-reaching ecological and social consequences. In addition, journalists, pedagogues, editors, artists, open-source programmers, independent managers, farmers, and members of ecological groups and fair-trade organizations are invited to work with Deconcentration International. A political economy of deconcentration can only come about when theoretical thinking is joined with practical experience in economics, stet.

Deconcentration International advocates the independence of universities from the large corporations, and is against the destruction of a democratic public by the concentration of media power. The freedom of thought is in danger: Obtaining research funds from large corporations is increasingly considered proof of productivity. At the same time, more and more often representatives of big industry are members of university boards. Thus questions that threaten the interests of corporations cannot even be formulated. Science that works in the interest of large corporations gives up its own scientific character. Science is only rational if it is critical of power. Corporate power destroys the power of free thinking, and the power of rational thought.

The so-called "Neoliberalism" has anti-liberal structures. The Neoliberals support the protection of large corporations by the state. This is the opposite of Liberalism, which originally opposed the concentration of economic power, state or private. What is presented today as a "modernization" of scientific activity is actually a relapse into mercantilistic thinking.

6

The Political Economy of Human Insecurity in Sub-Saharan Africa

As a paradigm, human security was popularised by the UNDP report of 1994. In this report, the UNDP sought to shift attention from the state to people as the key referent of security. This shift comes against a background of the dominance of a security concept that was defined in relation to the territorial state. It saw threats to security as primarily external in source and, by implication, relied on military might to respond to such threats. The obsession to protect the borders of the state against external aggression overshadowed the vast array of threats – social, economic, political and environmental – facing people within the territorial state. The thrust of human security is thus to shift the focus from the state to people and to make the latter the main referent of security. Thus at the heart of the human security paradigm is the security of people. Consequently, the definition of human security as expanded by the UN Commission on Human security is simply "freedom from fear, freedom from want and freedom to take action on one's own behalf". Establishing human security, according to the report, requires overcoming economic, health, environmental, personal, community and political insecurities.

Human insecurity has attained high levels in Africa, especially in Sub-Saharan Africa (SSA). Over 40 percent of its 800 million people live below the poverty line and this percentage is predicted to rise. Also, Africa has high incidents of conflicts and instability. Currently, Ivory Coast, the Great lakes region, Somalia, Darfur (Sudan), and the Horn remain highly volatile. Africa currently has the largest contingent of UN peacekeepers – 17,000 strong in the Democratic Republic of Congo (DRC). In addition, Africa is ravaged by various diseases, and is currently the global epicentre of the dreaded HIV/AIDS. Food and nutritional inadequacies have reached monumental proportions. Over 28 percent of all children in SSA are underweight as a result of malnutrition. And, while the average percentage of under nourishment in the developing world is 17, that for SSA is 33 percent. Southern, Central and the Horn of Africa continually remain vulnerable to droughts, painting a bleak scenario for food security. At the same time, environmental degradation is on the increase, reflected in deforestation, desertification, soil erosion, pollution, and depleting fish and game stocks. The ecological problems in Africa are compounded by the inability of African governments to establish credible environmental regimes and their willingness to trade the environment for scarce foreign exchange. The combination of all these disconcerting developments presents SSA as an indisputable region of high human insecurity.

While there is a great deal of consensus on the pervasiveness of human insecurity there has been scant analysis on its fundamental causes. In the case of SSA, the tendency has been to adopt the usual neo-classical formula and point to factors that are predominantly internal to the region. I have argued that what is frequently regarded as internal causes of insecurity such as poverty, conflicts, environmental degradation, food, health and educational insecurities are, in fact, manifestations of the crisis. In perspective, these are the product of more fundamental causes, including endemic structures and practices within the international system. Poverty is not natural; no child is born in Africa to be poor and destined to lead an insecure life. Neither does poverty descend from the skies like rain or hail; it is rather the consequence of a more fundamental cause. The same could be said of conflicts. No people in their right senses like to constantly live under conditions of violence and war that threaten their personal or community security.

There are always deep-seated causes that spark or predispose people to violence. It is therefore not enough to point to human insecurity without identifying its root causes, especially when the problem is menacing. Identifying the causes of a problem is necessary for a fuller understanding of its implications. Above all, understanding and mastering the causes of a problem enhances opportunities for effectively addressing it. Thus, in order to prescribe an effective antidote to a problem, it is imperative to diagnose its root causes. A deviation from this standard practice leads to a diagnoses of the symptoms rather than the root causes. In explaining the underlying causes of human insecurity in Africa, the study drew on the theoretical explanations outlined by Johan Galtung. According to Galtung, human insecurity is caused by violence, which can be direct or indirect. In the former the perpetrator of violence is visible. In the latter, variously referred to as "structural violence", or "social injustice", violence is built into structures in the form of unequal power relations and unequal life chances. This prognosis provides a good context for understanding human insecurity in SSA, given its relation with the industrial north.

For example, an asymmetrical trade pattern was established between Africa and the west since colonialism, which disadvantages the former. SSA has been unable to alter this pattern largely due to the operations of global institutions, structures and regimes. The dominant Breton Woods institutions, including the World Bank, the International Monetary Fund (IMF) and the World Trade Organisation (WTO) have functioned to maintain the structural imbalance between the north and south, leading to vast inequalities between the two regions. The reality of north-south relations fit into the explanation of both direct and structural violence. Although some may argue that the structural violence argument is deficient in failing to explain environmental insecurity, the study demonstrated that ecological insecurity in SSA is part of the structural crisis generated by globalisation and the international economy.

The study emphasises that globalisation has become a dominant force in the global economy. It imparts consequences that are both positive and negative. In the case of SSA, the negative impacts of globalisation outweigh its positive outcomes. Among other things, globalisation integrates SSA economies into the bigger global economy; it opens up Africa's economies to global competition in which the former are simply too fragile to successfully compete; Africa's economies have been delivered to multinational companies who flout environmental laws with impunity, while regional and social inequalities have been deepened by the different abilities of people and regions to respond to the challenges posed by globalisation or tap the opportunities it creates. Thus, while grafting SSA in to the global economy, the latter is simultaneously left at the margins, leaving Africa in a precariously ambivalent position. Globalisation has also inspired further sources of human insecurity through liberalisation, which came in the form of structural adjustment programmes (SAPs) and which requires Africa to open up its markets; democratisation, which has resulted in stage-managed elections that have resulted in conflicts and other forms of contestations. A further dimension of the globalisation trajectory is the escalation of SSA's debt burden, which has not only attenuated the ability of governments to deal with human insecurity, but also became a means of decapitalising Africa. The original purpose of SAP was to enhance Africa's ability to repay its external debts through the imposition of austerity measures.

Under the SAP regime credit lines were opened to countries judged to be rigorously implementing adjustment reforms. In the 1980s, Ghana and Uganda received large volumes of aid on account of their impressive adjustment record. However, such credit lines were never acts of charity. Rather, they were loans to be repaid with interest. The ultimate effect was that as African countries adopted SAPs and accessed new lines of credit, their external debt grew concomitantly. Once the debt emerged, it became a self-generating phenomenon and, worse of all, causing a reverse transfer of funds from Africa to the west. For example, between 1970 and 2002 SSA received $294 billion in disbursed loans. Despite paying out $268 in debt service, it still had a debt of $210 billion by the end of 2002. In total, during the 1970-2002 period Africa received some $540 billion and still shouldered a debt of $295 billion after paying back close to $550 billion in principal and interest. Even by 1996 arrears on Africa's debt had reached a whooping $64 billion, which was more than 25 percent of the total indebt. The debt crisis had spin effects on human insecurity in SSA.

Debt created the need for further external aid and this generated further indebtedness, imparting a funny scenario of digging a new pit to fill an old one. To be credit worthy and eligible for further loans, indebted countries needed to demonstrate an ability to service existing debts. This often required the commitment of large proportion of the national budget to debt service. In 1990, for example, Madagascar spent the equivalent of 7.2 percent of its GDP on debt service compared to just 2.1 percent and 1.2 percent on education and health respectively, while Congo spent nearly 4 times more on debt service than on education and over 12 times more than on health. Similarly, Zambia's debt service as a percentage of GDP in 2003 was three times and four times more than health and education respectively. Since the inception of the debt crisis, SSA countries have been devoting appreciable percentages of their national budgets to debt servicing. The pressure to repay debts thus diverts resources from infrastructure and services that are critical for alleviating poverty and human insecurity.

At the same time, foreign direct investments (FDI) and overseas development assistance (ODA), are on the decline. Although this has recently been increasing in certain countries (Angola, South Africa and Mozambique), and regionally in southern Africa, the flow of FDI to Africa has on the aggregate declined from $8.1 billion in 1996 to $6.1billion in 2000.

Although this rose to a high of $13.8 billion in 2001, it fell again to $7 billion in 2003. Similarly, net ODA has plummeted from a high level of $28 billion in 1990 to $16.4 billion in 2000. In spite of numerous international trade agreements promising Africa with access to world markets, its share of world exports remained at just 1 percent at the turn of the century although this was 4 percent in 1960, while its share of world trade has plummeted from 2.7 percent 1990 to just 2 percent in 2002. Against this background, Africa remains the most marginalised continent in the contemporary global economy. Its role has been limited to serving as a marginal market for northern industries. The little investments trickling down to SSA are concentrated in the capital-intensive extractive industries. While shunning Africa, the west has been giving more "aid" to farm animals in the form of subsidies. In 2000, the European Union's (EU) total aid to SSA amounted to $8.00 per African, while its subsidies to cows averaged $913 per cow. Japan's case was even more absurd. In that year Japan's total aid to SSA averaged $1.47 per African, while its subsidy to cows averaged a colossal $2,700. A moralist will argue from this evidence that industrialised countries price the value of cows above Africans.

Although terrorism is increasingly being recognised worldwide as a new source of human insecurity, this view is contested in Africa. Terrorism has historically not been an issue of concern to Africa although the continent displays conditions that should ideally inspire terror. Rather, what is emerging as a new source of human insecurity is the proliferation of anti-terror legislations, which are passed by African governments at the behest of the US. In the aftermath of 9/11 the US has evolved a policy of rewarding countries enlisting in the war on terror and punishing those apathetic or oppositional to the war. The dominance of the US in the post-cold war era, along with the associated benefits in the form of US aid, has presented involvement in the war on terror an irresistible offer for Africa. However, instead of securing citizens, anti-terror laws have rather provided leeway for the state to clump down on legitimate opposition, democratic forces and critical voices. In the process, these laws vitiate human rights, undermine human security and are rapidly reviving Africa's old and discredited practice of "constitution without constitutionalism." Thus, if anti-terror laws are becoming sources of human insecurity in Africa, they too are externally inspired.

The disconcerting development associated with terror and anti-terror legislation in Africa underscores the limits of the human security concept. This is particularly imperative in SSA where there is an ever increasing tendency for the concept to generate huge public expectations. Among other things, human security has so far not replaced the state as the dominant referent of security. There are still a number of intra- and inter-state conflicts whose resolution requires the active involvement of the state. Moreover, some of the internal conflicts, especially those involving rebels are targeted at the state. Also, the African state continues to be the author and the key determinant of security. All these mean the state's centrality in the security discourse in Africa may remain protracted and unchallenged for a long time. It has also to be noted that human security is not synonymous with development. Human security is rather an auxiliary factor of development. Thus, even attaining the goals of human security does not mean an improvement in the standard of living.

These limitations, along with suspicion among some countries that human security is an ideological tool or a pretext for humanitarian intervention by powerful states raise concerns not only about the efficacy of the concept but also about its universal acceptability. Ultimately, this perception may limit the utility of the concept, both in theory and practice in Africa.

However, even if the theoretical pretensions of human security are set aside, the practical side still needs to be addressed. Conflict, poverty, diseases, bad governance and human right abuses and environmental degradation needs to be halted. It is argued that this should be the challenge not only of Africans but also of the western countries who, have by their policies, contributed to the crisis in Africa. Western countries have to be part of the solution, moreover because they will contend with the consequences of the problem in the form of increased African migration to the west, inability to repay debt and even in an inability of Africa to continue to serve as a marginal market for the west. For these reasons the west should abolish the policies that have tended to hurt Africa, such as agricultural subsidies and aid conditionalities. They should also move speedily to curtail carbon and other green house emissions which are causing floods and droughts in Africa. As well the west, while increasing aid to Africa, should help establish a strong global environmental regime capable of controlling the activities of MNC.

While welcoming the contribution of the west to alleviate human insecurity, Africa should consider itself an integral part of the solution. To this end, it should reserve policies that tend to create conditions for conflict such as bad governance, marginalisation and exclusion of constituencies. The African Peer Review Mechanism (APRM), the initiative instituted under the New partnership for African Development (NEPAD) to promote better governance should be strengthened to make it more effective in achieving that objective. Civil society should be encouraged and strengthened as a partner both in governance and in development. While these progressive policies will not instantly transform the tattered character of Africa, they will doubtlessly be setting the region firmly on the path of human security and ultimately sustainable development.

Dramatised in deepening poverty; food and nutritional insufficiency; health and educational crisis; bad governance; violent and intractable conflicts; rising numbers of refugees and internally displaced persons; and environmental bankruptcy among other things, human insecurity has heightened in Africa in recent decades. While this fact is acknowledged, there is little discussion on the structural causes of the problem in the conventional literature. Importantly, there is little attribution of the problem to globalisation. While part of the causes of insecurity are admittedly internal, including bad governance, conflicts and self-destructive public policies, it is opined that external forces have played an unobtrusive, sometimes conspicuous, role in the escalation of the problem. Globalisation along with other external forces exerts pressures on Africa that attenuate the latter's capacity to alleviate human insecurity. Also, enmeshed in intrusive conditionalities, interventions by Africa's creditor community in the form of structural adjustment programmes (SAPs) and aid aimed at mitigating poverty and other adversities have often aggravated human insecurity. Accordingly, ameliorating human insecurity in Africa should be the responsibility not just of Africans but also of western states.

Human insecurity remains a global problem. The upsurge in the spate of terrorism, international crime, the spread of weapons of mass destruction (WMDs) and diseases such as HIV/AIDS, SARS, avian flu, etc, environmental degradation, the proliferation of conflicts cross the world all highlight the vulnerability of people both in the north and in the south. Moreover, over 1.3 billion of the 6.6 billion world population subsist on less than one dollar a day (Japan Ministry of Foreign Affairs 2006: 3). Yet, it is no exaggeration that human insecurity is most acute in sub-Saharan Africa (SSA)1, where a host of life-threatening developments persist and against which states have made little progress in averting, let alone reversing. Indeed, contrary to initial optimism about greater opportunities for human security and general development after the relaxation of East-West tensions, human insecurity has heightened in the post-cold war era for a number of reasons. Among others, Africa assumed an ambivalent posture in the international economy (Callaghy 1995). On the one hand, the continent was being marginalised in the global economy, while on the other hand it was increasingly being incorporated into the same economy through economic aid, structural adjustment programmes (SAPs), globalisation and recently through the New Partnership for African Development (NEPAD).

Marginalisation and incorporation have implications for SSA's external indebtedness, which has seen a dramatic escalation in the last two decades. Indebtedness and the pressures to repay in order to remain credit worthy have fed into the region's human insecurity dynamic. The abatement of the cold war has also been followed by a dramatic rise in the number and frequency of inter- but especially intra-state conflicts. Many of these conflicts reflect competition over the state and diminishing resources, making them seemingly intractable (Adedeji 1999; Laremont 2002). While undermining human security, conflicts also paralyse states and incapacitate them from addressing pressing human needs. In addition, conflicts have spawned refugees, internally displaced persons (IDPs) and migration all of which heighten human insecurity. And, notwithstanding the liberalisation of many hitherto closed political systems and the adoption of liberal constitutions, good governance has been far from established in many SSA countries. Various forms of dictators and unaccountable regimes exist whose corruption, ineptitude and neo-patrimonial policies have compromised basic human rights. Poverty has worsened in the region, pushing many more sub-Saharan Africans to the margins of survival. Together, conflicts, bad governance and poverty have combined to exacerbate the human insecurity dilemma in SSA.

The irreparable havoc caused by the HIV/AIDS pandemic in Africa has not helped the region's human security situation either. On the contrary, HIV/AIDS threatens not just affected populations, but in fact, the physical survival of countries where the epidemic has attained crisis proportions (World Bank 2000). In addition to being the global epicentre of HIV/AIDS, SSA is also ravaged by other communicable but relatively preventable diseases such as malaria, tuberculosis, ibola, diarrhoea and typhoid. All these are compounded by environmental degradation, which is accelerating with globalisation. Pollution, deforestation, soil erosion, floods, droughts and food shortages – manifestations of human insecurity – have marked the political economy of SSA. As a large proportion of the population depends on subsistence agriculture, environmental degradation and poverty have become mutually reinforcing making it difficult to distinguish cause from effect (Timberlake 1991). A distinguished feature of these threats is that they are neither posed by states nor by non-state actors. Hence they require counter-actions that are non- military. However, while the wide array of human security threats is acknowledged, there has been cursory analytical discussion on their causes.

This paper explores the causes of human insecurity in SSA. It argues that pressures unleashed by global forces in the form of liberalisation, privatisation, debt and globalisation undermine Africa's development in general and human security in particular. In advancing this argument the paper interrogates conventional assumptions on human insecurity in Africa and surmises that a heavily dependent region, Africa's fortunes are intricately tied to developments in the wider global economy. As such, human security in Africa cannot be realistically analysed in isolation from developments in the international system. Thus, in problematising human security, the paper explores the role of external factors in the aggravation of SSA's human security crisis. While part of the causes of human insecurity in SSA is arguably internal, deriving from among other things, conflicts, corruption, inauspicious public policies, leading to mismanagement, and sometimes from environmental factors such as famine, deforestation, desertification, etc, this paper surmises that the international environment plays a seemingly inconspicuous role in aggravating these factors. This hypothesis strikes at the core of conventional analysis, which tends to place less emphasis on the causes of human insecurity and even much less emphasis on the role of the broader international economic environment. Lacking a causal analysis, the discourse on human insecurity in SSA is conventionally cast as something with ontological status and which is both explainable and resolvable in isolation of other global developments. This paper contends that on the contrary, SSA economic, political and security fortunes are inseparable from wider extra-African developments.

The paper is broadly structured into five main parts with each, save the conclusion, having sub-sections. The general introduction constitutes the first part and sets out the context of the study. This section outlines the central argument, the objectives and the methodology of the study and ends with a rough classification of the literature on human security. The second part is conceptual and deals with the notion of human security – its origins, development, challenges and criticisms. Section two ends with a discussion on the causes of human insecurity. The third part, empirical, focuses on Africa. It analyses the causes of human insecurity, in particular demonstrating the role of the international political economy and globalisation. The fourth part makes recommendations for minimising and averting human insecurity, focusing on the role of Africa and the international community. The fifth section concludes the study by briefly recapping the salient issues raised in the paper.

A study on human security is timely not only because of the pervasiveness of the problem, but also because existing analysis on the subject remain inadequate and problematic. Typically, analysis on human security in Africa tends to ignore the role of the international system in the region's development. The main objective of the study is therefore to broaden the analysis on human insecurity in SSA by introducing an international political economy dimension to the discourse. More specifically, the study aims:

i. To review the literature and reconstruct the orthodox conceptions of security and human security in SSA with a primary objective of providing a deeper and holistic understanding of the nuances and trajectories of the phenomenon. The study dichotomises between the traditionally narrow and restricted notion of security of the cold war years on the one hand, and the broader and more generic view of security in the post-cold war era.

ii. To unravel the present causes and potential sources of human insecurity in Africa. The underlying objective here is to expand the frontiers of conventional explanations of Africa's human security threats beyond internal to include external factors, especially globalisation and pressures from the wider international system;

iii. Following from the above, to fill what is clearly a huge gap in the existing literature on the subject. External sources of insecurity are either unobtrusive or simply underemphasised. The significance of the study in this respect is its espousal of a holistic analysis of the sources and dynamics of human insecurity in SSA.

iv. To make prognosis on the prospects and challenges of human security in Africa. As well, to make recommendations on promoting human security, thereby augmenting the already bourgeoning literature on the subject in general and its relevance in Africa in particular; and

v. As the study cannot conceivably deal with all aspects of human security, given its multi-faceted nature, to lay the foundations for further research by identifying and mapping out new areas of interest on the subject.

Goals & anticipated impact

The study is expected to culminate into a research manuscript and later into a published peer-reviewed article, while the long-term goal is to develop it into a book. Exploring new dimensions and directions on the discourse on human security in Africa, such a publication is expected to receive wide readership among academics and policy makers. It is also expected to serve as a prescribed or recommended textbook in courses on African security and or development. Ultimately, it is expected to augment the growing body of literature on human security in Africa.

Research methodology

Focusing on the vast region of sub-Saharan Africa, the research did not lend itself to a detailed empirical study. Rather, it was predominantly library-based and relied on secondary sources –

books, journals, monographs, reports and internet sources. These sources were supplemented by contacts with identified Japanese institutions, scholars and researchers who had interest and expertise on the broader subject of human security. A few interviews and discussions were held with some Japanese on the subject. These included Professor Mitsugi Endo, the director of the Human Security Programme at the University of Tokyo; Shinichi Takeuchi of IDE who was part of team that worked on a project on human security and Professor Yoichi Mine of Osaka University whose research interest focuses not only on human security and development, but also on Africa and the developing regions. As well, interviews were held with JICA officials involved with implementing the Japanese government's human security programme in Africa. My experiences with researching and teaching in Africa also helped in developing the new outlook on the subject.

The body of literature on human security is huge, growing and often confusing. The confusion has been generated, and often deepened by the contested meaning, scope and utility of the concept (Oberleitner 2005: 186). For analytical purposes it is convenient, and indeed helpful, to classify the volume of literature on the subject into various dominant perspectives on the major elements of, and approaches to promoting human security. The classification is arbitrary yet necessary to underscore the wide scope of issues falling within the broader human security framework. In no particular order, these perspectives include the human rights, feminist, developmentalist, globalist and Marxist approaches.

The human rights perspective argues that the protection of basic liberties is the entry point to understanding and promoting human security (Hayden 2004, Sen 1999). It sees the protection of basic rights both as a cause and effect of human security. Peace, which is vital for security, is a critical human right requirement. Shue (1996: 38-39) notes that "a demand for physical security is not normally a demand simply to be left alone, but a demand to be protected against harm… [it] is a demand for social guarantees against at least the standard threats." The protection of human rights is not incompatible with human security. Rather, these are complimentary and mutually reinforcing. While acknowledging the various threats to human life, scholars writing from the human rights perspectives are concerned with the dangers posed to human security by recent developments in international relations, including the upsurge in humanitarian intervention and the war against terrorism (Robinson 2005). The imposition of economic sanctions on regimes has often worsened human insecurity of the larger population rather than the targeted regime. As well, overt military intervention in countries also often causes a sharp deterioration of human security as the examples of Afghanistan and Iraq clearly show. Similarly, the war on terror is causing great concerns for human rights across the world. This has prompted the International Commission of Jurists (ICJ) to devote its August 2004 biennial conference in Berlin to calling for the upholding of Human Rights and the Rule of Law in combating terrorism. Exponents of the human rights approach argue that the respect for human rights should not be compromised either by the fight against terror, or by the quest to promote state security.

Another body of literature addresses human security from the perspective of feminist thought. This literature is critical of the traditional notions of security as espoused by classical realism. It sees the state and military-based notion of security as exceedingly masculine, malebiased and exclusionist to female participation in global security structures. Moreover, feminism sees notions of national security, and concepts associated with traditional state security as socially constructed to perpetuate the social advantages of men (Tickner 2004). This perspective notes, moreover, that women are more vulnerable to security threats than men as such the former has suffered more from poverty, diseases, displacement, conflicts and post-conflict reconstruction than men. The feminist-based literature thus projects feminist thought as part of the grand human security agenda. Removing and averting the various threats to women, including marginalisation and exclusion should be central to a holistic human security paradigm (Fukuda-Parr 2004, Basch 2004).

Yet, another set of literature proceeds from a "developmentalist" angle. Taking a holistic approach to human security, this literature more or less conflates human security with human development, although the UNDP Report (1994: 23) warned that notwithstanding the link between them the two are discrete. It sees human security as subsuming the key indices of human development such as political and economic freedoms, education, poverty, incomes, conflicts, health, the environment and gender issues (Sen 1999, Gasper and Truong 2005, Mine 2007). This literature addresses a wide range of threats to decent human life. Unlike the human rights and feminist-based approaches, developmentalist literature does not disaggregate the components of human security; neither does it rank them in any order of importance. Rather, it treats all sources of threat to dignified individual and community life as important. Consequently, this scholarship recommends a holistic response to human security threats.

While, human right, feminists and developmentalist generally narrow the referent of security by shifting focus from the state to the individual, another set of literature expands it by focusing on the wider global system. This literature, which can conveniently be dubbed as "globalist" shifts from the traditional state-centred notion of security but argues that human security is inseparable from international security. Hence the former could not be pursued in isolation of the latter. Human security, globalists argue, could not be guaranteed in an insecure international environment. The absence of international security can potentially generate a "security dilemma", which undermines human security. The link between human security at the national level on the one hand, and global security on the other, is informed by the common threats faced by the "global village", including global warming, pollution, drugs, crime, viruses, and weapons of mass destruction. The globalist approach to human security thus proceeds from the truism that the traditional responsibilities of the state are changing and so are the sources of insecurity. Threats to state and people are no longer posed exclusively by its neighbours, but more generally from the international environment. Moreover, these threats are such that only through global efforts can they be averted. Globalists thus contend that human security is not just the responsibility of the state but also part of the broader agenda of global security. Thus, analysis of human security should focus on global security as well and not just on groups or individuals (Baylis 2005, Pettman 2005).

Marxist literature, however, differs radically from the above perspectives both on the causes of, and prescriptions for, human insecurity. Drawing on the analysis of Karl Marx, Marxists see the international system as polarised between two classes of people – the bourgeoisie who owns capital and other relevant means of material production on the one hand and the proletariat or workers who must sell their labour to make a wage. They contend that the relation between the two classes is one of exploitation of the latter by the former, which is facilitated by the state and its structures. Two key implications emerge from this dialectic: First, the proletariat remains insecure on account of its total dependence on the bourgeoisie and on wage labour; second, the dynamic of relation between the two classes, characterised by tension and conflict is a source of insecurity. Marxist literature generally highlights contradictions in class interests and sees this as a cause of human insecurity (Roth 2004). However, human security is achievable with the overthrow of capital and the bourgeoisie by a proletariat revolution. The revolution abolishes the oppressive state and its associated structures, social classes and hence the exploitation of one class by another. Marxists hold that the bourgeoisie-proletariat contradictions are evident at both state and international levels.

It has to be emphasised that the above classifications are neither exhaustive nor rigid. It is possible to have other brand of literature meandering between two or more of the noted perspectives while there are still others that remain uncaptured. Some may argue that the protection of the environment or the abatement of conflicts should be the starting point for a discussion on human security. Depending on one's approach, the above cluster of literature can be sub-classified, re-classified or even de-classified. Thus, rather than serving to espouse arguments and counter-arguments, these classifications are simply to serve an analytical purpose and hold less importance for the analysis on Africa. The classification merely stresses particular causes of, and prescription for, human insecurity. In the discussion on Africa, human security is taken as the aggregate of all the above perspectives. The analysis on Africa proceeds on the assumption that human security means more or less the "absence of threats to core values." How this is achieved could be a subject of debate between exponents of the various perspectives. However, the current project considers Africa as more concerned with the ends than with the means of achieving human security. In the next section, we examine the concept of human security – its meaning, scope and development.

HUMAN SECURITY- THE PARADIGM OF THE MOMENT

HUMAN SECURITY: SCOPE AND DEVELOPMENT

In the last two decades, human security has been elevated as an alternative to the statecentred security of the cold war years. The pre-eminence of human security suggests a departure from the traditional meaning of security, which focused primarily on the state. Until the abatement of the cold war, security was largely linked to the state. "National security" became a catchphrase and was conceived in militarised and territorial terms. In the context of bipolarity, threats to the state were seen as largely external and required military responses. This notion was widely accepted by states and international organisations. For example, based on such principles as the preservation of territorial integrity, respect for the sovereignty of states, non-interference in the domestic affairs of states, and the sovereign equality of states, the UN Charter defines security primarily in regards to the state (Oberleitner 2005: 189). Similarly, the notion of collective security advanced by the UN was conceived in relation to state security. Chapter VII of the UN Charter calls for collective action among states to promote collective security. However, this purely realist conception now referred to as the "old" or "traditional" notion of security, was ethnocentric, parochial and too narrowly focused (Henk 2005). Since the attenuation of East-West ideological tensions, interest has shifted dramatically from traditional security concerned with external threats, use of military force, and the security of national borders to "any major security issues, including without limitations those of a political, strategic, economic, social, or ecological nature" (Vale 1992: 100).

In essence, the human security concept challenged the idea of state dominance in international relations and subsequently as the main referent of security. The international system is no longer thought to be characterised exclusively by states. There are a vast numbers of non-state actors in the international system, who are sometimes successful in influencing the actions of states. Moreover, the contemporary international system is being shaped by globalisation, which is increasingly de-emphasising the sanctity of national borders. This, along with growing interdependence among states, means that protection of territorial borders can no longer be the ultimate goal of security. As Lodgaard (2000: 4) argues, "the constraints on state sovereignty, the mobilisation of international civil society in defence of international norms, the sharing of power between state and non-state actors in a globalising world .... leave a clear message: the state is no longer able to monopolise the concept and practice of security." In other words, these global developments have undermined the conventional assumptions of the Westphalia state system.

The ubiquity of poverty, the persistence of underdevelopment and general despondency in countries across the globe further highlight the state's inability to adequately address the vast number of issues posing threats to humanity. The 1994 United Nations Development Programme (UNDP) Report, the first official and multilateral articulation of the concept, outlined the limitations of the state-dominated security architecture and the justification for a broader, human-focused security paradigm:

The concept of security has so far too long been interpreted narrowly: as a security of territory from external aggression, or as protection of national interest in foreign policy or as global security from the threat of nuclear holocaust. It has been related more to nation-states than to people .... Forgotten were the legitimate concerns of ordinary people ... For many of them, security symbolized protection from the threat of disease, hunger, unemployment, crime, social conflict, political repression, and environmental hazards (UNDP 1994: 22).

The new security paradigm de-emphasises the state and focuses on people as the main referent. The post-cold war era has seen the emergence and persistence of new security threats generated, among other things by economic adversities, poverty, viruses, environmental decadence, and terrorism. Mostly internal and emanating from non-state sources, these security threats have rendered the traditional concept of security anachronistic and necessitated the formulation of an expanded and more relevant paradigm. Thus, at the heart of the human security paradigm is the security and safety of people. Specifically, the UNDP Report (1994: 20-24) identifies human security to involve two main components – "freedom from fear and freedom from want." These have been broadened into seven main areas, including:

- *Economic security* – this means access to employment and the earning of basic income on a sustained basis.
- *Food security* – this implies economic and physical access to food and balanced nutrition
- *Health security* – access to health facilities, medical care and basic drugs. It also means protection from all forms of communicable and non-communicable diseases.
- *Environmental security* – this means the protection of the environment and its natural resources upon which lives depend. Environmental security also means exploiting natural resources in such a way as not to compromise its use by future generations.
- *Personal security* – This means freedom from physical violence caused either by the state, groups or individuals. It also means freedom from threat to life, including suicide and drugs. Personal security is to be guaranteed both at home and at the work place.
- *Community security* – means the the freedom to belong to a community or communities, be they family, racial, religious, ethnic or others. Moreover, communities should be free from any forms of harassment, violence or intimidation.
- *Political security* – This includes the freedom of the individual to hold particular political views, subscribe to ideologies, belong to political formations and freely express political views.

The UNDP argued that human security prevailed when people were safe from acute instability in their social and political environments. It understood human security to mean "safety from such chronic threats as hunger, disease and repression [and] protection from sudden and hurtful disruption in the patterns of daily life – whether in homes, in jobs or in communities" (UNDP 1994: 23). The essentials of human security have been captured in a poetic yet practical way by Pettman (2005: 140). Human security, he writes is about the young child that did not die of neglect, the serious epidemic that did not break out, the job that was not cut, the gun that was not run, the ethnic prejudice that did not result in violence, the dissident voice that was not made silent, the landmine that was not sold and installed, the woman who was not trafficked across state borders and sexually abused, the agricultural product that was not dumped to the detriment of poor farmers, the short-term capital investment that was not allowed to wreck an infant industry, the addictive drug that was not produced and shipped, the refugee who was not forced to flee or remain abroad, and so on.

In short, human security is about eliminating threats to dignified life that characterise contemporary human society; it is about securing life free from threats.

Although articulated at the inter-governmental level in 1994, the notion of human security predated the abatement of the cold war and the UNDP Report. For example, in his State of the Union Address in 1944, American President Franklin Roosevelt argued that security "means not only physical security, which provides safety from attacks by aggressors" but also "economic security, social security [and] moral security". He argued further that "freedom from fear is eternally linked with freedom from want."2 However, little is known of the extent to which US immediate post-war foreign policy addressed or became consistent with the pillars of human security. It was certain though that in the context of American concerns with the "communist threat" and the determination to contain Soviet influence from the mid-1940s, Washington's human security pretensions, even if genuine, were quickly overshadowed by the practical demands of the cold war.

Two years after Roosevelt's address, the post-war constitution of Japan also articulated the concept of human security. The preface to the 1946 Japanese constitution states among other things that "We recognise that all peoples of the world have the right to live in peace, free from fear and want". The Japanese had just emerged from World War II in which their domination and colonisation of Asia had left a trail of destruction in Korea and China among other victims. The historic American bombing of Hiroshima and Nagasaki, two Japanese cities during the war, further exposed the country to the horrors of war. In the post-war era therefore, the Japanese adopted a pacifist constitution under which they resolved that neither they nor any people on earth should live in fear and want. The Japanese determination to shun war and adversities was reinforced by Article 9 of the constitution, which explicitly prohibits the engagement in war of the Japanese armed forces – naval, infantry or air force. For the Japanese, human security is to serve as a foundation of the country's post-war foreign policy. Although initially informed by war, the Japanese understanding of human security latter extended beyond conflict. In a speech at an international conference in December 1998, Keizo Obuchi, the Japanese Prime Minister, noted that human security "is the key, which comprehensively covers all measures that threaten human survival, daily life, and dignity – for example, environmental degradation, violations of human rights, transnational organised crime, illicit drugs, refugees, poverty, antipersonnel landmines and…infectious diseases such as AIDS – and strengthens efforts to confront these threats." The Japanese conception of human security thus covers all contemporary threats to human safety; i.e. both "freedom from fear and freedom from want".

Subsequently, human security began to feature as a theme of intellectual discussion towards the terminal stages of the cold war. In 1983 Barry Buzan produced a classic work, which added a human dimension to the predominantly cold war-informed meaning of security. Advocating a link with peoples' lives and survival experiences, Buzan focuses on the peace and security of people. He outlines a wider conception of security that transcends the narrow confines of the state to encompass the political, economic, societal and environmental threats to social well-being. The key point of departure of what was becoming a "new" concept from the traditional notion of security is the former's emphasis on the people rather than the state. Human insecurity defines critical threats to peoples' lives – what Buzan terms "social threats", that is, threats "arising from the fact that people find themselves embedded in a human environment with unavoidable social, economic and political consequences." Busan's work injected some momentum into the rise to prominence of a concept that was already establishing itself as a credible alternative paradigm in security studies. By the beginning of the 1990s, the concept had gained further grounds and was influencing international policy making. For example, *Common Responsibility in the 1990s*, the report of the Stockholm Initiative on Global Security and Governance (SIGSG), published in 1991 acknowledged the emergence of new security threats other than political. The report thus called for a new security paradigm that recognises threats from nonconventional sources such as environmental degradation, population growth and bad governance among others. Thus, before the celebrated UNDP report, human security had already become a familiar concept, featuring as a paradigm in academic circles and serving as a pillar of foreign policy for regional bodies.

In the post-1994 era, a series of unilateral and multilateral initiatives to articulate the concept of human security took place. In 1999 the Human Security Network (HSN), an intergovernmental movement dedicated to promoting human security, was lunched in Oslo, by a group of countries, including Canada, Norway and Japan. The HSN, which by mid-2005 had included no fewer than 13 countries drawn from Africa, Asia, Europe, the Middle East, North America and Latin America, was initially concerned with drawing global attention to the dangers of landmines. Yet, as an advocacy group, the HSN campaigned not just against landmines and the proliferation of small arms, but it was also concerned with promoting democratic governance; sustainable human development through the alleviation of absolute poverty; raising global awareness about HIV/AIDS; and promoting people-centred development, among other things, all of which it believed were critical prerequisites "for building human security."

The 1995 report of the Commission on Global Governance (CGG), *Our Global Neighbourhood* also stressed the need to broaden the concept of security from its territorial-based meaning "to include the security of people and the planet." By 2000 a number of industrialised countries who were members of the HSN including Canada, Switzerland and Austria had joined Japan in making human security a cornerstone of their foreign policies while some countries in the South, such as South Africa had incorporated the notion into mainstream domestic policy. At the highest multilateral level Kofi Annan, the Secretary General of the UN, was setting human security as a key objective of the world body. In a statement to the Foreign Affairs Committee of the Chinese People's Political Consultative Conference in 1998 Annan maintained that "the prevention of conflict begins and ends with the protection of human life and the promotion of human development. Ensuring human security is, in the broadest sense, the United Nations' cardinal mission." Annan, however, later cautioned that human security transcended the abatement of conflicts: "human security, in its broadest sense, embraces far more than the absence of violent conflicts. It encompasses human rights, good governance, access to education and health care and ensuring that each individual has opportunities and choices to fulfil his or her potential."

The lunching of the Commission on Human Security (CHS) at the UN Millennium Summit in 2000 was a further milestone in the promotion of human security. The CHS was tasked with, among other things, exploring the dimensions and trends of the new security threats to people and make necessary recommendations for averting those threats. The Commission was eventually established in 2001. Composed of eminent practitioners, the 12-member commission was co-chaired by Sadako Ogata and Amartya Sen and was referred to as the Ogata-Sen Commission. The CHS presented its report titled *Human Security Now* in May 2003 in which it outlined a comprehensive scope of human security and in many ways restated the calls of the 1994 UNDP Report. This ranged from basic freedoms of individuals and communities to social and economic empowerment – what the Commission called "the building blocks of survival, livelihood and dignity" (CHS 2003: 4). On this note the Commission called for the need to focus on security both at the macro (state) and micro (community and individual) levels. The Commission also noted that violent conflicts, poverty, ill-health, illiteracy and other socio-economic adversities are sources of human insecurity and therefore calls for the broadening of the security paradigm to include these non-conventional threats.

Unlike the 1994 UNDP Report, the CHS slightly expanded the components of human security to include "empowerment". Thus, it underscores the notion that human security involves "freedom from fear, freedom from want and the freedom to take action on one's own behalf." Protection and empowerment are two critical strategies identified by the report for ensuring people's freedom from want, fear and freedom to take action on one's behalf. Other highlights of the Commission's report include ways of stemming human insecurity. These, the report identified as protecting people from violent conflicts; the proliferation of arms; protecting people on the move such as refugees, IDPs and migrants; establishing a fund to cater for post-conflict situations; encouraging the establishment of fair trade among countries; ensuring minimum living standards everywhere; ensuring universal access to basic healthcare and education; establishing an equitable global system for patent rights; and recognizing the freedom of individuals to have identities and affiliations.

Finally, the CHS recommended the establishment of a Human Security Advisory Board (HSAB) to among other things follow up on the recommendations made in the report. The HSAB was subsequently established in 2003. Alongside the specific initiatives undertaken by some of its members, the EU incorporated human security into official regional policy in 2004. In its 36-page report, the *Human Security Doctrine for Europe* also referred to as the Barcelona Report, the EU acknowledged the numerous, yet new security threats facing people across the world. In particular, the report identified the scourge of conflicts and the devastating impact these have on human security. The Report was thus concerned with making recommendations on how best to implement the European Security Strategy (ESS), a multilateral preventive mechanism agreed upon by the European Council in December

2003. Alluding to the growing threat to humans posed by conflicts, failed states, organised crime, terrorism and the proliferation of weapons of mass destruction (WMD), the report recommended, among other things, the establishment of a "Human Security Response Force" (HSRF) composed of no fewer than 15,000 men and women to rapidly respond to conflicts and other forms of social disruptions in Europe. By 2003, therefore the concept of human security had been firmly established as a paradigm, shaping national, regional and international policy.

The contribution of Japan and Canada to the global promotion of human security deserves further discussion, not just because these countries are among the leading contemporary advocates of the concept, but also because both countries later focused on specific components of human security. As indicated already, Japan's initial conception of human security covered both "freedom from fear and freedom from want". Freedom from fear deals with threats to life such as conflicts, terrorism, etc, while freedom from want is concerned with deprivations caused by poverty, diseases, environmental degradation, etc. Consistent with its desire to promote human security, the Japan's Prime Minister Yoshiro Mori proposed the establishment of a human security fund (HSF) at the UN to finance human security-related programmes. The establishment of the HSF became one of the many recommendations of the Commission on Human Security (CHS). By March 2006, Tokyo had contributed 31.5 billion Yen to the HSF. In addition, Japan devoted 14 billion yen to the promotion of grassroots projects. Japan's ODA regime was also reformed in 2003 with the incorporation of a human security focus. Japan International Cooperation Agency (JICA) was given a new mandate in 2004 to serve as a key institution for implementing the country's human security agenda. JICA's activities, however, have focused mainly on empowering communities and alleviating poverty. In this wise, Japan focuses more on "freedom from want" than on "freedom from fear".

Similarly, Canada's initial holistic approach to human security has somewhat changed. In his address to the 51st United Nations General Assembly in September 1996, Lloyd Axworthy, the Canadian Foreign Affairs Minister, maintained that, Human security is much more than the absence of military threat. It includes security against economic privation, an acceptable quality of life, and a guarantee of fundamental human rights.....it recognises the complexity of the human environment and accepts that the forces influencing human security are related and mutually reinforcing.

At a minimum, human security requires that basic needs are met, but it also acknowledges that sustained economic development, human rights and fundamental freedoms, the rule of law, good governance, sustained development and social equity are as important to global peace as arms control and disarmament. It recognises the links between environmental degradation, population growth, ethnic conflicts and migration. Finally, it concludes that lasting stability cannot be achieved until human security is guaranteed" (Axworthy 1997: 184). Axworthy became well known for his advocacy for human security. He devoted considerable amounts of his time to advancing human security as a paradigm after leaving the Canadian Foreign Service. Consequently, the Canadian government invested enormous resources and energy into advancing its human security agenda.

However, following the increasing spate of political conflicts, religious contestations and ethnic violence across the world, the Canadians customised the concept of human security into a more circumscribed version, focusing on the protection of "individuals and communities from any form of political violence." In this wise, Ottawa defined human security succinctly as "freedom from pervasive threats to people's rights, safety and lives." This, Ottawa believes involves the protection of people and communities from conflicts and wars.

In promoting this particular human security agenda, five principal themes dominated Canadian foreign policy – protection of civilians; peace support operations; governance and accountability; public safety; and conflict prevention. To facilitate the implementation of these themes, a Peace and Human Security Division (PHSD) was created in the Ministry of Foreign Affairs and International Trade (Dorn 2001). The PHSD has produced several documents, setting out Canada's vision of a world free of fear and want.

CRITICISMS AGAINST THE HUMAN SECURITY CONCEPT

In spite of the wide acceptance of human security as an alternative to the state-based paradigm, and in spite of capturing the vast array of threats to human life, the concept and practice of human security has not been immune from controversy and criticisms. A great deal of the concern with the concept centres on its meaning, scope and methodological construct. Basing on the definition of the 1994 UNDP Report, Paris (2001, 2005) argues that the definition of the concept sets it to subsume every threat to human life. He contends that the concept is too expansive and includes "virtually any kind of unexpected or irregular discomfort."

For lacking a precise definition, the term is accused of being too inclusive to serve as a useful analytical tool. This charge is, however, rejected by another school of thought, which argues rather for broadening the concept. Pettman contends that focusing exclusively on humans as the referent of security is inadequate and problematic. He thus calls for a comprehensive account of human security to cater for "traditional" ways of living. The concept of human security is thus in a limbo; while one view denounces it as too broad and inclusive, another deplores it as too narrow and restrictive. Other concerns relate to methodology and question the feasibility of practically establishing human security. While acknowledging the desirability of a shift away from the state as the key referent of security, there is scepticism about the feasibility of truly meeting the goals of human security.

The two related questions posed by sceptics are: (i) Is human security practically achievable? (ii) Can human security supplant state security as a new dominant paradigm? In spite of the enormous amounts of funds and energy dissipated by states and statesmen towards promoting human security over the last ten years, there is no tangible evidence to suggest that a particular region or country has become humanly secured or is moving towards attaining human security. Sceptics doubt the practicality of meaningfully achieving human security. Moreover, despite coming into vogue for more than a decade, the human security concept has not established itself as an alternative to the state-based security. Human security has so far neither displaced nor replaced the state as the referent of security in practice. This reality confirms the argument that human security is not a substitute for national security.

There are still inter-state conflicts, terrorism and armed rebellions, which by their very nature, legitimately fall under the old state-centred security paradigm. The persistence of these threats means that the state will continue to be a referent of security. This is particularly so in Africa where intra- and inter-state conflicts remain a permanent feature of the region's politics. Moreover, in the African context, human security is arguably inseparable from state security as it is the state and its "institutions that ensure the physical protection and safety of their citizens, their equal access to law and protection from abuse." Having also remained at the centre of development, the state may resist efforts to dislodge it from this enviable position.

Again, the very nature of the human security paradigm and the manner in which it is being advanced sets it against the national interests of states. This, some argue, limits the foreign policy choices of states and in the process undermines national sovereignty. It is even feared that it could easily be used as a pretext by powerful states for humanitarian intervention or to subvert regimes considered unsympathetic with policy preferences of stronger states. Such concerns are held by a good number of "rogue" states in Africa. The Sudanese government's reluctance to accept a UN peacekeeping force, preferring rather an African Union force, to protect defenceless civilians in Darfur against government-backed militias, is largely motivated by fears that the US could use the mission to subvert it. This is against a background of US repeated accusation of Sudan of harbouring international terrorists. Similarly, the Union of Islamic Courts (UIC), the militia group that took control over Somalia in July 2006 after years of chaos, resisted proposals for the deployment of an African Union force in the country on grounds that the US could help install a westerninclined regime. However, the Islamic Courts was forcibly ejected by Ethiopian forces in mid- December 2006. The growing African scepticism over western/American paradigms and solutions for the continent's problems are not helping either. American and western dominance in global affairs in the aftermath of the cold war, along with their known desire to spread western values raise fears that human security could easily become an ideological policy instrument. Generally, the suspicion that the pursuit of human security goals could be used to further the foreign policy agenda of states could potentially lead to resistance by weaker states.

It is equally important to pose the question, especially in the case of Africa: who polices human security? Notwithstanding popular rhetoric, the state still remains dominant both as an architect and referent of security. By and large the state is at the centre of efforts to promote human security. The state informs, guides, and sometimes directs human security initiatives. Even initiatives towards human security regarded as non-state require the tacit approval and active cooperation of the state. The contemporary experiences in various parts of the world, especially Africa, suggests that while states are authors of human security, they can also engineer human insecurity (Oberleitner 2005: 196). The state can engage in domicide – the systematic intentional killing of its own citizens – either slowly but surely as in contemporary Zimbabwe, or speedily and violently as in Darfur. In undermining human security the state can as well thwart efforts of the international community or non-state actors to alleviate human suffering by obstructing their entry into the country as the Sudanese government is doing with Darfur. The state can also indirectly contribute to human insecurity in cases where it responds too slowly to assist victims of environmental catastrophes as, for example, was the case in the aftermath of hurricane Katrina in the American state of New Orleans in 2005 (Mine 2007). The African state in particular thus can severely erode citizens' freedom from fear and freedom from want. Similarly, non-state actors can also both promote and undermine human security. Just as humanitarian NGOs are dedicated to the course of human security so do armed groups, rebels and terrorists organisations endanger human security.

Further, given the euphoria about the concept and what it can achieve, it is imperative to signal caution about the limits of human security. Human security should not be projected to incite unreasonable expectations. It must be stressed that human security is not the ultimate panacea to all societal ills. Current discussions, especially at the international level, tend to create an impression that human security is synonymous with development. Often times, it is also depicted as though improved standard of living will follow inexorably with the attainment of human security goals. Nothing can be further from the truth. Human security is neither development nor can it spawn better living conditions by itself. As the UNDP (1994: 23) notes, development is about creating choices, while human security is about exercising those choices. Thus, the attainment of human security should be seen simply as a means to achieving broader developmental objectives. Human security ensures the prevalence of a serene environment within which citizens can peacefully and meaningfully exercise the choices available to them in furthering development. This involves attaining the necessary human instrumentalities to engage in agriculture, commerce, education and other critical industries of development. As a result of this difference, human security should be trumpeted with caution for it could easily usher in another era of disappointed hopes as did SAP and multiparty democracy in the 1980s and 1990s respectively, which generated optimism yet brought only vain promises of better living conditions to Africa. Some observers, in fact, caution that the very idea of securitising human beings creates false hopes for victims rather than addressing their genuine concerns. Feminist scholars are also critical of the human security concept. They are, for example concerned that the 1994 human security report did not treat women as a special disadvantaged category. This, they argue could mask the specific issues that predominantly affect women. Moreover, like the previous state-based security paradigm, feminists fear that the definition and content of human security still remains a largely male enterprise. What constitutes insecurity or violence against women is determined by men and not women. Thus, feminist literature is on the whole highly pessimistic on the prospects of human security and its constituents becoming a genuinely transforming paradigm (Basch 2004).

In spite of these criticisms, human security remains popular in theory and a seemingly unassailable global paradigm. It seems poised to guide the actions of national governments, NGOs and the international community at large. For Africa, it may well prove to be the path to genuine development that has remained elusive. This is more so because in contrast to previous paradigms such as structural adjustment (SAPs), democratisation and the Highly Indebted Poor Countries (HIPCs) Initiatives12, which focused on particular aspects of Africa's problems as the starting point for addressing underdevelopment, human security is holistic dealing with the political, social, economic and environmental aspects of human life. As such, it is worth experimenting. Yet, a comprehensive appreciation of human security requires a holistic understanding of the concept, including its structural causes and sources. In the next section we analyse the causes of human insecurity.

HUMAN SECURITY THREATS – CAUSES AND CONTROVERSIES

The overwhelming literature on human insecurity is muted on its causes. Not even the much celebrated 1994 UNDP Report or the 2003 UN Commission Report on Human Security came close to discussing the underlying causes of the problem beyond its symptoms. In the main, discussions on human insecurity have been limited to an acknowledgement of its existence and production of a chronology of its symptoms. Conditions such as poverty, health and food insecurity, conflicts and population displacements noted in the UNDP report, are symptoms of much more fundamental causes. Poverty is not natural; no child is born in Africa to be poor and destined to lead an insecure life. Neither does poverty descend from the skies like rain or hail; it is rather the consequence of a more fundamental cause. The same could be said of conflicts. No people in their right senses like to constantly live under conditions of violence and war that threaten their personal or community security. There are always deep- seated causes that spark or predispose people to violence. It is therefore not enough to point to human insecurity without identifying its root causes, especially when the problem is menacing. Identifying the causes of a problem is necessary for a fuller understanding of its implications. Above all, understanding and mastering the causes of a problem enhances opportunities for effectively addressing it. Thus, for the purpose of addressing human insecurity, it is helpful to explore the root causes of poverty, conflicts, environmental degradation, among others, which tend to exacerbate human insecurity in SSA.

Attempts at understanding the causes of human insecurity often focus on the domestic politics of states. For example, in her analysis of human insecurity, Robinson (2005: 5) notes that the twin concepts of disempowerment and marginalisation of communities are at the heart of the problem. She contends that "the underlying causes of practically all human insecurity are an absence of the capacity to influence change at a personal or community level, exclusion from voting or participating in local and national decisionmaking, and economic or social marginalisation." As a solution, therefore, she suggests the need to empower people and to include them in mainstream decision making. While this prognosis has some validity for Africa, it only provides partial insights into the larger human insecurity problematique. In the main, it adds to the growing voices that point to human insecurity as a phenomenon caused primarily by factors internal to states. Even so, it neither captures the causes of marginalisation nor exclusion, thus vitiating the usefulness of the argument. The utility of the analysis is limited, moreover, in its inability to explain human insecurity caused by environmental bankruptcy. As earlier noted, the Japanese and Canadian governments have been hailed for pioneering the incorporation of human security into their official foreign policies. They view human insecurity in terms of poverty and conflicts respectively. Accordingly, they advocate poverty alleviation and conflict-prevention measures as solutions to human insecurity. Yet, these approaches only partially explain the complex and deepseated causes of human insecurity, especially in Africa. What, then, are the causes of human insecurity?

So far, the most influential causal explanation of human security relevant to the current study is the structural violence argument associated with Johan Galtung. According to Galtung, human insecurity is caused by violence, which is "…. harm done to human beings as a process, working slowly as the way misery in general and hunger in particular, erode and finally kill human beings" Galtung. In an earlier work Galtung argues that violence takes two main forms. First, there is personal or direct violence, i.e., "where there is an actor who commits the violence." In this wise, direct violence generates insecurity when, for example, a robber hijacks a car; a woman is abducted, smuggled or raped; in conflict situations civilians are injured, maimed or killed; an unscrupulous individual deliberately sets the forest on fire or when a rebel group poisons a river, which is a community's source of water, etc. This part of Galtung's explanation is similar to the "human agency" argument made by Bajpai, which traces human insecurity directly to human or human-made factors.

The second form of violence is structural or indirect. Galtung also refers to this as "social injustice". In this form, "the violence is built into the structure and shows up as unequal power and consequently as unequal life chances." In distinguishing between personal and structural violence, Galtung notes that, ...if people are starving when this is objectively avoidable, then violence is committed, regardless of whether there is a clear subject-action-object relation, as during a siege yesterday or no such clear relation, as in the way world economic relations are organised today. ..... Violence with a clear subject-object relation is manifest it is visible as *action*. It corresponds to our ideas of what *drama* is, and it is personal because there are persons committing the violence. ...... Violence without this relation is structural, built into structure. Thus, when one husband beats his wife there is a clear case of personal violence, but when one million husbands keep one million wives in ignorance there is structural violence. Correspondingly, in a society where life expectancy is twice as high in the upper as in the lower classes, violence is exercised even if there are no concrete actors one can point to directly attacking others, as when one kills another" – italicized words in the original.

Galtung thesis on both direct and structural violence provides a good context for understanding human insecurity in SSA given its relation with the industrial north. For example, an asymmetrical trade pattern was established between Africa and the west since colonialism, which disadvantages the former. Africa has been unable to change this pattern largely due to the operations of global institutions, structures and regimes. The dominant Breton Woods institutions, including the World Bank, the International Monetary Fund (IMF) and the World Trade Organisation (WTO) have functioned to maintain the structural imbalance between the north and south, leading to vast inequalities between the two regions. The reality of north-south relations fit into the explanation of both direct and structural violence. Although critics may argue that the structural violence argument is deficient in failing to explain environmental insecurity, it will be argued subsequently in the case of SSA that ecological insecurity is part of the structural crisis generated by globalisation and the international global economy. To be sure, others have built on the structural violence thesis, linking it directly to the global economy. This school argues that structural oppression and violence are endemic in the global economic system.

This view suggests that human security is in part determined by human inhabited structures, including political, social and ecological conditions. Pushing the argument further, Hampson notes that human security at national levels have direct relationships with international security and that "international order cannot rest solely on the sovereignty and viability of states." Similarly, Thakur notes the presence of "structural coercion so severe as to turn human beings into chattels...." The collective structuralist view reflects a notion that human insecurity is caused by oppressive structures. Hettne and Soderbaum contend that the need for broadening the security discourse beyond the state was necessitated by the structural transformation in the international system, characterised by interdependence and the new global divisions of labour and power. Positioned at the periphery of the international economic system, the global division of labour and power has generated implications for human security in Africa. The international division of labour, along with pressures unleashed by globalisation adversely affects Africa's ability to address the various human security threats identified by the UNDP Report. How globalisation and external factors promote human insecurity in SSA is analysed in the next section.

SOURCES OF HUMAN INSECURITY IN SUB-SAHARAN AFRICA

In July 2003, the University of Cambridge in the United Kingdom organised an international seminar aimed at exploring the root causes of human insecurity.13 Although the overwhelming focus of the deliberations was on terrorism considered to be the main source of security threat to western countries, the seminar arrived at certain conclusions that are relevant for understanding the causes of human insecurity in other regions, including SSA. Among other things, the seminar identified four interrelated categories of causal factors of human insecurity:

(a) causes that are unobtrusive and hence not easily acknowledged and explained;
(b) causes that have historical origins;
(c) causes that are systematically reproduced through existing social, political and economic institutions; and
(d) causes that reflect the immediate consequences of existing institutional conditions.

These factors were further collapsed into two main headings – internationalized causes (factors emanating from the western-inspired state system and values, including the globalization of western democracy); and localized causes – those that are specific to local situations such as terrorism, inequalities, inauspicious state policies, conflicts, etc. Although the geographical focus of the conference was on Western societies, the typologies of causes have relevance in SSA, where many of the causes of human insecurity are unobtrusive and historical. Also, some of the causes of human insecurity are either directly or indirectly incited by the globalisation of western values. Thus, the typologies of causes are consistent with the structuralism argument in that most of the causes of human insecurity in Africa are externally-inspired. The question is how unobtrusive, historical and externally-inspired are the causes of human insecurity in SSA, and what role do states and existing social institutions play in the human insecurity dynamic in SSA? In addressing these critical questions, it is imperative to explain globalisation, even if cursorily, to identify some of its salient features and consequences as a gateway to understanding how it directly affects or indirectly provides the context for contemporary human insecurity in SSA.

GLOBALISATION AS A DIRECT AND PROXIMATE SOURCE OF HUMAN INSECURITY

As a concept, globalisation remains contested, devoid of any intellectual consensus on its definition. It has therefore been variously defined based on its visible characteristics and impact. For example, Hettne *et al* (1999: 7) define globalisation as "the vision of a borderless world in which territory has lost all importance and functionalism is predominant". McGrew (1992) conceives of globalisation in two senses: first as "the multiplicity of linkages and interconnections that transcend nation-states and societies, which currently make up the modern world system" and second, as "a process through which events, decisions, and activities in one part of the world can come to have significant consequences for individuals and communities in quite distant parts of the globe." Giddens (1990) puts this idea more succinctly as "the intensification of worldwide social relations, which link distant localities in such a way that local happenings are shaped by events occurring many miles away and vice versa."

Others see globalisation in terms of the re-ordering of social relations at the global level. Thus, Held *et al* (1999: 16) perceive globalisation as a process (or set of processes), which embodies a transformation of the spatial organisation of social relations and transactions – assessed in terms of their extensity, intensity, velocity and impact-generating transcontinental or inter-regional flows and networks of activity, interaction and power." A set of basic and incontrovertible attributes of globalisation can thus be discerned from the above definitions. These include internationalisation i.e., the intensification of cross border interaction between countries and economies; liberalisation, i.e., emphasis on deregulation of the political and economic spaces; universalisation, i.e., its capacity to spread experiences of one region to various parts of the globe; and deterritorialisation, i.e. the capacity to undermine state borders (Scholte 2001).

An equally visible feature of globalisation is the close connection between countries, economies and peoples, shrinking the world into what is now euphemistically described as a "global village" (McGrew 1992: 63). The linkage of economies and countries is being facilitated by the advances in technology seen in at least two ways: First, the processes of flow and dissemination of information has been revolutionarised by satellite television and radios, enabling people in one part of the world to watch events live in another part. In addition, communication has been improved by the internet and cellular phones. This information superhighway has ensured that residents of even the remotest part of the world where these facilities exist are able to communicate with other parts of the world several thousands of kilometres away. Secondly, the way people travel has seen a dramatic revolution.

The use of jumbo and supersonic jets has considerably reduced the time required, for example, to cross the Atlantic from Europe. Moreover, the production of larger and more spacious aircrafts has made it possible for more people to be flown at a time. The faster mode of travel has facilitated interactions and the conduct of business several thousands of kilometres away. Thus, as Giddens (1990: 19) observes, globalisation has radically re-ordered our social and economic life in that "locales are thoroughly penetrated by and shaped in terms of social influences quite distant from them." Consequently, it has become possible for "the decisions and actions of the powerful [to] readily acquire a transnational impact affecting the welfare and security of people across the globe."

Similarly, the global financial system has been reshaped in such a way that capital can easily be invested across borders. In other words, the movement of capital is now faster than ever and multinational corporations (MNCs) have become the key agents of this process. A global trade regime such as the World Trade Organisation (WTO), which advocates for the removal of trade barriers, has provided fresh opportunities for capital to move and to find niches across the world. The rules of WTO are being reinforced by other multilateral pacts such as the multilateral agreement on investment (MAI). This agreement was originally negotiated among OECD beginning from 1995 but latter offered to developing countries. Essentially, MAI calls for the removal of trade barriers and empowers investors and MNCs to sue host governments deemed to be pursuing discriminatory policies against capital. In a sense, the power conferred on capital by MAI erodes the already tenuous sovereignty of host states in Africa. In turn, the loss of sovereignty to capital and markets means that globalisation impacts negatively on human security while at the same time truncating the ability of host states to redeem themselves.

A further disconcerting consequence of globalisation is the engendering and deepening of inequalities both at the international and national levels. Mainly due to the differing abilities of regions and states to confront its challenges or tap its associated advantages, globalisation has widened the already disturbing gap between the industrial north and the agricultural south. This gap is seen, among other things, in the disproportionate distribution of global infrastructure and wealth between the two poles. It was observed at the turn of the century that the bulk of the global communication infrastructure was concentrated in the north, which with only a fifth of the world's population had access to 74 percent of all the world's telephone lines while the poorest fifth of the world had access to a paltry 1.5 percent. Similarly, at the beginning of the 1990s, the North received over three-quarters of total global foreign direct investments (FDI), compared to a mere one percent by the South.

In his memorable Reith Lectures on globalisation at the turn of the century, Anthony Giddens (1999) noted that the share of the richest fifth of the world's population in global income rose from 70 percent to 85 percent, while that of the poorest fifth dropped from 2.3 percent to 1.4 percent over the preceding decade. The asymmetry in the distribution of the gains and pains of globalisation is also visible at the regional level. In SSA, the effects are overwhelmingly negative. In the same lecture, Giddens observed that the income per head in 20 SSA countries fell below what it was two decades ago. The pattern of the inequitable distribution of the benefits of globalisation is also perceptible at the national level, which in many cases has led to tensions and conflicts, thus undermining human security. Globalisation essentially reinforces liberal assumptions on development and the implementation of these assumptions has compounded the human security problematique in SSA. To understand how this happens, we need to carefully analyse some of the known sources of human insecurity in Africa, including conflicts, poverty, the debt crisis, political liberalization, environmental degradation, food insecurity and social inequalities.

CONFLICTS

There is absolutely no doubt that conflicts present one of the most daunting threats to human security in Africa. Africa's conflicts are, however, unique in the sense that they have become much frequent and intense. For example, a good proportion of the 80 conflicts recorded in SSA between 1960 and the 1990s occurred in the post cold war era. Also, majority of the conflicts are intra-state. Of the 16 wars occurring on the continent between 1990 and 1997, only two – the Chadian/Libyan and the Rwandan/Ugandan conflicts were interstate. So far, only few countries in the region have been spared of war. In 1994, no fewer than 12 of the 48 countries in sub-Saharan Africa were at war; two countries were at the post-war phase while 14 had a previous or current experience with political violence. To confirm its preeminence as a theatre of conflicts, Africa had the largest UN peacekeeping contingent – 17,000 strong in the DRC – by the close of 2006; while there are calls for additional international peacekeepers in Darfur and Somalia, where conflicts have been raging unabated for the past 5 and 16 years respectively. Ivory Coast, once the epitome of economic development in Africa is now war-torn. Similarly, Zimbabwe which was until 1990 full of promise for political stability is now teetering dangerously on the brink of violent inter-party conflict.

Generally, these conflicts have devastating impact on human security. First, many of the conflicts have drafted children as combatants. This is especially the case in conflicts involving rebel and militia movements. In Uganda a good number of the forces of the Lord Resistance Army (LRA), fighting the government in Kampala are children, and so were the cases with the Revolutionary United Front (RUF) in Sierra Leone and the National Patriotic Front of Liberia (NPFL), once led by Foday Sankoh and the now captured Charles Taylor respectively. Yet, the most appalling part of Africa's child soldiering is the forced manner in which the children are abducted and incorporated into the fighting force. In Uganda, the LRA invades villages at night and abducts children, some as young as six. While the boys are immediately initiated and grafted into fighting, the girls are made "comfort women" and beast of burden. Moreover, during raids adults who resisted or showed signs of sympathy with government forces were maimed with an ear, the nose, arm or limb brutally cut off. This cruelty, meant to elicit maximum cooperation with rebels, heighten the human insecurity not just of children and women who are most often brutally abused and raped, but also among the populations among and around whom rebels operate.

Secondly, conflicts generate refugees and internally displaced persons (IDPs). The UNDP noted that by 1992 conflicts in various African countries had spawned large numbers of refugees, including 870,000 in Somalia, 850,000 in Ethiopia, 670,000 in Liberia, 400,000 in Angola and 270,000 in Sudan (UNDP 1994: 32). According to the Internal Displacement Monitoring Centre (IDMC), the Norwegian-based international body monitoring conflictinduced internal displacement worldwide, Africa had more than 50 percent of the 23.5 million IDPs worldwide and was home to 3.2 million of the 12 million refugees worldwide at the end of 2005. This figure includes some estimated 570,000 people internally displaced in Zimbabwe by the government's "clean up" operation, but excludes IDPs from less publicised inter-communal violence such as those flaring up intermittently in Nigeria.

Human insecurity is manifested not only among the people on the move, but also in the regions and among the communities in which refugees and IDPs take temporal refuge. Thirdly, conflicts induce human suffering with the more vulnerable – women, children and the elderly – the most affected. The vulnerability of these sections of the population, especially women is even more glaring in refugee and IDP camps. The absence of law and order provides salutary conditions for the unscrupulous to prey on the vulnerability of women. Moreover, the general adversity, scarcity and lack of proper sanitation expose IDP and refugee camps to epidemics. Aside of humans whose human security is evidently compromised, conflicts also induce infrastructural destruction – roads, hospitals, schools, water supply systems, etc, which should traditionally provide supportive conditions for human security. Similarly, conflicts undermine agriculture, commerce and industry. Even under normal conditions, food resources, medical, employment and educational facilities are barely adequate in SSA and conflicts only worsen the situation. Although difficult to adequately quantify in monetary terms, it has been estimated that a local civil war costs a low income country like Uganda about $54 billion on the average. Human rights violations are worse under conflict situations. Much more pressure is exerted on the environment under conditions of conflict. Ultimately, conflicts heighten food, health, community and personal insecurity.

The causes of conflicts in Africa have been well discussed in the literature. Some link conflicts to political and governance-related factors such as ethnicity, the fragility of the postcolonial state, and the struggle over the state, others locate it in environmental factors, pointing to competition for farming and grazing lands and other natural resources, while others see conflicts as reflecting the artificiality of the African state. However, less perceptible are the conditions and pressures from the international system and the indirect, but also direct role of external actors that tend to either create, ripen or exacerbate conditions for conflict. It is common knowledge that economic crisis is a good recipe for conflict, and Africa's economic malaise is too familiar to be recounted here. One of the most visible highlights of Africa's economic crisis is the debt overhung, which has been known to be conflict-inducing. Smith has noted that about 50 percent of the 25 most indebted Third World countries were at war in 1990 or early 1991.

Similarly, Brown notes that of the 33 highly indebted countries in SSA only four – Niger, Sao Tome, Senegal and Tanzania – have escaped destructive conflicts and wars of one form or another. The correlation between poverty and general economic despondency on the one hand and conflict on the other was most poignantly stated by Therese Paquet-Sevigny (1990), the former UN Under-Secretary General for Public Information: Deepening poverty is already leading to mounting instability. The widespread unrest, turmoil and violence which is now afflicting an unprecedented number of countries is linked to one common thread of growing economic malaise, regardless of the ethnic and political guises it adopts. In Liberia, Rwanda, the Horn of Africa.....poverty is the tinder which ignites the resentments and fears that all people and communities harbour.

The inescapable reality is that conflicts linked to distribution are often exacerbated by economic crisis typified by unemployment, inflation and prolonged periods of recession. The role of external players in sparking or escalating conflicts in Africa is also wellknown. During the cold war, proxy wars were fought on behalf of the US and the Soviets. As a proxy for the US, Apartheid South Africa, for example, destabilised neighbouring states in a bid to destroy African National Congress (ANC) bases, but also to check the spread of communism in the region. Similarly, Ethiopia and Somalia served as allies for the Soviets and the Americans respectively during the cold war and received military assistance from their respective patrons. The abatement of the cold war severed relations between patrons and clients but the weapons, missiles and tanks remained, which were used in post-cold war internal conflicts. The involvement of the US in post-cold war conflicts is, however, still provable. In 1998, the Clinton administration gave $20 million in aid to the Sudan People's Liberation Army (SPLA) and its supporters – Uganda, Eritrea and Ethiopia – to help overthrow the Islamic regime in Khartoum.15 And, as recently as December 2006, the US encouraged and aided the Ethiopian invasion of Somalia to dislodge the Union of Islamic Courts, a regime the former believes provides haven for international terrorists. The Ethiopian military campaign has heightened insecurity in the Somali capital of Mogadishu in particular and the country in general. The new friendship between the US and Ethiopia – previously implacable ideological enemies – and the aid the latter receives from Washington has helped it to prosecute its seemingly intractable border conflict with Eritrea.

Africa's conflicts are now known to be fuelled by "conflict" or "blood" diamonds, defined by the UN as "...diamonds that originate from areas controlled by forces or factions opposed to legitimate and internationally recognized governments, and are used to fund military action in opposition to those governments, or in contravention of the decisions of the Security Council."16 Proceeds from the sale of conflict diamonds have been known to have sustained the conflicts in Angola, Sierra Leone, Liberia, Congo, and to a limited degree, in Ivory Coast. For example, between 1992 and 1998, UNITA, the Angolan rebel group, earned over $4 billion from the illegal sale of diamonds. The UN also estimates that by 1999, the RUF of Sierra Leone had sold about $125 million worth of rough diamonds to the diamond industry in Europe alone. And, Charles Taylor is believed to have sustained his war and regime for long because of proceeds from diamond sales. Access to diamond mines helped sustain brutal conflicts.

The question often sidelined, however, is who buys the blood diamond? Although some of the diamond does find market on the African continent, it has been estimated that the bulk of the so-called conflict diamonds find its way into the store house of the diamond cartel, De Beers in the US. The cartel, however, insists that it is nearly impossible to determine the origin of diamonds. On the whole, about 40 percent of the world's diamonds, all of them believed to come from Africa, is sourced by De Beers. The point is no one trades in merchandise that has no ready market. As long as there is a diamond market in London, New York and Tokyo, the illicit trade will persist to the detriment of Africa. The sale of illegal diamonds persists because there is a market with high demand for them and sadly, that market is located in western countries.

Poverty

The preponderance of poverty in SSA is beyond question. Over 40 percent of the 800 million people in SSA live below the poverty line – earning less than 2 dollars a day (UNDP 1999). Africa is the only region in which absolute poverty is expected to increase over the current level (UNDP 2000). The gravity of poverty is exemplified in nearly all the indicators of human development. For example, as of 2002 the percentages of sub-Saharan Africans with access to improved sanitation, water sources and literate were 36 percent, 58 percent and 61.3 percent respectively. These figures were just slight improvements over those recorded in 1990 (UNDP 2005: 243). Moreover, SSA is the only region where overall human development index (HDI), a composite indicator that covers three dimensions of welfare – income, education and health – has been declining since the 1990s UNDP (2005: 21). These have spin implications for human security, especially on the ability of people to influence their own lives. Poverty can be cyclical and may be passed on to one's children or even the next generation once unbroken. Poverty also increases the vulnerability of people to abuses and violations. In many countries in SSA, including South Africa poverty has driven the youth into various social vices such as prostitution, drugs, gangsterism and crime. Additionally, poverty limits access to health and nutrition where these are available and thus increases the susceptibility of people to diseases. While acknowledging the various mode of transmission, the South African government has maintained that poverty is a proximate cause of the rapid spread of HIV/AIDS that is rocking the country. A virus like avian flu may spreads rapidly in SSA as poverty disinclines people to report cases fearing the curling of birds. The lack of adequate equipments further limits the ability of poor countries to quickly detect and track down such a disease.

The adverse implications of poverty for human security, however, transcend the vulnerability of people. To be sure, poverty limits access to the new information highway. Such innovations as satellite television, the internet, cellular phones, among the key features of the global village, remain beyond the reach of the majority of the population in Africa. As of the mid-1990s, there were more telephones in the Japanese capital of Tokyo alone than in the whole of the SSA African region (*The Financial Times* 7 June 1996: 3). Similarly, the UNDP notes that, as of 2003, only 9 out of every 1000 and 54 out of every 1000 sub-Saharan Africans had telephone mainlines and cellular phone subscription respectively compared to 567 of every 1000 and 705 of every 1000 in high income OECD countries (UNDP 2005: 265). Access to the internet is still limited in SSA even in many universities, which are supposed to be institutions of knowledge production. And, because of its prohibitive cost many more Africans lack access to satellite television. Information is a source of power under the current global dispensation and drives development. Globalisation has shifted the basis of a country's comparative advantage from tangible natural resources to access to knowledge and information. Missing out on the information super highway is thus not only a mark of disempowerment in the globalised world, but it is also just as detrimental as the lack of access to food.

Political corruption and abuse of human rights by governments are high under conditions of poverty as people become more preoccupied with basic survival. Under such conditions impoverished people see human rights as a luxury. The quest to survive leads to intense, often violent, competition among communities over diminishing resources such as farming and grazing lands and may result in conflicts, which as noted already, is a major source of human insecurity. Also, because of the uneven urban-rural terms of trade the former has been the more active in national politics partly because many urban workers are educated and are relatively better off economically than their rural counterparts. By contrast, many rural dwellers are illiterate and unable to analyse national issues. The ignorance of the poor is often exploited by the predatory state, which misinforms them and compounds their vulnerability to insecurity. Thus, in general poverty is not only a symptom but also a catalyst of human insecurity. On the whole, poverty is on the increase in SSA, the determination of states to meet the Millennium Development Goals (MDG) notwithstanding. The causes of poverty, however, remain debatable. Too often, fingers have been pointed to conflicts as a factor creating impoverished conditions, or undermining opportunities for poverty alleviation. Often, too, inauspicious and self-destructive public policies have been blamed. In its 1981 Report, which set the stage for the introduction of the ubiquitous SAP, for example, the World Bank blamed SSA escalated poverty and general underdevelopment on the adoption of statist and patronage policies (World Bank 1981). Such neo-classical explanations, pointing to mainly internal factors as causes of poverty and underdevelopment, have remained dominant and continue to inform western aid packages to the region. SAPs, and their fleet of conditionalities were meant to undermine that state's dominance in economic activities by transferring its central role in the distribution of resources to the market.

While the responsibility of internal factors in causing underdevelopment and human insecurity is undeniable, it can be argued that external factors have been partly responsible for their exacerbation although this is often hidden and not easily observable. Although poverty in SSA predated the introduction of SAPs, the implementation of these IMF and World Bankstyled neo-liberal economic policies from the late 1970s exacerbated, rather than ameliorated, the problem and consequently heightened human insecurity. Everywhere, the hallmarks of SAPs included desubsidisation, deregulation, devaluation, decontrolling and privatisation. These policies deepened poverty and human insecurity. Desubsidisation, for example, placed the prices of basic food, health and education beyond the reach of the majority of the population. Devaluations also eroded purchasing power and pushed people down below the poverty line, while privatisation and liberalisation hastened the demise of nascent industries with the textile and leather industries being the hardest hit. Moreover, liberalisation brought in cheaply produced western rice and maize, which drove many rural farmers out of job. Together, liberalisation and privatisation aggravated the already worse unemployment situation in the region, worsening human insecurity.

While unemployment is increasing, FDI and overseas development assistance (ODA), which would have injected some life into SSA economies and help alleviate unemployment, are on the decline. Although this has recently been increasing in certain countries (Angola, South Africa and Mozambique), and regionally in southern Africa, the flow of FDI to Africa has on the aggregate declined from $8.1 billion in 1996 to $6.1billion in 2000. Although this rose to a high of $13.8 billion in 2001, it fell again to $7 billion in 2003 (Harsch 2003: 16). Similarly, net overseas development assistance (ODA) has plummeted from a high level of $28 billion in 1990 to $16.4 billion in 2000 (Asante 2003:16). In spite of numerous international trade agreements promising Africa with access to world markets, its share of world exports remained at just 1 percent at the turn of the century although this was 4 percent in 1960, while its share of world trade has plummeted from 2.7 percent 1990 to just 2 percent in 2002 (UNCTAD 2004). Against this background, Africa remains the most marginalised continent in the contemporary global economy. Its role has been limited to serving as a marginal market for northern industries. The little investments trickling down to SSA are concentrated in the capital-intensive extractive industries. Consequently, the rate of job creation has remained negligible.

The intrusive and strict austerity conditions imposed on adjusting countries caused a massive erosion of the already tenuous economic sovereignty even in making domestic policy choices.

Under adjustment, even a country's annual budget had to be approved by creditors in the latter's bid to ensure the judicious use of aid money. The effect of such scrutiny and surveillance has been to undermine the state's ability to determine and implement priority programmes that seek to address human insecurity. The drive to cut down on public expenditure, for example, has necessitated a reduction in state's budget for education and health which are thought to make only long-term returns. Ultimately, a pool of illiterate and unhealthy population is created whose safety and security is far from assured. Indeed, the Cambridge seminar on security warily noted that the plethora of conditionalities imposed on developing countries by the dominant international financial institutions (IFIs) have become a source of human insecurity, fuelling conflicts and defeating the original intention to alleviate poverty.

Moreover, as it is with every public policy, SAPs produced winners and losers but in a much disproportionate way. While a minority, mainly the capital owning class, benefited from the liberalised market and financial environment, the majority were losers who suffered increased economic adversities. A consequence of this development was to widen further the disconcerting gap between social classes. The widening disparity was also visible even within particular industries. The agricultural sector was a typical example. A study in Ghana found that that the gap between large and small scale cocoa farmers widened dramatically under SAP. The former, constituting 32 percent of cocoa farmers, received 94 percent of total cocoa revenue, while the losing majority of 68 percent received a meagre 6 percent (US Government 1989: 8). In nearly every SSA country, SAPs left a trail of social inequality between a small minority of winners and the vast losing and exasperated population. Such grotesque inequality, aggravated by the maldistribution of the costs and benefits of adjustment undermined human security.

As the Cambridge seminar on security noted, inequalities have a potential to generate disaffection especially in situations where the losers are the more numerous. One of the predictable responses to the adversities generated by austerity is migration, which has both short- and long-term impact on human security. **Migration** follows two patterns. First, there is the massive movement of destitute youth from the rural areas to the urban centres in desperate search for employment, which is often non-existent. The ultimate effect of this is the swelling of cities' population and the exertion of additional strains on the already over-stretched urban infrastructure. Pushed further by desperation, many of the youth enter into the informal sector, characterised by legal and illegal activities. The latter includes drugs, prostitution, money laundering and other vices inconsistent with human security. Second, economic adversities serve as "push" factors, instigating international migration especially among professionals. While some professionals migrate to relatively affluent African countries such as South Africa, Botswana and Namibia, the majority head for western countries, causing a massive brain drain on the continent.

Although international migration of professionals is historical, it intensified with the introduction of SAPs in the 1980s. For example, while it was estimated that 27,000 skilled Africans left the continent for industrialised countries between 1960 and 1975, the figure rose to 40,000 between 1975 and 1984. The Economic Commission for Africa (ECA) and the International Organisation for Migration (IOM) estimate that at least 20,000 skilled Africans left the continent each year since 1990. According to the international NGO, Doctors without Borders, Malawi produced 44 nurses in 2005. That year 86 nurses left the country causing a shortfall. The NGO laments further about the ratio of doctors to patients. In Malawi, Mozambique and Lesotho, for example, the ratios are 2, 2.6 and 5 respectively compared to the World Health Organisation's (WHO) standard ratio of 20 doctors to 100,000 patients. The exodus of nurses and other health professionals leaves hospitals and clinics without the requisite manpower and worsening an already serious problem. Freedom from want is undermined where medicines are available in hospitals but without doctors or nurses to dispense them. In recent years young unskilled Africans also risk their lives in dangerous journeys across the Sahara and on the Atlantic to reach Europe in a desperate attempt to escape economic adversities in their home countries.

DEBT - A SOURCE OF HEALTH AND EDUCATIONAL INSECURITY

A further consequence of SAP is the escalation of Africa's debt crisis. While the region's debt crisis is mounting, it has never been formally linked to SAP or external actors. Hence, the debt crisis remains hidden as a cause of human insecurity. Whereas SSA debt is partly blameable on self-destructive internal policies, such as massive investments in unprofitable public enterprises, subsidies, corruption and mismanagement, etc, external factors have contributed to its escalation.

Majority of SSA countries rely on primary agricultural exports, whose prices are controlled by external market forces. Collapsing world prices (usually during periods of increased production) create balance of payment problems, which in turn spawns a need for external borrowing to finance budget deficits. At the same time the supply of these agricultural products are inelastic such that producers cannot immediately take advantage of rising world prices. Cocoa, for example, takes five years from nursery to yield fruits. And when producers eventually increase production, the prices fall, creating further need for borrowing and ultimately indebtedness. Africa's loss of its comparative advantage in the supply of raw materials, following the emergence of biotechnology, the production of cheaper genetically modified and synthetic substitutes, has worsened its situation.

Globalisation and the skewed international trade regime offer little opportunities for SSA to reverse its declining economic fortunes. Under the current free trade regime, SSA is to liberalise its markets, exposing its nascent industries to destructive global competition. At the same time, Northern governments continue to subsidise their farmers, giving them a competitive edge over their SSA counterparts. From Cancun, Mexico in 2003 to Doha, Qatar in 2006, the World Trade Organisation (WTO) has consistently failed to resolve the impasse between the North and South over agricultural subsidies. Northern subsidies mean that talks about granting Africa access to northern markets would yield practically nothing, given the former's ill-placed position to compete. Africa is not an exporter of computers, digital cameras, TVs or cars; its competitiveness lies not in industrial products, but in agricultural goods. Subsidies on agricultural commodities by western countries mean the global market is effectively closed to Africa.

The refusal of western governments to compromise on subsidies reveals a fundamental contradiction in their policies. While they hide under globalisation to preach free trade, they simultaneously subject Africa to conditions of unfair trade. The collapse of the recent WTO negotiations in Doha means that the question of establishing fair trade among countries is no longer an issue on the agenda of the industrialised countries. Indeed, in its report, the UN Commission on Human Security recommended the institution of fair trade practices among countries and regions as a way of helping weaker and vulnerable countries to better cope with the challenges of human security.

To be sure, the original purpose of SAP was to enhance Africa's ability to repay its external debts. It was thought that this could be achieved by imposing austerity measures on African countries under which the state would be prevented from subsidising or engaging in patronage politics. Under the latter, the state used scarce public funds as reward for political loyalty. Under the SAP regime, therefore, credit lines were opened to countries judged to be rigorously implementing adjustment reforms. In the 1980s, Ghana and Uganda received large volumes of aid on account of their impressive adjustment record (Herbst 1993). However, such credit lines were never acts of charity. Rather, they were loans to be repaid with interest. The ultimate effect was that as African countries adopted SAPs and accessed new lines of credit, their external debt grew concomitantly. Once the debt emerged, it became a selfgenerating phenomenon and, worse of all, causing a reverse transfer of capital from Africa to the west. For example, SSA received $294 billion in disbursed loans between 1970 and 2002. Despite paying out $268 in debt service, it still had a debt of $210 billion by the end of 2002. In total, during the 1970-2002 period Africa received some $540 billion and still shouldered a debt of $295 billion after paying back close to $550 billion in principal and interest.23 Even by 1996, arrears on Africa's debt had reached a whooping $64 billion, which was more than 25 percent of the total indebtedness.

Debt created the need for further external aid and this generated further indebtedness, imparting a funny scenario of digging a new pit to fill an old one. To be credit worthy and eligible for further loans, indebted countries needed to demonstrate an ability to service existing debts. This often required the commitment of large proportion of the national budget to debt service. In 1990, for example, Madagascar spent the equivalent of 7.2 percent of its GDP on debt service compared to 2.1 percent and 1.2 percent on education and health respectively, while Congo spent nearly 4 times more on debt service than on education and over 12 times more than on health. Similarly, Zambia's debt service as a percentage of GDP in 2003 was three times and four times more than health and education respectively (UNDP 2005: 286-287). Since the inception of the debt crisis, SSA countries have been devoting appreciable percentages of their national budgets to debt servicing. The pressure to repay debts thus diverts resources from infrastructure and services that are critical for alleviating poverty and human insecurity.

The current initiatives to ease Africa's debt under the highly indebted poor countries' programme (HIPC) have proved illusory. Almost all SSA countries are still indebted over 10 years after the introduction of the programme. In 2006 Ghana, along with 16 other developing countries, was granted access to the US-managed Millennium Challenge Account (MCA) valued at US $547 million. The MCA is a credit facility reserved for developing countries judged to "rule justly, invest in their people, and encourage economic freedom" – literally promoting good governance.25 Other SSA states are striving to gain access to the MCA as well. But, here again, nothing could be further from the truth. The MCA is not a gift and countries accessing it know that it is a loan that is repayable in the future with interest. As such, it compounds their external indebtedness and attenuates their ability to address human insecurity. Overall, SSA foreign debt has played a role, even if indirect, in aggravating human insecurity.

POLITICAL LIBERALISATION AND DEMOCRATISATION

The process of democratisation, accompanying globalisation has generated mixed results in SSA. On the one hand, democratisation helped to liberalise many of Africa's hitherto closed political systems by sweeping away one-man and one-party dictatorships. On the other hand, however, it has tended to create conditions for human insecurity. In retrospect, the importance of democracy for development cannot be overemphasized. The World Bank Report of 1981 blamed Africa's lingering crisis on bad governance. This view was shared by several leading scholars on African development (Nyong'o 1987; Ake 1994, 1996; Mkandawire 2001). In a recent work, Guest (2004) also argues that Africa's economic crisis is mainly caused by bad leadership and bad governance. On their part Africans have acknowledged the importance of democracy in development reflected in their collective adoption of the African Charter for Popular Participation in Development and Transformation, in Arusha, Tanzania in 1990. The charter underscored the importance of popular participation and inclusivity in the development process.

However, the relevance of democratisation for the current discussion on human security in Africa stems from the manner in which the project was instituted and executed. With the exception of a few countries – Botswana, Senegal, Mauritius, South Africa and Zimbabwe – the majority of SSA liberalised their political systems in response to IMF/World Bankimposed conditionalities. Often referred to as second generational conditionality, the demand for political liberalisation and democratisation was supported by Africa's leading bilateral creditors, who have made democratisation a cardinal condition for aid and investment. The emergent global disdain for undemocratic governance after the demise of the communism made it difficult for countries to circumvent the conditionality.

In many respects, however, the process of democratisation has become a source of tension among competing constituencies as incumbents organised stage-managed elections to satisfy the creditor community. In many cases such practices have generated post-election tensions, which did not only deepen existing social fractures, but led to full scale conflicts. Recent post-election violence in Nigeria, the Ivory Coast, Togo, Lesotho, the Democratic Republic of Congo (DRC), to name a few, have all cost human lives and destruction of property. In the same vein, the pressure to democratise has in many cases led to the emergence of truncated or election democracies variously described as "pseudo democracies", "virtual democracies" (Joseph 1999), or "incomplete metamorphic democracies" (Udogu 1997). These are systems, which hold elections but follow policies that are anything but democratic, thus creating conditions for violent contestations. To this extent, the imposition of democracy from above rather it developing organically from below has become a source of conflict and consequently human insecurity.

Environmental Insecurity

There is little doubt about the escalation of environmental degradation in Africa. The threat to human security posed by this phenomenon is dire as over 70 percent of sub-Sahara Africans depend on the forest for livelihood. The extent of environmental decay in the region is too familiar to be recounted here. However, suffice it to mention that the region's ecology has been plagued by rapid deforestation, desertification, soil erosion, pollution, drought and famine. In addition, SSA is faced with an intractable population growth rate of about 3.1 percent, the highest in the world, despite the prevalence of the HIV/AIDS pandemic. The pollution of land and rivers by multinational companies is on the increase, while drought and famine have repeatedly hit SSA in the last four decades. Fish stocks are rapidly being depleted from rivers as fishermen leave little time for stocks to replenish. With the destruction of forests for farming and grazing, the natural habitat of wild game is increasingly being encroached upon, while poverty compels the rural folk to poach animals for food, thus causing the extinction or near extinction of game species.

Ultimately, the environment in SSA is unsustainable, imparting severe threats not only to the present but also to future generations. The causes of such rapid environmental degradation can be broadly classified under two main headings – natural and human-induced. Natural occurrences such as earthquakes are beyond human control. These occur unceremoniously at the discretion of Mother Nature and what governments and aid agencies do is simply to provide assistance to victims. Luckily, earthquakes are infrequent in SSA. The second set of causes is human-made and includes deforestation, soil erosion, pollution, poaching and population growth. Deforestation leads to desertification and soil erosion; air and water pollution negatively affects public health and aquatic life; poaching threatens the survival of game; while population growth exerts additional pressures on over-stretched resources. At times, the responsibility for environmental collapse rests with the African states for failing to establish or enforce strong environmental regimes. Yet, while acknowledging the role of humans and the state in the decay of the environment, it is possible to identify the indirect, but also direct contribution of globalisation and other external pressures to the crisis. First, the role of poverty in inducing conflicts has already been noted. However, as argued earlier, poverty which is partly caused by external interventions, facilitates environmental degradation. The inability to access fertilizers, for example, drives rural farmers into shifting cultivation as a dominant agricultural practice. This systematically reduces the fertility of land within a short period of time, causing further impoverishment. Similarly, pastoralists herd cattle over large plains of land and when this is overgrazed, they are forced to cross borders, sparking skirmishes and sometimes violent conflict with rival pastoral communities. Poverty and environmental decline are thus mutually reinforcing.

Second, beyond community level, the state is often forced by external pressures to compromise environmental conservation. At the July 1992 Earth Summit in Rio, delegates were concerned with African states' vulnerability in trading the environment for scarce foreign exchange in a bid to revive their ailing economies and to repay external debts. This concern was vindicated by the pursuit of environmentally-hostile policies in SSA. In a bid to increase foreign exchange earnings, Ghana increased its timber exports causing it to loose 25 percent of its tropical forest during the ten-year period between 1984 and 1994. The Ghana Forestry Commission (GFC) estimates that the country currently looses 75,000 hectares of forest annually. The GFC is concerned that at this rate Ghana's entire forest could disappear by 2010.27 Similarly, encouraged by a spectacular revenue of over $300 million from timber exports in the 1960s, Ivory Coast embarked on a logging spree that caused a 67 percent declined in its closed forest area in 20 years – from 12 million hectres in 1956 to just 4 million in 1977. Also, desperate to earn foreign currency, Benin is on record to have accepted the dumping of toxic wastes into its oceans for compensatory payments of as little as $2.50 per tonne when this would have cost the company $400.00 per tonne in the US.

Moreover, the determination to attract fresh foreign investments and to dissuade existing investors from leaving has inclined the state towards capital vis-a-vis its domestic constituencies. The state has thus tended to relax environmental rules to encourage MNC operations. Thus, Shell and other oil companies can abuse the environment and impoverish surrounding communities in the Niger Delta while enjoying state support. In Ghana, too, communities in the vicinity of gold mines are witnessing increased mercury pollution, land degradation, air and noise pollution, which together impart harmful consequences, including spreading inexplicable skin diseases. Yet, no firm state measures have been instituted against the concerned mining companies. In Uganda, state police have shot and killed protesters opposing government plans to lease forest land to an Asian sugar plantation company in April 2006. While environmentalists argue that the plantation farm would endanger the existence of rare species of animals and birds, the government contends that it will bring in much needed revenue. The pressure to liberalise national economies and create space for MNCs in response to the dictates of globalisation, along with the enhanced powers of capital to tame the state, has forced the latter to relax or even waive environmental laws. In following environmentally bankrupt policies, African states seem to be oblivious to the intricate connection between environmental protection, sustainable development and human security. Thus, although unobtrusive, external factors play a role in the escalation of environmental insecurity in SSA.

Food Insecurity

Sub-Saharan Africa's food insecurity, reflected in growing hunger, famine, malnutrition, along with its implications for development is also a familiar story. A ministerial conference of the African Union (AU) in 2005 noted that over 11 million people in the Horn of Africa and 3.5 million in Kenya were hit by food crisis; 71 percent of the population in the Democratic Republic of Congo (DRC) were undernourished, while the lives of 48 percent of children in Northern Uganda were threatened by chronic food insecurity (AU 2005). Similarly, a UNICEF report notes that 28 percent of all children in SSA are underweight (UNICEF 2006). A 2006 Oxfam briefing paper – *Causing Hunger: An Overview of the Food Crises in Africa,* – provides graphic details of the scale of the region's food insecurity. The paper notes that while the average percentage of under nourishment in the developing world is 17, that for SSA is 33 percent. Southern Africa and the Horn are particularly prone to drought raising further concerns about food safety in these regions. Oxfam is on the whole pessimistic about the food situation in SSA and the prospects for the region meeting its Millennium Development Goals (MDG) of halving hunger by 2015.

The causes of Africa's food insecurity are complex, but can generally be linked to a combination of internal, external and unpredictable environmental factors. Poverty is often identified as a cause of food insecurity. This argument stems from the fact that in most cases, food may be available but remains unaffordable. While, poverty is itself the product of other factors, the argument sounds plausible in a region where the percentage of the population living below $1.00 a day has doubled since 1981. For example, in 2005 northeast Kenya was hit by a food crisis, which severely affected pastoralists while the country experienced a 15 percent increase in harvest and a 5 percent rise in GDP. By that year, the proportion of Kenyans living below $1.00 a day had risen to 66 percent from 40 percent in 1990 (Mason 2006). Generally, the wealthy are least affected by food shortages as they are able to afford even under conditions of rising prices. In this sense, poverty is a noticeable cause of food insecurity. However, as noted earlier, poverty in SSA is often exacerbated by globalisation and other externally-inspired pressures.

Often, too, food insecurity results from inadequate investments in the agricultural sector. According to Oxfam (2006), while food aid to SSA has been increasing, there has been a 43 percent drop in aid for agricultural production in the periods between 1990-92 and 2000-02. Oxfam estimates that Africa requires $18 billion a year in investments in rural infrastructure, including agriculture, to achieve the region's MDG on hunger reduction. The lack of investment in the food sector has been worsened by the region's heavy dependence on natural rain, which has become erratic in recent decades due to climatic changes. Unpredictable rainfall patterns, along with extremities of weather conditions have left Africa vulnerable to the effects of famine, drought and floods. Unlike Europe, and North America, Africa has a limited capacity to control its environment. As one observer warily notes, "when the rains fail [Africans] go hungry. And when the rains are too heavy....they lose their homes." Irrigation in SSA is on a small scale and concentrated on large commercial estate farms. Only 7 percent of Africa's arable land is irrigated compared to 38 percent in Asia.32 Sub-Sahara Africa is thus highly vulnerable to declines in food production during conditions of drought. It will be helpful to SSA agriculture and food security if external donors give equal attention to investments in irrigation as to food aid. The familiar oriental aphorism that teaching a child how to fish feeds him for his entire life than merely giving him fish, should guide agricultural aid policies to Africa.

Africa's incessant and intractable conflicts have also compounded its food insecurity. Agricultural activities, which require a serene environment, are undermined by conditions of violence, instability and uncertainty. In Sudan, prolonged conflict between the southern-based Sudan People's Liberation Army (SPLA) and the Khartoum government has left the arable lands in the south to waste, leaving southern Sudanese to depend on food aid. Uncertainty about the future also disinclines farmers to invest in food production even after the ending of conflicts. Other times, conflicts divert public resources away from investments that avert food shortages and enhance poverty alleviation. A report of the Technical Cooperation Department of the UN Food and Agricultural Organisation (FAO) noted in 1997 that the seven Intergovernmental Authority on Development (IGAD) countries – Djibouti, Eritrea, Ethiopia, Kenya, Somalia, Sudan and Uganda – which are highly susceptible to drought and food shortages, allocated $2 billion to military expenditure as a result of conflict and instability in the Horn. This, the report worried, could discourage donors whose aid aim at alleviating poverty.

An additional cause of food insecurity in SSA is the growing HIV/AIDS scourge. By 2005, SSA had over 26 million cases leading to 2.5 million deaths. HIV/AIDS and other diseases such as malaria and tuberculosis significantly undermine food production by reducing the man-hours available for agriculture. The negative effects of HIV/AIDS on agricultural production are already evident. Oxfam notes that the production of maize, the staple food of much of SSA, has seen a 54 percent decline between 1992 and 1997 as a result of HIV/AIDS.

Studies also estimate that by 2020 HIV/AIDS will claim the lives of 20 percent or more of the population engaged in agriculture in many of the southern African countries, where the epidemic has assumed crisis proportions. One adult death is estimated to correspond to a 15 percent drop in food security. This scenario is certain to worsen the food situation as about 70 percent of the population in the worse HIV/AIDS-hit countries is engaged in agriculture. The devastating impact of HIV/AIDS is fed by poverty, which incapacitates affected families from accessing medication and the necessary nutritional food to supplement their diet. Similarly, the negative impact of malaria on development has now become palpable. It was estimated in 2000 that economic development in Africa would have been 32 percent higher had malaria been eradicated 35 years ago. It is also noted that the GDP per person in malaria-infected countries averaged 3 percent lower than malaria-free countries. Moreover, the learning abilities of children with cerebral malaria (a severe type of malaria) are reduced by 4.5 percent even after they have been cured.

Environmental factors such as drought and floods also compound the food crisis in SSA. In the main, however, such environmental catastrophes are related to global climate changes, especially global warming, which has altered the normal patterns of rainfall. Droughts and floods, which used to occur at approximately 50 years intervals, now occur much more frequently. Thus, while there were only 16 major disasters in the 1960s, there were 29 and 70 in the 1970s and 1980s respectively, caused by droughts, cyclones, earthquakes and floods. As well, regions which normally receive rainfall crucial for planting and sowing no longer get this at the right time. These climatic changes have heightened uncertainty about food security. A research by the UK Department of International Development, cited by the *Independent* newspaper predicts that by 2050, the effects of climate change will severely affect southern Africa, the Sahel, the Great Lakes, the coastal strips of western and eastern Africa and would worsen agriculture in general and food production in particular.35 Already, the Sahel and Southern Africa in particular have been devastated by recurring droughts and floods and this report could only bring more bad news. Further rises in global temperatures will put an estimated 60 million people in Africa at risk of hunger. In addition, such climatic changes would worsen the energy crisis of the many SSA countries depending on hydro-electricity and subsequently undermine industrial production.

While the causes of Africa's food insecurity appear overwhelmingly internal and ecological, a careful examination of the factors reveals the hidden responsibility of external interventions. The role of external factors in the accentuation of poverty and conflicts has already been noted. Besides, international NGOs like Oxfam, Jubilee 2000 and Christian Aid, attribute Africa's food crisis to a combination of inauspicious policies followed by industrialised towards the region. Oxfam bemoans that "inadequate debt cancellation, declining and poor quality development aid, flawed advice from donors, conditions attached to aid that forced [recipient] countries to adopt damaging agricultural policies, and unfair trade rules..." are fundamental to understanding of SSA's food insecurity. Oxfam is also critical of the slow manner in which the north has traditionally responded to Africa's food emergencies. As well, various reports link SSA's food problems to the north.

It is, for example, worthy of note that much of the global warming giving rise to environmental calamities in SSA is caused by industrialised countries, which emit the bulk of the global carbon dioxide and other greenhouse gases. Although the north has only 20 percent of the world's population, it is responsible for 80 percent of the world's emissions. The US is particularly culpable. With a population of 300 million, the US alone produces carbon dioxide to the combined equivalent of 135 developing countries with a total population of 3 billion. In other words, 22 percent of the world's emission of greenhouse gases is accounted for by 4.5 percent of the world's population in the US, while India, for example, with 17 percent of the world's population emits 4.2 percent of the world's greenhouse gases (Christian Aid 2005). If climate changes are the major causes of droughts and floods, then it can be argued with little risk of error that external agents are partly responsible for food insecurity in Africa.

Terrorism and Insecurity

Terrorism is a source of human insecurity for the simple fact that it breads fear, uncertainty, destruction and death. As such, it has since 9/11 elicited international attention. International conferences have been organised to examine its root causes and to explore ways of averting it. One of the contentious issues, however, relates to its definition. While there is consensus that hijacking and crushing civilian aircrafts into soft targets, or turning oneself into a bomb and blowing up civilians at a crowded market place amounts to terrorism, there is by no means agreement on whether the term is applicable to methods used by subject people legitimately resisting foreign occupation. As Clapham argues, terrorists are compelled "to operate within territory that is effectively controlled by their enemies." The familiar axiom that "one man's terrorist is another's liberation fighter" is an indication of how long away an intellectual consensus on the definition of the concept is. Since 9/11, however, there has emerged a tendency for any violent or non-conventional mode of grievance articulation to be branded as "terror". Beyond the unending controversy about who is a "terrorist", it is clear that the use of violence of any form leading to the spread of fear among people is a threat to human safety and security.

Some African states have been victims of terror. Countries with radical Islamists such as Algeria, Egypt and Morocco, have had to deal with terrorists acts, perpetuated by groups opposed to the state or its policies, on a regular basis. Although such violent acts are common, and indeed frequent in North Africa, they are by no means confined exclusively to that part of Africa. Some countries south of the Sahara, including Somalia, Ethiopia, and

Nigeria have in recent decades witnessed various forms of terrorist acts. The most publicised terrorist acts in Africa were the near simultaneous attacks on the US embassies in Nairobi, Kenya and Dar Es Salaam, Tanzania on 7 August 1998 that claimed 213 and 10 lives respectively. The casualties in the Nairobi attack were predominantly Kenyans, including 34 who were employed by the embassy and 167 who were either passing or working near the embassy at the time of the blast. As well, another 5,000 people received medical treatment while extensive damage to buildings and other infrastructure were recorded. Similarly, in the Dar es Salaam attack, 70 additional people were injured.

It is, however, imperative to distinguish between domestic and international terror. The former is localised and targets the state and its institutions within specific state boundaries, while the latter refers to the perpetration of terror outside their countries. International terrorism targeting Africans or African targets in Africa is rare. It was apparent in both the Nairobi and Dar es Salaam attacks that the target was US interests and not Kenyans or Tanzanians, although regrettably more Africans than Americans were killed. Historically, terrorism has never been considered as a major security threat in Africa. It has been noted, for example, that Africa ranked fifth in the total international terrorist attacks by region after Latin America, Asia, Western Europe, and the Middle East between 1997 and 2002. Africa's casualties for that same period were comparatively insignificant to elevate terrorism as a major security threat. Also, while Africa displays extreme poverty, high levels of state failure and colonial control, factors generally known to breed terrorism, the phenomenon has remained foreign in its political traditions. Thus, the global war on terror declared by the US as part of the pursuit of al Qaeda and its operatives should ideally have little appeal to Africa. Rather than terrorism, there are direr sources of human insecurity towards which energies should be dissipated. As Robinson (2004: 13) argues, for those afflicted by absolute poverty, "....insecurity is equated not with where a terrorist might strike next, but instead with where tomorrow's only meal will come from, or how a job will be found that provides enough income to ensure shelter for a family or purchase life-saving medicines for a dying child." In spite of this truism African states have joined the post-9/11 global war against terror.

In enlisting in the terror war, SSA countries have passed anti-terrorism legislation under the behest of the US. Such legislation is designed to give sweeping powers to the state to act swiftly and decisively against suspected terrorists. The broader rationale is to create a less permissive operating environment for terrorists within their borders. African countries have passed this legislation because American post-9/11 foreign policy has focused on increasing aid to and directly supporting countries that are committed to the war on terror. At the same time it cuts down, even cancels, assistance not only to countries apathetic to the war, but also those crippling Washington's freedom at pursuing terrorists. Thus, for supporting the establishment of the International Criminal Court (ICC), South Africa, a known regional ally of the US, was denied $7.6 million in military aid.37 Besides directly withholding its aid, the US also blocks, where possible, assistance from other western states destined for countries in Africa considered passive in the war against terror. Scandinavian aid agencies, which use US banks, have seen their funds destined for Liberia and other countries engaged in post-conflict reconstruction frozen apparently because those recipients are slow in passing anti-terrorism laws. The US, however, claims its action is to prevent such monies from financing terrorism (Anderssen 2007). The American argument seems implausible as it is unthinkable for a northern NGO to directly fund a southern organisation dedicated to perpetrating terror against western countries.

As it obstructs, even cuts, aid to non-supporters, Washington also rewards states which publicly demonstrate commitment to fight terror. Consistent with this policy, the US has recently provided Kenya, which has become one of its strongest regional allies, with $14 million in training and equipment to enhance the capacity of the Nairobi regime to fight terror. Part of the funds is to be used in the construction of a Guantanamo Bay-styled detention facility to hold suspected terrorists. Kenya received this package against a background of its efforts at arresting and repatriating suspected Somali and Ethiopian terrorists to Mogadishu and Addis Ababa respectively.38 Disturbing, however, is that such incentives and rewards are extended even to undemocratic and human rights and human security-threatening regimes. In 2003, for example, the US sold military weapons to 18 of the 25 countries it branded as "undemocratic". The war on terror has provided a pretext for the US to establish friendship with previously despised Pakistani President, Pervez Musharraf, who ascended to power through a military coup in 1999 and who has since established an authoritarian regime in his country. The US provides military and financial assistance to Pakistan and is also currently the source of arms to Angola, Chad and Ethiopia – countries that are at war or have a recent history of war. It is a huge policy contradiction for the US to continually vilify Robert Mugabe who was elected into office and compliment Pervez Musharraf who came to power by forcibly dislodging a constitutionally elected government. In recent years, both Mugabe and Musharraf restrict human freedoms in their respective countries.

In context, the individual state initiative to pass anti-terror legislations was inspired by the AU's collective stance on terrorism. Following from the Algiers convention of 1999, which obliged member states of the Organisation of African Unity to accede or rectify the protocol on preventing terror, African leaders specifically entrenched an anti-terror clause in the Constitutive Act of the successor organisation, the AU. According to Article 4(o), the AU shall be guided by certain principles, including "respect for the sanctity of human life, condemnation and rejection of impunity and political assassination, acts of terrorism and subversive activities."39 The US cannot be said to have influenced the insertion of this clause into the Constitutive Act since chronologically speaking the promulgation of the Act in 2000 predated 9/11. Rather, its inclusion in the Constitutive may have been inspired by the spate of terrorist acts in North Africa and in Nairobi and Dar es Salaam two years earlier. Nevertheless, an organisation in constant need of western financial assistance, the AU was happy to dance to American tunes on the war on terror. The ending of the cold war and the emergence of the US as the dominant global power made the argument even more logical. Largely as a result of the aid incentive, nearly all member states of the AU have passed or are in the process of passing anti-terrorism legislation. 40 However, this development has engendered critical implications for human rights in particular and human security in general in several African countries.

While the passing of anti-terror legislation was hailed in some countries as an assurance of the state's commitment to secure the personal security of people, there are concerns on the other hand about the sweeping powers being assumed by the state under those legislations. Such powers make it easier for governments to manipulate the rule of law to crush and annihilate legitimate opposition or people agitating for democratic reforms. In Uganda, opposition elements have criticized the country's anti-terror bill on grounds that it "seeks to lower the standard of proof on which one can be held and convicted on a terrorism charge"

Uganda's anti-terror laws have enabled the state to arrest and detain Dr. Kizza Besinge, who poses the strongest challenge to the presidency of Yuweri Museveni. As part of the anti-terror drive, moreover, a controversial bill is currently being debated in the largely rubber-stamp parliament of Uganda to legalise the tapping of phone calls by security agents. This is ostensibly to "monitor communication between suspected terrorists" but in reality to suffocate opposition and critics of the increasingly authoritarian Museveni regime. There are also fears in Nigeria that the revival of the anti-terror squad originally set up by former strongman, Sani Abacha, will be used to terrorise the media and pro-human rights activists; in Ethiopia, a number of anti-poverty activists, opposition politicians and journalists have been detained since December 2006 under the country's anti-terror laws; the Eritrean Movement for Democracy and Human Rights has appealed to the AU to intervene in the arbitrary arrests and systematic detention of individuals suspected of being critical of government under the pretext of clumping down on terrorists; in Zimbabwe opponents of the beleaguered Mugabe regime are simply branded either as agents of imperialist forces or "terrorists"; while in Kenya there is a growing feeling of vulnerability by the Muslim community under the country's anti-terror laws. In an attempt to fight terror, anti-terror legislations have turned many African regimes into tyrants, making the solution part of the problem.

In addition to the human security threat posed by counter-terrorism legislations, there have occurred a number of military strikes on suspected terrorists which have caused population displacements, deaths and fear. For example, in early January 2007, the US launched an aerial attack on "suspected Islamic terrorists" in Somalia. Although the strike killed a number of suspected terrorists, it also claimed the lives of no fewer than 20 civilians and wounded many more. The occupying Ethiopian forces in Somalia have also caused severe civilian casualties in their efforts to eliminate terrorists. Somalia is still far from being secured. The threat from Islamic "terrorists" has not receded while the determination of the American and AU-backed Ethiopian forces to rid Somalia of terrorists remains as strong as ever. This scenario is set to prolong the conflict between "terrorists" and Ethiopian forces and also set to cause human insecurity especially as the former has in recent times adopted a tactic of using civilians as human shields. In general, it is getting increasingly clear that the mechanisms used to prosecute the war on terror in Africa are threatening human security, perhaps more seriously than terrorism itself. Importantly, Africa's anti-terror legislations are externally-inspired.

In short, the scale of human insecurity in Africa is enormous, but the causes of the phenomenon are traceable not wholly to internal factors as is often hastily assumed, but also to external interventions. Poverty, debt, conflicts, food insecurity, educational and health insecurities as well as environmental degradation are all largely progenic of conditions inspired by forces external to Africa. Mitigating human insecurity in SSA should therefore be the collective task of Africa and the international community.

MITIGATING HUMAN INSECURITY IN SUB-SAHARAN AFRICA

Clearly, the human security challenges facing Africa are enormous, ranging from conflicts, refugeeism, poverty, bad governance, food and health insecurity, to environmental degradation. The enormity of the human security challenges requires the collective effort of Africa, MNC, NGOs, Africa's creditor community and the international community at large if they are to be effectively addressed. The popular aphorism of "African solution to African problems", which came to vogue at the beginning of the century has limited relevance in the context of human insecurity. The axiom was evoked in the context of conflicts on the continent and was meant to galvanise African states to assume responsibility for preventing, containing and managing conflicts on the continent. However, given the sheer magnitude of the human security crisis, the international community has to be part of the solution. Thus, in analysing the specific responsibilities of constituencies, this section discusses two levels of response – Regional (Africa's response) and the role of the international community.

Regional Initiatives – the Role of the African Union (AU)

The AU is engaged in various fronts to mitigate human insecurity. One of these is through diplomatic protocols. A number of protocols have been signed since 1980, including the charter on Human and People's Rights (1981), Charter on Popular Participation (1990), Protocol of the Rights of Women (2003), the Charter on Youth and Development (2006). While they target particular constituencies, the protocols were in the main meant to promote freedoms and above all to empower people to be involved in decisions affecting their lives. There are also important sub-regional initiatives such the ECOWAS Declaration on political Principles (1991) and the ECOWAS principle on Democracy and Governance (2001). These principles are meant to improve upon the standard of governance, with a view of deepening democracy and popular participation and ultimately empowering citizens. In practice, however, many of these protocols have remained only on paper for many countries.

However, the dominant focus in promoting human security has been on mitigating and containing conflicts. In addition to being a source of insecurity, conflicts also feed and exacerbate other threats to human security. Once heightened, insecurity is a recipe for further conflicts, making the two complimentary and mutually reinforcing. Accordingly, international and regional attempts to address human security challenges in SSA have mostly focused first and foremost on conflicts prevention and resolution. The 2005 report of the UN Office of the Special Advisor on Africa

(OSAA) noted that addressing Africa's conflicts is the key to establishing human security.46 The AU has therefore been exploring ways of dealing with conflicts. At the 2000 AU Summit in Sirte, Libya, the organisation discussed human security as part of the grand agenda to install comprehensive security architecture in the continent. The broader AU security plan includes crisis prevention, peacekeeping, programmes to curb the proliferation of small arms, and the recruiting of child soldiers. The climax of the initiatives towards security was the inauguration of Peace and Security Council (PSC) in 2004 as stipulated in the Constitutive Act of the AU. The establishment of the PSC was informed by Africa's need for more robust approach to conflict resolution. With more or less comparable powers with the UN Security Council, the PSC of the AU has a primary responsibility for maintaining peace and security.

The PSC is also responsible for taking critical decisions regarding the raising and deployment of AU peacekeeping forces. In addition, the PSC is to perform mediatory and reconciliatory roles. The PSC is to be complemented by other conflict preventing mechanisms such as an African Standby Force (ASF) and a continental Early Warning System (EWS). A critical requirement, meanwhile, is for the AU to strengthen its peacekeeping capacities. This requires, among other things, the commitment of troops towards peacekeeping efforts. This is particularly crucial because the response of African states to the call by the AU in early 2007 to send an 8,000-peace keeping force into Somalia has been paltry. As at mid-2007 only Uganda had contributed a small force of 1,500 troops. As already noted, conflicts are not the only sources of human insecurity. Bad governance and poor human right cultures also lie at the heart of human insecurity in SSA.

To this end, regional bodies and especially the AU should be doing more to promote transparency, empowerment and the active participation of citizens in the formulation and implementation of decisions that affect their lives. So far, official protocols, charters and declarations have done little to substantially improve upon these principles in practice. The AU should be bold to institute tougher action against recalcitrant states, including Zimbabwe, Sudan and Swaziland, which are known to be stifling liberties and democracy. Such action could include diplomatic isolation, exclusion from attending AU summits and participation in regional sports tournaments. In the meantime, the AU should shift radically from the traditional practice of fraternalising and empathising with fellow heads of state to a posture of openly criticising and denouncing those leaders whose regimes fall short of meeting the standards of good governance established by the AU.

Also, as part of the process of promoting good governance and democracy, the AU should seek to ensure the credibility of elections. This, it should do by, among other things, providing the necessary logistical and expert assistance to countries undertaking elections. While assisting countries, the organisation should be bold to condemn fraudulent elections that are becoming the norm, not the exception in many countries in Africa. In April 2003 the AU wasted no time in congratulating president Olusegun Obasanjo on his re-election in a sham Nigerian election. Two years latter (May 2005) the AU showered congratulatory messages on Faure Gnassingbe, after emerging from a stage-managed poll in Togo that was anything but free and fair. Then, again, in April 2007, president John Kuffour of Ghana, the chair of the AU, together with President Thabo Mbeki of South Africa, a leading architect of the AU, sent warm congratulatory messages to Mr. Umaru Musa Yar' Adua on his election as the new Nigerian president in a poll which both local and international observers dubbed as seriously flawed. As a natural consequence, these polls spawned post-election conflicts, claimed scores of human lives, undermined confidence in the country's electoral process and, above all, vitiated the legitimacy of the "elected" regimes.

The AU needs to move away from the largely ineffective secret diplomacy used to chastise leaders to openly condemning such elections and if not re-run to de-recognise leaders who emerge from such visibly flawed polls. NEPAD remains Africa's current blueprint document for development. Adopted in 2001, it provides a framework within which Africa is to be aided by industrial countries to address its developmental challenges. Essentially, it aims at eradicating poverty as a precondition for sustained development; encourage employment creation; diversify production to increase Africa's access to western markets; promote cooperation and integration in Africa; and accelerate the empowerment of women. In pursuing these objectives, NEPAD identifies three areas needing priority attention: peace and security through good governance; increased investments in agriculture, communication, tourism, health and education; and the mobilization of resources through resource transfer to Africa via ODA, FDI and debt reduction.48 Theoretically, these are noble objectives that can potentially alleviate human insecurity but practically NEPAD may produce the opposite effect. This prognosis stems from its excessively neo-liberal posture and conformity with the dictates of economic globalisation. NEPAD calls for increased dependence on western aid and greater incorporation into the global capitalist economy, which are poised to cause an escalation of Africa's external indebtedness. As well, its emphasis on liberalisation and free markets are certain to open up Africa's economies to largely extra-African companies and consequently imperil the survival of nascent industries. This is a recipe for compounding the already bad unemployment situation in Africa. NEPAD therefore requires some re-formulation; it has to be re-cast as a counter-hegemonic policy framework truly dedicated to addressing Africa's development and human security challenges.

This said, Africa remains a vulnerable and dependent continent, with a vastly diminished ability to single-handedly reverse its declining economic and human security fortunes. It thus requires the assistance of western countries and the international community in general to deal with its current quagmires, not only on humanitarian grounds, but also on moral grounds. As noted earlier, the causes of human insecurity in Africa are partially, if not wholly externally- inspired, hence western countries, whose policies have caused the escalation of the crisis, have to feel morally obliged to assist Africa. The west should assist Africa, moreover, because the latter will likely bear the brunt of inaction in the form of increased African migration to the west, crime, drug peddling, money laundering, and terrorism if the deteriorating human security situation in Africa continues unabated. Thus, some of the various ways in which the international community can assist Africa are discussed in the next section.

THE ROLE OF THE INTERNATIONAL COMMUNITY

The west and the broader international community can assist in alleviating human insecurity through efforts in resolving conflicts, addressing health and educational insecurity; promoting good governance, resolving the asymmetry in international trade and helping Africans to protect the environmental. This objective can be achieved in various ways:

Conflicts

The international community should seek to augment the efforts of the AU and regional organizations in SSA in conflict prevention, management and peacekeeping. Already, the US and the European Union (EU) have been providing financial and logistical assistance to regional organizations. British, French and the US assisted ECOWAS peacekeeping efforts in Liberia, Sierra Leone and recently in Ivory Coast. In 2002 the US helped to establish the African Crisis Response Initiative (ACRI) to train approximately 9,000 African soldiers to speedily respond to peacekeeping demands on the continent. ACRI has been replaced by the African Contingency Operations Training Assistance – ACOTA (Hardy 2003). In the same year, it pledged training assistance to ECOMOG as well as setting up military bases for the deployment of troops to conflict spots. In June 2004, the US established a $600 million Global Peace Operations Initiative (GPOI) fund to support African peace operations (Malan 2004: 27). In the same way the EU has supported AU peacekeeping efforts in Darfur, the Central African Multinational Force and capacity-building for the AU Commission's Peace and Security Department through its annual grant of 250 million Peace Facility for Africa (CCR 2005: 49). Japanese assistance to peacekeeping operations (PKOs) in Africa is also noted. In 2004 approximately 20 percent of the total operation cost of eight PKOs in Africa, amounting to $550 million, was borne by Japan. As well, in April 2004 Tokyo pledged an aid package of $100 million in the near term to the government of Sudan and the Sudan People's Liberation Movement following their signing in January of the Comprehensive Peace Agreement. Over $10 million of this has already been disbursed.

However, given the general trend towards the withdrawal from Africa's conflicts by the west, in the aftermath of the cold war, some are critical of the motives behind such international assistance. With the exception of Japan whose pacifist post-war constitution prohibits the engagement of its military in combat operations, other western countries, in particular the US and the EU are being suspected of using their various assistances to exclude their troops from physically participating in PKOs on African soil. The previously strategic importance of Africa during the cold was has waned, leaving no compelling reasons for Americans and western soldiers to die in Africa in what is often considered as needless intra-state conflicts. This thinking was helped by America's terrible, perhaps humiliating, experience in Somalia under the United Nations Operations in Somalia (UNOSOM II) in 1993, during which international television screens featured a killed American soldier being dragged on the street of Mogadishu by Somali militiamen. The US eventually withdrew from the operation in March 1997. A key consideration here is for such international support to be dictated not by the strategic or ideological considerations of the west, but rather by the genuine commitment to enhance the conflict resolution capacity of the AU and its regional bodies.

A further contribution is for the west, and especially the US to cease clandestine arm sales and military support to conflict-prone countries such as Chad, Angola and Ethiopia. While doing this the international community should master courage to intervene in situations in which human right abuses and human suffering are glaring and grotesque. A case in point is the Darfur region of Sudan, where the international community seems to be procrastinating while civilians are brutalised and killed by government-backed militiamen. In a situation of this kind, an authorisation by the UN should be enough to warrant a humanitarian intervention. An approval from the Sudanese government should not be the deciding factor neither should sanctions be an option as these have almost always ended up hurting civilians more than sanctioned regimes.

Aside of the military dimension, which targets conflicts and post-conflict situations, the west can assist in forestalling conflicts.

One way of achieving this is to help promote and strengthen good governance. Internal mechanisms such as the much heralded African Peer review Mechanism (APRM) instituted by the African Union offers little promise to promote good governance. This is not only because submission to the review process is voluntary, but also because the APRM lacks the instruments to compel recalcitrant regimes to meet standard governance practices (Akokpari 2004). Rather than relying on the APRM, the west could take tougher stance on stubborn regimes.

Examples of these include Zimbabwe, Sudan, and Swaziland whose continued obstruction of democracy is a potential source of conflict. In this regard, even supposedly "friendly" regimes to the west such as Kenya and Ethiopia who display governance-related problems should not be let off the hook. Kenya and Ethiopia should be prevailed upon to curb rampant corruption and gross human rights abuses respectively. The US should not use its newly forged strategic friendship with these countries over the war on terror to protect them as it did with Mobutu Sese Seko and Siad Barre of Zaire (Now Democratic Republic of Congo –DRC) and Somalia respectively during the cold war. The painful lesson has been learnt; when these regimes fell after the cold war, DRC and Somalia became theatres of intractable conflicts.

A disconcerting trend emerging in Africa is the phenomenon of stage-managed elections, which provide pretexts for armed conflicts. As indicated already, the AU has so far lacked the courage to condemn such feign elections, let alone isolate resultant leaders. The Nigerian presidential elections of 2003 and 2007, the Togolese election of 2005, and the Ugandan presidential election of 2006, for example, did not meet minimum electoral standards. Yet, in its characteristic style the AU warmly welcomed the new leaders into its fold, setting the stage for post-election contestations in these countries. The international community should openly denounce such elections and completely isolate leaders who emerge from such fraudulent elections. The resolution by the European Union (EU) parliament on 24 May 2007 to withhold aid to the federal government of Nigeria if the flawed elections of April 2007 were not re-run is a good step. Over the last five years the EU earmarked 500 million (US$674.5 million) for various projects on governance, health, water and sanitation in Nigeria. Aid withdrawal by other bilateral creditors such as Japan, Canada and the US will further exert the needed pressure on Nigeria to meet minimum electoral standards. Also, new threats by Nigeria's major investors to withdraw can help regenerate sanity in the electoral and general governance performance of the country. In other words, the international community should do what the AU is failing to do.

Health and Education

Health and educational security can be significantly bolstered by the international community at large and in particular by Africa's major creditors through the easing of intrusive conditionalities attached to aid. While conditionalities are necessary in some cases, e.g. preventing aid towards poverty alleviation being diverted into military budgets, they should not be made universal. The fact is that conditionalities have attenuated the efforts at addressing poverty in general and health and education in particular that aided the development of Asia (Stein 1995). There is no doubt that the health and educational sectors require reforms to make them more efficient; but these should not be placed beyond the each of citizens through privatisation. Other services such as the provision of water and sanitation should also be reformed and not privatized. These services and amenities provide foundations for human security and should therefore be both available and affordable. Alongside the above, African governments should begin to devote large percentages of the budgets to health and education. These can be achieved by scaling down the allocations for defense and the large number of cabinet ministers and special advisers to presidents.

Furthermore, creditor countries should move debt remission beyond rhetoric. Very little has been achieved by SSA by way of debt cancellation since the institution of the HIPC initiatives in 1996. The July 2005 G8 meeting in Gleneagles, Scotland from which Africa had hoped for massive concessions turned out to be a disappointment. At the conclusion of the meeting, the G8 only adjusted aid figures from the current $25 billion a year to $50 billion by 2010. Experts, however, estimate that Africa requires $100 billion in development aid and a minimum annual growth rate of 7 percent (more than double the current growth rate of between 2 and 3%) if it is to meet the UN millennium goals (Short 2002). Moreover, of the 18 countries which received some debt cancellation only 14 were African in contrast to the AU's expectation of total and unconditional remission of the region's debt. While debt cancellation does not automatically or instantly translate into improvements in human security, it nonetheless enables the proportion of national budgets currently being devoted to debt service to be ploughed into other human security-enhancing areas such as education, health and infrastructure.

Debt remission should be accompanied by more aid. Here, again, it is disheartening to note that since the mid-1980s the north has consistently failed to deliver on aid promises to Africa. In 1986 the UN developed a four-year recovery programme, the United Nations Programme of Action for African Economic Recovery and Development (UN-PARRED) 1986–1990. This programme embodied pledges by the international creditor community to provide assistance to Africa. However, the tepid response from the international community condemned UN-PARRED to a premature demise. Again, in 1991, the United Nations New Agenda for the Development of Africa in the 1990s (UN-NADAF) was adopted under which the international creditor community was to commit 0.7 percent of its GNP as ODA to Africa. Only a few countries, including the Netherlands and the Scandinavian countries met this target by the end of the decade. Consequently, overall ODA to Africa plummeted from $28.6 billion in 1990 to $16.4 billion in 2000 (Bentsi-Enchill 1997; Asante 2003: 16). While shunning Africa, the west has been giving more "aid" to farm animals in the form of subsidies. In 2000, the EU's total aid to SSA amounted to $8.00 per African, while its subsidies to cows averaged $913 per cow. Japan's case was even more absurd. In that year Japan's total aid to SSA averaged $1.47 per African, while its subsidy to cows averaged a colossal $2,700 (UNDP 2003: 155). This morally disheartening reality means that the west has to do more in terms of aid if it is to be seen to be genuinely promoting human security in Africa. The war on terror should not eclipse aid towards poverty alleviation as it seeming to be the case with US aid policy.

International Trade

The Commission on Human Security identified trade imbalances between regions as a worrying source of economic insecurity (CHS 2003). Trade imbalance with the north remains one of Africa's most daunting challenges to development.

One reason is SSA's overwhelming dependence on primary agricultural exports. With the exception of the short-lived and ill-fated import substitution industrialisation (ISI) strategy of the 1960s, successive development strategies have done little to change the structure of SSA's production. Neither have Africa's post-colonial elite made any concerted efforts towards transforming or diversifying the inherited colonial economy (Ake 1996).

In fact, by its emphasis on export agriculture, SAP, which dominated Africa's development landscape, helped to perpetuate the existing international division of labour and production. Another reason is that whereas the prices of SSA's primary products are determined by impersonal market forces, the prices of industrial goods are determined by producers, placing Africa at a disadvantage vis-à-vis its northern trading partners. The asymmetry in Africa-northern trade is compounded by the former's limited access to western markets and state subsidies to western farmers.

The 1975 Lome Convention gave African, Caribbean and Pacific (ACP) countries some limited access to EU markets.51 This has not been enough and some countries such as South Africa have had to negotiate separate trade agreements with the EU. The essential requirements of the west are first, to grant Africa greater access to its markets, and second to stop subsidies to its farmers. The perplexing paradox is that while Africa is being urged to desubsidise and liberalise under a plethora of conditionalities, western governments are increasingly subsidising and protecting agriculture. Desubsidisation of northern farmers must complement African access to western markets. To this end western countries need to be considerate in their negotiations at the WTO, as Africa and the developing world are the ultimate losers in a failure to compromise on agricultural subsidies. Fairer international trade among regions is a good starting point for reducing poverty and its associated insecurities.

Food

Although poverty limits access to food, one of the major causes of food insecurity is inadequate supply. Often, this is due to failures in rain. The international creditor community can help rectify this in the long term by assisting Africa to reduce dependence on rain through invests in irrigation. Large scale irrigation projects will not only create employment but will also ensure a fairly constant supply of food. Moreover, timely interventions by the international community when food-related crisis erupt in Africa is required. According to Oxfam, food insecurity in Africa partly stems from the slow response of the international community. Citing the case of Niger, Oxfam notes that "although the earliest warnings came in late 2004, it was only when pictures of suffering children were shown on television in June 2005 that the international community was galvanized into action. By the time aid arrived, 3.6 million people were suffering from hunger." Slow responses from the international community are frequently complimented by the paltry response to humanitarian appeals to help victims of food crisis in Africa. For example, an appeal by the UN for $225 million emergency food aid for Kenya in February 2006 yielded only $79 million during the first month in April 2006 (Oxfam 2006: 6). Such delays by the international community in meeting food aid targets have often caused and escalated preventable food shortages.

Moreover, concrete measures need to be put in place to curb the emission of carbon dioxide and other greenhouse gases. It is now known that China will soon overtake the US in emissions as a result of the former's rapid economic development. As such the curbing of emissions should not be seen as the sole responsibility of the US and western countries. China, India and indeed all countries in both north and south should consider themselves part of the anti-global warming campaign.

The attainment of food security may remain a mirage without concomitant assault on the HIV/AIDS pandemic, which both undermines production and access to food in many communities. The fight against HIV/AIDS should be intensified. The pace at rolling out antiretrovirus drugs should be intensified with new commitments by the international community to donate funds.

President George Bush announcement in early June 2007 to commit $30 billon to fight HIV/AIDS over the next five years is encouraging.52 Critics argue that this is still inadequate. However, for Africa, this represents a step in the right direction. Similar commitment by other western countries could significantly boost the campaign against HIV/AIDS. Alongside this, the campaign to educate people especially rural dwellers on AIDS should remain relentless. A strategic partnership between the state, NGOs and the international community at large is necessary to mount a concerted effort against HIV/AIDS.

The Environment

It was noted that environmental insecurity in SSA is primarily caused by three main factors – natural disasters, poverty and international pressures. The frequent occurrences of natural disasters such as droughts and floods have been linked to the activities and policies of western countries. Similarly, the role of external factors in the exacerbation and mitigation of poverty was also noted. Thus, by and large a great deal of responsibility rests with external in addressing environmental insecurity in SSA. In this regard, industrialized countries have to do more to alleviate poverty as a way of easing pressure on the environment. As well, the north should assist SSA in establishing stronger environmental regimes that are capable of limiting, even controlling the exploitation of resources by MNCs. One way of achieving this is through the establishment of a new global environmental regime that holds MNCs accountable for ecological damages and obliging them to compensate affected communities. Since the north is culpable for some of the environmental catastrophes experienced in Africa, it should see it as a moral responsibility to speedily assist countries faced by such calamities.

MNCs, should assume responsibility for causing environmental damages. To this end, companies operating among communities should compensate communities for lost land and other resources. MNCs should engage in environmental and infrastructural development. Since African states are presiding over diminishing resources, companies should compliment the efforts of the state by investing in infrastructure such building schools, roads, hospitals and clinics, as well as the provision of sanitation and drinking water. In order words, MNC should endear themselves to communities by investing in the development of the latter. In doing this not only will MNCs be helping in addressing poverty, but also creating a nonviolent environment conducive for their own operations. One observer lamented about the situation in the Niger delta, "down by the coastline, the Ogoni people live .... 500 thousand people. They sit right on top of the oil. When you go through this territory, you go through towns that have absolutely no electricity. There's no hospital and no school. People [are] very frustrated [and] very angry." Such frustration and anger have been reflected in community protests and various attempts to sabotage the oil industry in the region through illegal perforation of oil pipelines and the kidnapping of foreign oil workers. Consequently, by early 2006, oil production has fallen by a fifth, i.e. by 450,000 barrels per day (bpd) out of about 2.5 million bpd (*New York Times* 21 February 2006). Oil companies in the Niger delta and MNCs in SSA in general could better secure their investments through corporate social responsibility in the countries and especially in the communities where they operate.

Conclusion

Africa's insecurity crisis is enormous and visible. Its poverty levels are high and set to increase. Poverty feeds into the HIV/AIDS pandemic, which is rocking the region. In addition, intra-state conflicts have become frequent and protracted, while environmental degradation has become rapid. Together, these have both heightened human insecurity and stymied efforts at reversing these conditions. The emergence of the human security concept was aimed at shifting the hitherto overwhelming attention from the state to people who face silent, grave but largely ignored threats. The dominance of the state and the logic of the cold war marginalised people in the discourse on security. The thrust of the 1994 UNDP report is to highlight the risks and threats facing people that have remained uncaptured by public policy at state and international levels.

While there is global consensus on focusing on "human" as opposed to "state" security, there has been scant analysis on the fundamental sources of human insecurity. In the case of SSA, the tendency has been to adopt the usual neo-classical formula and point to factors that are predominantly internal to the region. It has been argued that what is frequently regarded as internal causes of insecurity such as poverty, conflicts, environmental degradation, food, health and educational insecurities, are in fact manifestations of the crisis. In perspective, these are the product of more fundamental causes, including endemic structures and practices within the international system. It is common knowledge that in order to prescribe an effective antidote to a problem, it is imperative to diagnose its root causes. A deviation from this standard practice leads to a diagnoses of the symptoms rather than the root causes.

The study emphasises that globalisation and other related global forces such liberalisation, democratisation and debt, among other things have been fundamental source of human insecurity in Africa. Not only do these external factors spawn human insecurity, but they also engineer fresh conditions, including conflicts, and environmental degradation that exacerbate the problem. Although terrorism is recognised worldwide as a new source of human insecurity, this view is contested in Africa. As argued, terrorism has historically not been an issue of concern to Africa although Africa displays conditions that should ideally inspire terror. Rather, what is emerging as a new source of human insecurity is the proliferation of anti-terror legislations, which are passed by African governments at the behest of the US. The US has evolved a policy of rewarding countries enlisting in the war on terror and punishing those apathetic or oppositional to the war. The dominance of the US in the post cold war era, along with the associated benefits in the form of US aid, has presented the war on terror an irresistible offer for Africa. However, instead of securing citizens, anti-terror laws have rather provided leeway for the state to clump down on opposition, democratic forces and critical voices. In the process, these laws vitiate human rights, undermine human security and are rapidly reviving Africa's old and discredited practice of "constitution without constitutionalism." Thus, if anti-terror laws are becoming sources of human insecurity in Africa, they too are externally inspired.

The disconcerting development associated with terror and anti-terror legislation in Africa underscores the limits of the human security concept. This is particularly imperative in SSA where there is an ever increasing tendency for the concept to generate huge public expectations. Among other things, human security has so far not replaced the state as the dominant referent of security. There are still a number of intra- and inter-state conflicts whose resolution requires the active involvement of the state. Moreover, some of the internal conflicts, especially those involving rebels are targeted at the state. Also, the African state continues to be the author and the key determinant of security. All these mean the state's centrality in the security discourse in Africa may remain protracted and unchallenged for a long time. It has also to be noted that human security is not synonymous with development. Human security is rather an auxiliary factor of development. Thus, even attaining the goals of human security does not mean an improvement in the standard of living. These limitations, along with suspicion among some countries that human security is an ideological tool or a pretext for humanitarian intervention raise concerns not only about the efficacy of the concept but also about its universal acceptability. Ultimately, this perception may limit the utility of the concept, both in theory and practice in Africa.

However, even if the theoretical pretensions of human security are set aside, the practical side still needs to be addressed. Conflict, poverty, diseases, bad governance and human right abuses and environmental degradation needs to be halted. It is argued that this should be the challenge not only of Africans but also of the western countries who, have by their policies, contributed to the crisis in Africa. Western countries have to be part of the solution, moreover because they will contend with the consequences of the problem in the form of increased African migration to the west, inability to repay debt and even in an inability of Africa to continue to serve as a marginal market for the west. For these reasons the west should abolish the policies that have tended to hurt Africa, such as agricultural subsidies and aid conditionalities. They should also move speedily to curtail carbon and other green house emissions which are causing floods and droughts in Africa. As well the west, while increasing aid to Africa, should help establish a strong global environmental regime capable of controlling the activities of MNC.

While welcoming the contribution of the west to alleviate human insecurity, Africa should consider itself an integral part of the solution. To this end, it should reserve policies that tend to create conditions for conflict such as bad governance and marginalisation. The APRM should be strengthened to make it more effective in reversing practices of bad governance on states. Civil society should be encouraged and strengthened as a partner both in governance and in development. While these progressive policies will not instantly transform the tattered character of Africa, they will doubtlessly be setting the region firmly on the path of human security and ultimately sustainable development.

7

Human Rights and International Finance

Combining the human dimension with finance (in general and not necessarily international at this stage) we can conceive of different outcomes. At one extreme we are presented with financing for profit with little human consideration. But along the line we will find occasions when the affectional may, or may seem to, condition finance's functional nature.

Take, for instance, the financing of a friend or one's own child without interest—in a way giving ones money away. The motivation for the act, however, is more important than the altruistic appearance. The child may even be charged interest or be required to reimburse the capital; not because of a desire for direct material gain by the parents, but in order to make the child socially responsible. In this case despite the functional appearance of the transaction, the motivation is affectional. Inversely, a friend or a protégé may be advanced funds without interest, "out of the goodness of ones heart," yet the motivation may be a functional investment in the future and expectation of the return of the favor based on an evaluation of the recipient's potentials for success. The operation is functional.

Transferring these interpersonal instances of the affectional and the functional to the socio-political arena, we may find that the functional extreme of financial gain may reduce the human factor to a mere tool; producing the phenomenon of slavery. In such a situation, the relationship of the human factor to the capital is that of servitude. On the other hand, the human consideration may reduce capital to a tool whose use is not to produce profit but to serve social welfare irrespective of financial cost effectiveness. In the extreme case of the claim of social welfare on the capital the relationship of the human factor to finance will be that of entitlement. This situation may be approached in a social democracy with strong egalitarian labor unions or in a totalitarian state capitalism with centralized democracy.

While the interpersonal affectional/functional and the sociopolitical servitude/entitlement tendencies can be traced in time and space to different cultures, when they are transferred to the international domain, they acquire a patently Western characteristic. It is that international finance is associated with capitalism and the human dimensions translated into human rights and identified with democracy: both developments of modern Western culture. To some extent, this Western association of the proposition is a distorting factor; because it projects the interaction of capitalism and human rights into societies and cultures whose historical evolution has been different from the West. In order to better grasp the proposition it may be useful to briefly scrutinize the development of capitalism and human rights within the Western culture and see whether the two were interrelated and, if so, what the nature of this interrelation was and to what extent it can be transferred to modern international relations. The developments we are concerned about here are those of post-reformation Europe. The Calvinist and puritan concept of the "elect" did not, as such, contain a direct human rights component. God had chosen the "elect" to become rich probably because they were pious, hardworking and frugal and did not indulge in the joys of the tavern. By the very fact of the godly distinction between the "elect" and the others, the elect did not have to feel guilty for the lot of the downtrodden. Of course, as they amassed wealth and their reputation as conscientious craftsmen and businessmen grew, the elect could expand their activities and provide employment for the poor.

In the course of the centuries, however, riches became the measuring rod dissociated from the pious characteristics which were to bring it about. Indeed, as Protestant ethics metamorphosed into social Darwinism in the nineteenth century, social institutions, notably the churches, tried to attenuate its impact by emphasizing Christian charity and creating charitable foundations.

Human rights, however, were not originally developed in reaction to this state of affairs but as another concern of the emerging bourgeoisie and as a complement to capitalism. Locke's life, liberty and property . were safeguards that the bourgeois capitalism wished to wrestle out of the monarchs. These ideas inspired the English Bill of Rights and the American and the French Revolutions. The human rights they proclaimed were civic and political, leaving free rein to liberal economy.

This free rein, combined with social Darwinism and the industrial revolution, caused economic and social disruptions in the nineteenth century. Christian charity was not enough to counter balance the encroachments of free enterprise capitalism. Trade unionist and socialist ideas and institutions emerged to counteract and interact with the free enterprise and the government to secure social and economic justice. Conflict, compromise and cooperation between the four dimensions (government, capital, labor, and, to some extent, the church) provided economic, social and political settings oscillating somewhere within the spectrum going from servitude to entitlement.

In the process, the intrinsic characteristics of most of these dimensions within the national boundaries of Western countries were compromised: governments assumed more and more social, economic and regulatory responsibilities beyond their political, military and judicial authority. Labor movements, originally inspired by Marxism, eventually sat down to negotiate with capital and government instead of wiping them out by revolution. And capital moved from sweatshops to unemployment and health insurance for the workers. These evolutions did not take place because they were intrinsic to the characteristics of each of these social dimensions but because of the presence and potentials of the other dimensions within the national boundaries and their input within the legal system.

SERVITUDE OR ENTITLEMENT: INTERNATIONAL

In the course of the colonial and imperial expansions of the West, each of these dimensions produced different impacts on the penetrated territories. In general, and naturally, they reverted, circumstances permitting, to their intrinsic characteristics. The interactions in the new non-Western environments produced different complexes. The Western Governments, for example, while essentially political and military powers, were creating frameworks for the international economic penetration of their national capital. We thus could encounter home countries with well-developed human rights conditions whose international financial arms extending into other parts of the world needed not occupy themselves with human rights considerations.

Capital moved to non-Western regions of the globe in search of profit: its intrinsic characteristic. One of the incentives for the capital to move was the absence of the restraints encountered in the home country—notably in the domain of economic and social human rights. Of course, in some cases some residual developments of the interactions within the home country did move on with the capital. For instance, during the nineteenth century industrial revolution, capital had come to realize that the Malthusian misery of the workers was not cost-effective and that providing some standards of hygiene and housing were more efficient both for better production and better control of the workers.

Of course, the introduction of such standards in traditional societies could, at times, disrupt local ways of life and cultural patterns. Thus, in addition to possible lack of Western style civic, political, economic and social human rights in the countries penetrated by international finance and other dimensions of Western culture, such penetrations had the potential of disrupting the local traditional cultures.

In the aftermath of World War II, human rights became one of the major concerns of the United Nations. With the moral implications of decolonization the United Nations' efforts to improve human dimensions through international finance were inspired by affectional factors defined earlier. Governments were to contribute, with little or no interest, to such programs as the Special United Nations Fund for Economic Development or in later years finance arrangements made by the World Bank and IMF to help developing countries. Contributions to these international programs and institutions and aids and grants provided through bilateral arrangements between governments did not have profit or interest or capital as their direct functional goal. Their goals were economic and political and each government had its own ideological rationale to contribute to it. The indirect functional goals of such programs have become more apparent in the recent role played by the IMF in bailing out developing countries with huge debts which are unable to meet deadlines on their payments.

In 1948 the UN General Assembly adopted the Universal Declaration of Human Rights which served as basis for the "International Covenant on Civil and Political Rights" and the "International Covenant on Economic, Social, and Cultural Rights," adopted by the General Assembly in 1966. The two covenants came into force in 1976. As the title of these covenants indicates, they are aimed at securing the two different kinds of human rights discussed earlier. But the forms and the circum-stances in which they have been formulated are far different from the evolution of these rights within the Western culture. At the UN, it is the governments of different countries who proclaim principles with little or no enforcement instruments at the international level. They can, of course, enforce the principles they proclaim within their national boundaries; although this is not always the case.

For international finance an international covenant or any other principle of behavior is only effective to the extent that it is enforced by the governments of the countries within which they operate. This applies to the home as well as the host countries. International finance seeking gain on the international market place is not in charge of enforcing human rights. If the government of the United States forbids, under penalty, the U.S. firms to deal with the Soviet Union because the Soviet Union is helping the Polish government to suppress human rights in Poland, the U.S. firms will find it difficult to disregard such law—unless they can find some international trade practice or legal loophole permitting them to go around the prohibition. Similarly, where a host country has laws on minimum wage, workers insurance or taxes for welfare and education, international finance will find itself obligated to abide by those laws—unless it can negotiate concessions from the government. The side comments in the last two sentences above are, for some, the crux of the problem.

The Church

So far, we have touched upon the international projection of the attitudes of the governments and the capital towards human rights. A look at the international projection of the other dimensions, namely, the church and labor, which we discussed in the context of the development of human rights within the Western countries will throw light on other human rights restraints on international finance.

The church has, of course, an involved relationship with international finance; too extensive to delve into within the limits of this study. Suffice to say that over the centuries, while saving the souls of non-Western people, the church in general created favorable grounds for the international movement of capital and at times served, more or less, as the conscience of international finance in cases of flagrant abuses. Churches have played important roles in influencing international capital in the field of human rights in the last two decades. They have, in fact, taken the lead in the popular pressure on multinational corporations to respect human rights.

As distinct from other popular protesters, such as civic and student groups which act on the outside and around international capital by such tactics as demonstrations, lobbies, boycotts and using the mass media, the churches have had leverage within multinational corporations and financial institutions as shareholders and investors. Together with such other institutional investors as universities, they have been able to influence corporations and financial institutions by threatening to withdraw their investments and accounts. Above all, as shareholders, churches have brought human rights issues in the corporate policy making process through proxy resolutions.

In the domain of human rights the impact of churches on international finance can be significant due to the parallelism of church structures with those of international finance, extending from within the home and host countries into an international network. Some, such as the Catholic church, have been inherently international. When the Pope tours Central America and tells the campesinos of their human worth, international finance and the government with which it works will have to cope with the new political awareness. When the Central Committee of the World Council of Churches adopts a resolution, as it did in 1977, considering multi-cultural corporations as oppressors and exploiters, it is addressed to its nearly 300 member churches and over a billion adherents around the world.

TRADE UNIONISM AND SOCIALISM

The internationalization of institutions, which emerged as a consequence of trade unionist and socialist ideas, has had a checkered history. In the course of its evolution the trade unionist dimension did not lend itself to an integrated international growth. It enmeshed with the government and capital within the national frontier to gain job security, social benefits and favorable wages. This, of course, happened in those Western countries where negotiation—not always without conflict—among labor, capital and government was possible. In these contexts, labor movements recognized capital as a legitimate component of the social and economic process and distinguished between their claims on capital as syndicalist action for improvement of labor conditions and their political action for influencing the government through social democratic parties. As the symbiosis between labor and capital developed, more often than not, it pitted the national labor against foreign labor.

Where cultural, economic and political conditions were not favorable for symbiotic evolution, such as Southern and Eastern Europe, and later other parts of the world, the socialist dimension inspired by Marxism turned into militant political action. These evolutions can be traced through the history of the international labor and socialist movements. The International Secretariat of National Trade Union Centers created in 1901 fell apart in 1913, precisely because of the conflict between the pragmatic social democratic unionism and revolutionary socialism. When World War I started, workers of Western industrial nations picked up arms to defend their "bread baskets" against each other. But the end of that War was marked by the implantation of Revolutionary Communism in Russia where international and national capital was nationalized. The conditions surrounding the Russian revolution, however, did not lend themselves to putting capital at the service of entitlement programs. Eventually a state capitalism was instituted which, under Stalin, brought human rights conditions closer to the servitude end of the spectrum.

The 1917 Bolshevik Revolution further crystallized the differing characteristics of trade unionism and militant socialism. The post WW1 Western inspired international trade unions, whether the International Federation of Trade Unions (IFTU) founded in 1919, or the International Trade Secretariats of various crafts and industries, remained conglomerations of national trade unions. Among the international labor organizations, the International Confederation of Christian Trade Unions created in 1921 by Catholic workers unions was probably, in aspiration, more universal because of its religious orientation. The Comintern as an international political arm of Soviet communism was to mobilize the proletariat under the slogan of "Workingmen of the world unite." In that spirit it created in 1920 the Red International of Labor Unions (RILU) to counteract Western inspired trade unions. It is interesting to note that RILU was dismantled in 1935 to permit its national units to act more freely within their respective countries. The brief cooperation of the Soviet Union and Western democracies during WW2 saw the end of the Comintern in 1944 and IFTU in 1945. By the end of WW2, however, the Marxist socialist ideology had consolidated its home and widened its sway. The countries of Eastern Europe that had embraced it, despite the fact that they were not practicing it, had become the official standard bearers for the emancipation of the proletariat and in that role condemned international finance as the new form of Western imperialism.

Soon after the end of WW2 the trade unionist and ideological dimensions of labor reorganized in modified forms reflecting the new realities at the international level; but with little change in their intrinsic characteristics. (International Confederation of Free Trade Unions (ICFTU) created in 1949 can be reasonably considered a successor to IFTU while World Confederation of Labor (WCL) was the post-WW2 de-confessionalized merger of ICCTU and some Protestant unions.)

The World Federation of Trade Unions (WFTU) provides an interesting case. Despite its trade union appellation, it contained within it the two trade unionist and ideological characteristics with striking emphases. Created in 1945 under the influence of the Soviet Union, WFTU is mostly composed of workers' organizations within the Eastern European countries. The national trade unions within these countries are enmeshed with the state capitalism of their government beyond recognition. An Italian trade union delegation to Moscow—having in mind Fiat automobile corporation which has factories in the Soviet Union—inquired from the Soviet unionists whether they would take solidarity action, if asked, against a multinational corporation within which workers in a Western country were on strike. The answer of the Soviet workers was that "... this is a political question and trade unions in the USSR are not involved in politics."

Inversely, the relatively small portion of the member organizations of WFTU which are outside Eastern Europe have been the more militant unions in the West and the developing countries such as CGT in France, CGIL in Italy CUTch in Chile, or CNT in Uruguay—the latter two suppressed by military regimes.

UNDERDEVELOPMENT AND NATIONALISM

The main international thrust for the ideological promotion of human rights, however, has not been the use of trade unions—precisely because of their intrinsic characteristics of symbiosis with the national government and the capital. The international setting has not lent itself to the Marxian scenarios of proletarian consciousness and revolution in the highly industrialized societies. Instead, the consciousness has been that of underdevelopment and nationalism, and in some extreme cases, that of religious fanaticism. The methods have been those of militancy, creation of national liberation fronts, guerrilla warfare, coup d'états and terrorism. And the target has been imperialism and its manifestation in the form of international finance. If there needed to be any proof for the justification of this scenario, Allende's attempt at gaining control through democratic process in Chile and the circumstances of his overthrow provided it.

The threat of national liberation fronts and other forms of disruption have become a check on international finance for consideration of human rights; but usually they are perceived too late, basically because of capital's primary intrinsic characteristic of profit making and also because where the international finance does promote human rights in the host country, it generally does it according to Western standards which often disrupt the cultural pattern of the host country and accelerate the process of social change. Unfortunately, when the political and social unrest become serious, consideration of human rights by international finance further precipitates the process. By trying to improve the economic and social conditions, it admits pate shortcomings and points the way. And by supporting the ruling class, yet nudging it to ease the situation by granting some civic and political human rights, it creates contradictions within the established order, thus weakening its position against the militant elements. The past history of these events, from the Soviet Revolution to Nicaragua has shown that once the process begins, the compromise between international finance and militant factors is unlikely.

Past history has also shown that once the revolutionary elements have succeeded, the regime they install is not that of entitlement. They invariably call international finance back in. By suppressing and controlling civil and political rights and by standardizing economic and social human rights they create favorable and predictable conditions for international finance to follow its natural goal to seek profit which, at the same time, helps develop the economy of the authoritarian "socialist" or "state capitalist" host country. This transition process has not yet fully taken shape. In the early seventies a number of Eastern European countries and more recently China passed laws to facilitate the influx of international finance. Some efforts were made in that direction. But the economic and political upheavals since the seventies have brought that movement to a practical halt. For other more recent regimes issue of revolutions, wounds are still too fresh for accommodation.

We thus return to the realities of symbiosis between international finance and the government, and by doing so to their intrinsic characteristics. Governments are, in the last analysis, political, military and legal entities. International finance is a balance sheet. Balance sheets don't have a soul. Whether it is Romania, Honduras, South Africa or Haiti, for the international finance to move across frontiers, its forecast printouts should show that the balance sheet will be in the black. The human dimensions of international finance lie outside of it, affecting and being affected by it.

HUMAN RIGHTS' IMPACT ON INTERNATIONAL FINANCE

The shareholders invest capital in a corporation for return and banks make loans for interest. If the shareholders do not know or do not care what happens in South Africa or Haiti, the corporation calculates the price of labor—in combination with raw material, capital layout, management, energy costs, etc.—and comes to the conclusion that it is profitable to invest in those countries. If, however, the shareholders do know and do care about human rights conditions in these countries and make a point of it as shareholders, then the corporation may have to take human dimension of the operations into consideration.

As mentioned earlier, interestingly enough, the church is the dimension which provides national and international structures parallel with the international finance and is actually intertwined with it, therefore having a leverage on it for the observance of human rights. The church has the intrinsic characteristic of saving human souls. It is true that it has been known to promise only post-mortum salvation and thus appease the downtrodden without chastising the profiteers. But in the present international conjunctures the church seems to have also taken the direction of promoting earthly human rights among private as well as state (e.g. Poland) capitalists. The structure and intrinsic characteristics of the church thus single it out as one of the more likely national and international dimensions to sensitize international finance to human factors.

It must, however, be noted that the churches themselves were largely sensitized to human rights issues by "radical" movements of the sixties and the seventies which, from within the universities and student movements, were trying to mobilize the public opinion. Although the "radical" movements subsided or became more institutionalized—such as the Greens in the German Federal Republic—they helped develop the intellectual components of the public opinion concerned with international human issues. The intelligentsia/public opinion dimension runs through the social fabric beyond the structured institutions so far covered.

International trade unions, despite the national orientation of their member organizations have taken some critical stands against international finance. It is, of course, in the interest of trade unions in the developed countries to promote social and economic human rights in the less developed countries. The more the labor force in the developing countries moves towards entitlement claims the more expensive the price tag for that labor will become and the less interested international finance will become to move away from its home country labor market.

Governments do have components within their intrinsic characteristics, notably the political and the legal, which do reflect human dimensions. Elected officials, and even authoritarian leaders are sensitive to the intelligentsia/public opinion dimension mentioned above. Thus, the home country may try to become the soul of international finance by, for example, prohibiting it from moving to another country because according to its criteria the target country does not respect human rights or forbidding certain practices such as bribing officials of other countries. In terms of international realities, these policies are subjective and peculiar to the home country's policy. To the extent that they are not universal practices, they may handicap the movement of international finance. Host countries, as we have already discussed, can also establish standards for human rights. This latter phenomenon, however, can be better observed from the other perspective

INTERNATIONAL FINANCE'S IMPACT ON HUMAN RIGHTS

We pointed out that the international finance is a balance sheet. On the face of it, unskilled labor at $0.10 per hour in another country compared to $3.35 in the home country is attractive. Of course, it has to be fed into a complex of other factors to determine the feasibility of its use. The labor may be in the Andean Altiplano or Central Australia and when combined with such factors as transfer of capital goods, transportation, access to market, etc., may be found not to be cost effective.

In addition to these obviously functional factors, international finance will need to look into the political and legal structure of the potential host country in terms of foreign exchange convertibility, repatriation of capital and interest and other pertinent laws. These considerations should per force lead into other questions. It is appropriate for the international finance to find out why labor is at $0.10 per hour. The variables here will be enormous. For example, we may find that labor is cheap due to an archaic feudal social pattern where a small oligarchy of families exploits the masses. It would be quite disruptive and absurd if the international finance getting into the host country took upon itself to improve the lot of the people by offering the workers the minimum wage of its home country.

It may equally be the case that in order to have access to the labor, the market or the raw material in the host country, or simply to make its capital available there, the international firm may have to make some donations to the official oligarchs and power holders of the country. Indeed, the word "bachshish" usually used to imply bribe means donation. It is true that acceptance of favors by the prince consort of the Netherlands or the prime minister of Japan to influence a deal in the context of what we know as a modern culture can be considered reprehensible. But in our own culture, for many centuries, when the King bestowed titles to his officials, they were to collect tributes for their services and even pass on some to the King. The process is feudal and still in practice in some developing countries. It is not for the international finance or its home country to impose their own value system on other countries.

It is, however, a fact of social dynamics that the introduction of a foreign agent into a body will influence it. Whether it is by "donation" to the ruling class or competing with local job givers for labor, international finance will contribute to the process of change; and as a factor, will acquire a certain image. The image, in the long run, is that of superiority and aggressiveness. The nineteenth century mandarins who looked down on the Western mercenary commerce soon came to realize its potency.

The influx of international finance does not only awaken a general sense of alienation but contributes to new radii of identification. The labor in developing countries working for foreign industries, when receiving special treatment, becomes, so to speak, a separate class. It may be considered lower by traditional societies which have pride in their own identity as was the case in China earlier, or it may be considered superior in cultures which do not have respect for their own identity.

Usually there is a combination of both because some segments of the society may remain traditional while others may aspire to modernism. At the same time, those who work for foreign firms, despite the fact that they may be better treated than the rest of the indigenous population, may become more conscious about the discrepancy between themselves and the foreign personnel and resent the discrepancy. Inversely, some, recognizing the discrepancy, become loyal to their foreign employers in that context and try to imitate the culture of the latter.

These phenomena, and others, such as the collusion between the ruling class and international finance, can trigger social upheavals which will use the concepts of human rights to justify their cause and in doing so will find international finance and its home country the appropriate villains. As past events have demonstrated, this process spirals into confrontation between the discontented elements and the international finance. The government of home country—especially when it is the USA—gets involved, and the market mechanisms by which international finance was attracted into the host country get distorted.

For example, the home country will provide military and economic aid to the government of the host country to suppress the social unrest and secure the continuation of the privilege of the international finance. The beleaguered host government will suspend whatever human rights which may have existed in the country and the international finance and its home country by association become implicated in the process.

At some point the situation loses its cost effectiveness in the overall picture of the home country. Whatever its international finance may be gaining in the host country may be offset by the expense to the taxpayers of the home country to maintain the government of the host country. Unfortunately, at this point the situation is no longer evaluated in terms of sound financial considerations but gets marred by ideological and political exigencies. Where social upheavals end up in successful revolutions, international finance takes a loss during the revolution and its usual aftermath of nationalization. Further, the antagonism and resentments between the new regime and international finance handicap the resumption of the activities of the international finance in the host country for a time.

CONCLUSION

If international finance is to survive the wave of state capitalist totalitarian governments with claims of putting capital at the service of entitlement, it should make sure that not only its own balance sheet is in the black, but that the overall outcome of its operations is profitable. In terms of free enterprise capitalism, bombs, tanks and helicopters which go up in flames in "national wars of liberation," and for which the taxpayers foot the bill, are economic hemorrhage. They produce inflation and reduce our competitiveness. We are still suffering from the economic consequences of the Vietnam War. In our own enlightened self-interest, there comes a time when we should cease to prop up unpopular regimes. For that, we need awareness on the part of the people, governments, and the international finance. In short, we need broader and deeper education about international realities, and better political analyses put at the service of international finance. We can start by offering seminars and internships in international relations for corporate managers.

Equatorial Guinea into the literature linking natural resource abundance poor development performance, authoritarianism, and civil conflict, respectively. The paper concludes by arguing that oil has exacerbated already present pathologies in Equatorial Guinea's political economy, paving the way for future problems of underdevelopment, instability and authoritarian rule, problems that could all be alleviated to some degree by changes in U.S. foreign policy towards the region.

In March of 2004 the government of Equatorial Guinea arrested nineteen soldiers accused of plotting a coup in this tiny, oil rich African country. Meanwhile, the Zimbabwean government arrested another seventy soldiers supposedly en route from South Africa to support the coup. Led by South African mercenary Mark du Toit and financed by, among others, Sir Mark Thatcher, the coup plotters hoped to replace President Obiang Nguema with the long-exiled opposition leader Severo Moto.

This dramatic turn of events highlights the renewed interest in this former Spanish colony in west Central Africa. The recent discovery of massive oil reserves just off the country's Atlantic shores has already made Equatorial Guinea Africa's third largest producer of oil, with an estimated 181,400 barrels producing each day. Foreign investment has flown in from around the globe, especially from the U.S. Economic growth has been the fastest in the world and the IMF predicts a staggering 45.1 percent rate of growth for 2005. This rapid growth, coupled with the country's miniscule population of less than 500,000, has brought GDP per capita estimates (PPP) to an astounding $50,240, the second highest in the world after Luxembourg. Equatorial Guinea's oil wealth could transform the country from an impoverished backwater into an economic powerhouse. Yet few benefits have accrued to the masses—rampant poverty, disease, and inequality persist. Life expectancy has stagnated at a dismal 49 years while unemployment exceeds thirty percent. Oil rents have consolidated President Nguema's brutal, authoritarian regime and helped further criminalize one of the world's most criminal states. Growing ethnic and regional tensions, the recent coup plot, and an earlier such attempt in 2003 point to rising political instability in the years to come.

This combination of poor development performance, entrenched authoritarianism, and political instability mirror the experiences of other natural resource abundant countries throughout the world. The so-called "resource curse" has thwarted the hopes of many poor, primary commodity exporters and spawned an extensive academic literature intent on explaining this seemingly paradoxical outcome. This diverse literature can help explain Equatorial Guinea's current plight and shed light on what lies ahead—further underdevelopment, few opportunities for democratization, increased political instability, and violence. As the best work from the resource curse literature acknowledges, however, the political economy of oil in Equatorial Guinea will follow its own, often idiosyncratic, path. Equatorial Guinea's tiny size, the extraordinary pervasiveness of criminality at high levels of government, the unique nature of its regional and ethnic cleavages, its history of extreme personal rule, its strategic importance to the United States, and the offshore nature of its oil reserves will condition the country's experience of the resource curse in important ways. Ultimately, Equatorial Guinea's predicament lends further credence to the central arguments of the resource curse literature and offers an extreme example of the pitfalls associated with resource-led development in very weak states.

This paper analyzes the political economy of oil in Equatorial Guinea with special attention to the academic literature on the resource curse. It begins with a brief history of the country and its recent experience with oil-led development. The paper then moves on to integrate the experience of Equatorial Guinea into the literature linking natural resource abundance to poor development performance, authoritarianism, and civil conflict. The paper concludes by arguing that oil has exacerbated already present pathologies in Equatorial Guinea's political economy, paving the way for a future of underdevelopment, instability and authoritarian rule, problems that could all be alleviated to some degree by changes in U.S. foreign policy towards the region.

EQUATORIAL GUINEA: FROM TROPICAL BACKWATER TO AFRICA'S KUWAIT

Equatorial Guinea remained until quite recently one of Africa's backwaters. Rio Muni, a small sliver of the African mainland between Congo-Brazzaville and Gabon, and Bioko Island make up this tiny country of less than half a million residents. Under Spanish colonization cocoa exports dominated the economy and foreigners, mostly Spanish and Nigerian, controlled the small service sector. The vast majority of Equato-Guineans remained subsistence farmers with little or no integration into the market economy. Limited health and education services and almost no infrastructural development outside the main towns left the colony in a state of gross underdevelopment. Colonialism, therefore, created neither a unified national market, nor effective state institutions and left the masses egregiously impoverished.

Unfortunately, independence heralded an even worse period

marked by economic decay and brutal dictatorship. Macias Nguema, the country's first president, came to power in 1968 through relatively democratic means. He then installed one of post-colonial Africa's most oppressive regimes, rivaled only by Idi Amin in Uganda. Nguema's rule combined the worst characteristics of the Latin American caudillo and the African "Big Man," centralizing power and cultivating a menacing cult of personality. He executed a classic purge of the opposition, especially targeting traditional leaders and intellectuals. His reign of terror killed or forced into exile between a third and a half of the country's population. The purge also drove the country into economic free-fall: the expulsion of Nigerian and Spanish expatriates triggered a ninety-percent drop in GDP as the cocoa industry virtually disintegrated.

Nguema filled most government posts with members of his family and his Esangui clan, a subset of the Fang people who dominate mainland Rio Muni. He discriminated openly against the Bubi people, the dominant ethnicity on Bioko and killed almost all of Bioko's Bubi politicians. (11) This widespread brutality and favoritism bred ethnic tensions between the Fang and Bubi, who together make up ninety-percent of the country's population, and also fostered divisions between the various Fang clans. Because the Fang dominate the mainland and the Bubi the island, these tensions took on a decidedly regional component.

Eventually, Nguema began murdering increasing numbers of his own clan and family, alienating even his closest supporters. Teodoro Obiang Nguema, Macias' nephew, initiated a violent and successful coup in 1979 and came to power under the title "liberator." His regime ended the reign of terror but continued the police state and dictatorial apparatus installed by Macias. Obiang remains in power to this day, his ruling Esangui clan retaining almost complete control of the country. Human rights groups routinely describe him as one of the world's worst dictators, pointing to gross human rights abuses and tight restrictions on civil and political freedoms.

Under Obiang, Equatorial Guinea became a classic criminal state, with many top-level institutions involved in various illicit behaviors. Bayart, Ellis and Hibou, in their seminal work on the criminalization of the African state, list Equatorial Guinea as one of only three African countries already worthy of the moniker 'criminal state' in that the apparatus of rule had become intimately intertwined with wide-scale criminal activity. Robert Klitgaard's Tropical Gangsters describes his years working there for the World Bank. It depicts an amazingly impoverished people led by corrupt and ultimately inept gangsters engaged in massive criminal activity and human rights abuses. Criminal industries already known to flourish in Equatorial Guinea include toxic waste dumping, drug trafficking, pirate fishing, arms and aircraft smuggling, and forced labor of children.

By the mid-1990s Equatorial Guinea had become a quintessential criminal state, retaining its autocratic political system, witnessing ethnic and regional tensions, and continuing to suffer from extreme under-development and human rights violations. Great hopes for a change came in 1995 when Mobil struck offshore oil at its Zafiro prospecting site. Since then, oil has been found in many other sites off the coasts of both Bioko and Rio Muni, making Equatorial Guinea Africa's most important new oil producer. Economic growth has averaged around 41 percent per-annum, and a building boom has gripped the capital of Malabo and the oil towns of Luba on Bioko and Bata on the mainland. Energy companies have invested billions of dollars in the country over the past decade, and the weekly "Houston Express" flies directly from Malabo to Texas. The benefits of development remain concentrated in the hands of a very small elite, however, with very few trickle-down effects for the masses. The oil industry only employs approximately 10,000 people, mostly expatriates or migrants from the U.S., Nigeria, the Philippines, and Cameroon. Furthermore, few oil rents have been invested in programs to improve the quality of life for the people, with spending on health services averaging a mere 1.23 percent of GDP. Clearly, the boom has done little to improve life for the majority of Equato-Guineans.

While of limited importance to most of the country's people, oil has certainly brought massive wealth to Obiang's ruling clique. Misallocation of oil rents for lavish personal expenditures have grown to ridiculous proportions. Obiang just bought a multimillion dollar mansion outside Washington D.C. His son Teodorin has become a regular in Manhattan, Hollywood and Paris, where he is famous for driving his many fancy cars up and down the Champs-Elysses. He has even begun his own Los Angeles-based music company. A recent corruption scandal involving Washington D.C.'s Riggs Bank implicated the bank and Obiang for illegally siphoning off millions of dollars from Equatorial Guinea's treasury into personal accounts. Furthermore, most of the money Obiang spends inside the country goes to seemingly misguided huge projects, such as building a new capital, Malabo 2, rather than for roads between villages, new schools, or new hospitals.

8

Rethinking the Global Political Economy

For a quarter of a century, it has been conventional wisdom among policy makers, academics, and journalists that the neo-liberal policies that have governed the global economy are a great success. We have been assured that the costs of global deregulation of capital, labor and commodity markets - including the dislocation of workers and communities - are "transitional" and more than compensated by the benefits in overall economic growth, rising standards of living and a narrowing of the income gap between rich and poor. Indeed, poor nations have been told that their only hope for prosperity lies in opening all national markets and pursuing an export-led growth strategy.

Yet there is no convincing proof that the so-called "Washington Consensus" has delivered on its promises. Most of the claims are based on anecdotal evidence and typically count just the benefits and ignore the costs. More systematic efforts to find a positive net impact by comparing economic performances of countries according to some crude assumptions of "openness" have met with skepticism from honest professionals (Rodriguez and Rodrik 2000). On the other hand, there is a strong prime facie case that the net impact of neo-liberalism has been negative. For example, in a study for the United Nations, British economist John Eatwell (1996) pointed out that financial liberalization of the 1970s was supposed to:

- move savings from developed to developing companies
- lower the costs of borrowing

- increase economic growth

Instead, by 1992:

- savings flowed from developing to developed countries
- interest rates generally rose
- economic growth slowed down

Since Eatwell's study, we have experienced the Mexican peso collapse, the East Asia financial crisis and, now a worldwide recession, all of which have diminished performance of the neo-liberal regime even further. One recent study compared the rate of growth in real GDP from 1960-1980, with the growth from 1980 to 2000 for 116 countries divided into quintiles according to per capita income. It found that the growth rate fell for every quintile from the earlier to the later period. Among the poorest countries in the lowest quintile, the 1980-2000 growth rates turned negative (Weisbrot et al. 2001). Ironically, those nations that have grown the fastest over this period, were those that most resisted the advice of the "Washington Consensus."

Inequality has also gotten worse. As Christian Weller, Robert Scott, and Adam Hersh (2001) have shown, the median income of the richest ten countries was 77 times that of the poorest ten countries in 1980, and 149 times in 1999. The incomes of the richest 10% of the world's people were 70 times that of the poorest 10% in 1980, and 122 times in 1999. Within nations, inequality also seems to have worsened. Certainly in the countries where the data are most reliable, the trend is clearly toward more inequality. Even World Bank president James Wolfensohn in 1999 was moved to admit, "At the level of people, the system isn't working."

INADEQUATE GLOBAL INSTITUTIONS

The history of successful national economies tells us that markets need to be regulated by political institutions in order to work effectively. Government regulation is necessary to enforce contracts, assure transparency, and protect citizens from the brutalities of the unrestrained market. Central banking and discretionary fiscal policy are essential to maintain macroeconomic growth and stability. But today, the leadership of the world's advanced nations, driven by multinational financial interests and rationalized by an extremist "free market fundamentalism," are attempting to create a global marketplace without the political institutions needed to make it work.

The International Monetary Fund (IMF), for example, is not a central bank for nurturing global growth and stability. It is rather a lender with an ideological agenda, conditioning its loans to troubled nations with austerity and anti-labor policies aimed at giving priority to debt repayment through exports rather than domestic growth. Although it demands that individual client nations open their financial markets to competition, the IMF itself is the center of a credit cartel; it has agreements with other financiers to assure that projects it does not like will be blacklisted from receiving assistance from the World Bank and other international lending institutions, as well as governments and large private lenders. Like all cartels, the IMF uses its oligopolistic power to pursue political objectives. It therefore has a decided bias toward countries whose leaders are in sync with the bank's major supporters. A former chief economist of the IMF has openly acknowledged that the staff of the IMF make no important decision without checking with the U.S. Treasury.

Moreover, the staff is inadequate for its task. Stanley Fischer (1997), then first deputy managing director of the IMF, told the New York Times in December 1997 that his agency - despite its army of a thousand economists - did not have the capacity to monitor the global banking system effectively: "The amount of detailed knowledge it takes to understand a system is beyond the capacity of a single multinational organization to deal with."

The assumption that the G-3, the G-7, or the G-8 can some how provide overall management for the global economy is likewise misplaced. The leadership of these advanced countries have even less capacity to plan for global stability than does the IMF or World Bank. Thus, despite the expressed concern of the world's great economic powers after the Asia crisis of the 1997 that a new financial "architecture" was needed, very little reform has taken place.

In reality, the global financial system is governed by ad hoc crisis management, characterized by late-night phone calls from U.S. Treasury officials to the world's financial tycoons, IMF officials flying to Third World capitals in disguise, and Wall Street lectures to recalcitrant politicians in developing nations. The crisis-management style has one big advantage for those who attempt to manage the global economy. It avoids the politically difficult questions of accountability and sovereignty. When the world faces a crisis, issues of fairness, economic sustainability, and democracy are brushed aside as secondary to the emergency task at hand: restoring investor confidence. When the crisis is over, the global policymakers turn to other issues, and the opportunity for serious public debate is lost - until the next crisis, which must be managed again at still higher levels of risk.

In the absence of institutions that can maintain and stabilize global demand, the deliberate encouragement of export-led development strategies places the fate of the global economy on the willingness and ability of the large advanced economies - Japan, the European Community and the United States - to provide the markets and capital investment needed to accelerate growth in the rest of the world.

With the Japanese economy currently mired in its crisis of finance and consumer confidence, it is an unlikely source of economic stimulus. Indeed, it well may be that in order to solve its problems; Japan will have to go through a financial restructuring that in the near term will further reduce its domestic growth.

Europe is in better shape. It has idle capacity and its capital account is in balance. But the Euro zone is constrained by a macroeconomic conservatism that is built into the Maastricht Treaty and other political arrangements and will be hard to dislodge in the near term. Moreover, for now, Europe's economic policies will focus on easing its eastward expansion.

This leaves the task to the United States, which during the 1990s, particularly the last half, has provided much of the stimulus for world demand.

9

Prospects for the U.S. Economy

The U.S. economy appears to be at the end of a mild recession. The recession was in large part a natural outcome of the ten-year economic expansion that ended in March of 2001.

During its first five years, this expansion was at best ordinary. After having fallen in 1991, the GDP rose at an average of a little above 3% annually through 1996, about the same as the previous two expansions and considerably less than earlier upturns. What made this recovery different was its "second wind," averaging 4% for the first quarter 1996 to 2001.

The most important contributor to this second wind was what did not happen: an inflation shock that would have induced the Federal Reserve Board to raise interest rates. The absence of inflation in the 1990s should not have been such a surprise. In modern times, all significant bouts of inflation have been generated by a war or exogenous oil price shocks, not by a peacetime economy that expanded beyond its sustainable limits. The last price flare-up was generated by a short-lived panic in oil markets when the 1990 Gulf War was launched. Global oil prices also sparked the inflation of the 1970s. The previous price run-up was kicked off in the late 1960s by then President Lyndon Johnson's refusal to raise taxes to pay for the Vietnam War. The inflation spell before that was ignited by the Korean War, the one before that by the lifting of price controls after World War II, and the one before that, by the impact of World War I (Faux 2001).

The absence of price inflation in the 1990s allowed the Federal Reserve to accommodate economic growth. But the prospect of continued growth and the availability of cheaper credit fueled an inflation in financial asset values, causing the U.S. stock market to rise over 350% between October 1990 and January 2001(Council of Economic Advisers 2002). Despite the obvious speculative excess, the Federal Reserve declined to use its ability to impose credit restrictions targeted at the stock market. Instead it waited until 1999, when it tightened credit in the entire economy and helped precipitate a recession.

Once the recession began the Federal Reserve quickly reversed itself and lowered interest rates 11 times, driving short-term rates down from 6.5% in June 2000 to 1.8% by December 2001. Long-term rates fell as well, but much less. Moreover, the Bush Administration, despite its conservative rhetoric, was quick to apply a Keynesian fiscal stimulus in the form of a tax rebate. The result was that consumer spending, after a temporary drop in the wake of the September 11 attacks, was maintained. By early 2002 it appeared that a slow recovery was beginning.

No one can predict the future. Nevertheless, current conditions allow some educated guesses about the capacity of the U.S. economy to act as the locomotive for the revival of rapid global economic growth.

In the short term (one year), we can expect the U.S. unemployment rate - which is a lagging economic indicator - to rise, even in the face of a recovery. The unemployment rate in February 2002 was 5.5%, up from a low of 3.9% in October 2000. Based on past history we can expect the rate to rise to somewhere around 6% by the end of the year.

The impact of a rising unemployment rate will be felt on consumer incomes - particularly for those at the bottom of the wage distribution. The U.S. experience shows that below 5% to 5.5% the labor markets tighten and the benefits of growth begin to be shared by those at the bottom. Thus, the end of the 1990s expansion, earnings for low-wage workers were rising faster than those for high-wage workers.

Similarly, when the unemployment rate rises, real income growth among U.S. workers slowed down. Chart 1 shows the estimated losses among family income quintiles of a rise in the overall unemployment rate from 4% to 6.5%.

In the medium term (2-4 years), even with a recovery, it is not likely that the United States will return to the growth rates that it enjoyed in the late 1990s.

First, the impact of the recent stock market decline will dampen a return to what Alan Greenspan called the "irrational exuberance" of those years. Some $5 trillion in U.S. households' financial assets evaporated between third quarter 2000 and third quarter 2001. (U.S. Federal Reserve System 2001) and it will take time for the small investors to forget the pain of that loss, and for new money to come into the financial markets. Moreover, the price-earnings ratios in the U.S. stock markets are still above historical averages.

Second, the impact of the Enron and related scandals has yet to run through the economy. Banks, for example, have become more conservative in their lending. And the easy financing through the stock market that U.S. companies enjoyed over the last decade has diminished. Together with the collapse of the "dot.com" sector of the stock market, the Enron scandal is having a negative impact on the confidence of investors - particularly small investors and workers with defined contribution pension plans. Already it is estimated that U.S. companies will have to come up with cash for about $30 billion in convertible securities coming due in the next 18 months that they had assumed they would be able to pay for with stock.(Business Week 2002).

We also know now that the profits of a number of large corporations in the technology sector were overstated. For example, Enron's profits between July 2000 and October 2001 were overstated by at least one billion dollars, or 78% of the total profits claimed (Madrick 2002). Estimates are that that the profits of all U.S. corporations in the late 1990s were falsely inflated by between 20% and 25%. If so, this suggests that the stock market bubble was even larger than we thought.

Third, overcapacity in a number of technology sectors will continue.

Fourth, new cost pressures on U.S. companies will come from rising health care costs. After several years for stability, these costs are now expected to accelerate once again.

Fifth, the capacity of American consumers to spend faster than they earn may be reaching its limit. As Chart 2 shows, relative to disposable income, both domestic consumption and consumer debt in the U.S. are at their highest levels since the end of World War II. The risingvalue of residential real estate is now the consumer sector's main support. If the United States were to experience a deflation in housing prices, consumers would be forced to retrench.

Finally, the long-term problems of U.S. manufacturing will persist. There is, of course, a tendency in most advanced countries for manufacturing's share of total employment to shrink because of higher productivity rates in manufacturing relative to the service and commercial sectors. But the weakness in the U.S. manufacturing sector does not reflect a simple secular trend. As Chart 3 shows it is directly connected to the chronic and persistent trade deficit.

Despite the persistent U.S. trade deficit, there is a widespread assumption that the U.S. economy is highly competitive. The heart of this claim is that the relative unregulated state of U.S. markets, especially labor markets, has led to a productivity "miracle." A closer look at the productivity makes this proposition doubtful.

As Table 1 shows, real GDP per worker has grown faster in the United States than in the Euro zone. But output per worker is not as accurate a measure as output per hour *worked*. When that adjustment is made, the U.S. performance still leads, but by a smaller margin.

Table 1: Productivity(1996-2000)

	U.S.	**Euro zone**
GDP/worker	2.5	1.2
GDP/hours worked	2.1	1.6
Net domestic product / hours worked	1.8	1.5

Productivity(1993-2000)

	U.S.	**Euro zone**
Net domestic product / hours worked	1.4	1.8

Moreover, as a recent report by Credit Suisse (2001) First Boston points out, international comparisons of Gross Domestic Product are distorted by differences in the way depreciation is measured. Therefore Net Domestic Product, which subtracts capital depreciation from the calculation of GDP, is a better measure of economic progress. When the two economies are compared on that basis, the1996-2000 performances narrow considerably. When the longer period, 1993-2000, is examined, the Euro zone performance is superior. It should also be noted that by 1997, at least five European economies (Belgium, Norway, France, West Germany, and the Netherlands) had reached productivity levels that were at or above more of the United States (Mishel, et al 2001). The illusion of faster U.S. productivity growth may have contributed to the willingness of the Federal Reserve to keep monetary policy loose even as the unemployment rate reached and went below "NAIRU" levels.

In the long term, the U.S. economy is clearly headed for a financial crisis. In 2000, the U.S. current account deficit was a record $450 billion, 4.5% of GDP. The recession reduced the current account deficit in 2001, but it was still above $400 billion. When the economy recovers, the deficit will continue its relentless expansion because U.S. consumers and businesses now have an inordinate propensity to import as income rises. According to last year's report of the U.S. Trade Deficit Commission (2000), "For an equal increase in national income in the United States and foreign countries, the United States increases its purchase of imports proportionally more than foreigners increase their exports."

Nobel prize-winning economists Franco Modigliani and Robert Solow (2001) recently characterized the large and growing deficit in the U.S. international trade balance as "the greatest potential danger facing the economy in the years to come."

In order to finance this deficit, the United States has had to borrow from other countries and sell them more of its assets. Thus, each year its economy must devote more of its income to interest on the debt and the transfer of profits to investors in other countries. After 1988, these payments began to exceed foreigners' remittances to the United States.

This net foreign "debt" is now 22% of GDP. Assuming a recovery, the U.S. economy is on a trajectory to a debt burden of roughly 40% of GDP within five years.

The United States is, of course, not Argentina. The dollar is the world's most important reserve currency and America has better credit and more assets to sell. But it is a matter of simple arithmetic that it cannot forever borrow in order to buy more from the rest of the world than it sells. The interest burden will eventually be so heavy that foreign investors will be unwilling or unable to keep financing the rising debt. When that happens, the dollar will drop and interest rates will spike upward. The United States will then be forced to run a trade surplus with a drastic devaluation of the dollar and/or a draconian deflation in real incomes in order to reduce demand for imports and make U.S. goods cheap enough to run a surplus in world markets. The costs of balancing trade through deflation would be considerable; according to an earlier calculation, bringing a 2% current account deficit into balance would require a 10% drop in GDP and a jump of 5 full percentage points in the unemployment rate (Godley 1995). At today's deficit share of 4% and more the required contraction is even greater.

Getting to a trade balance will be even more difficult because U.S. manufacturing capacity may well have shrunk below the level needed to eliminate the trade deficit through expanding exports. Given the relentless import competition, investors are reluctant to make long-term capital available to medium-sized and small manufacturing firms - and some large ones as well. The grim outlook for manufacturing also reduces the incentive for young people to invest in becoming skilled workers.

The low savings rate also contributes to the current account problem but it is now a function of a deficiency in private rather than public savings. This is a much harder problem to solve. In fact, we do not know how to raise the private savings rate. And under current conditions increasing the saving rate would reduce consumer demand, upon which the U.S. economy - and the world - depends.

Another imbalance driving the trade deficit is the overvalued dollar, whose price against other major currencies may be as much as 25% too high. By making U.S. exports more expensive and imports cheaper, the high-value dollar has been a major cause of the erosion of U.S. manufacturing capacity.

Whether one believes that the trade imbalance is caused by low savings, a high dollar, slower growth in Japan and Europe or some combination of all of these factors, the fact is that the U.S.

government is not attempting to solve any of these problems. Indeed, the Bush Administration is deliberately moving in the opposite direction on all fronts. Its ten—year, $1.3 trillion tax cut will further reduce the national savings rate, and it has repeatedly declared opposition to any effort to significantly reduce the value of the dollar. Neither does it have a credible industrial strategy; its recent decision to raise tarriffs on steel imports will do little to solve the industry's fundamental problems. It has also been unwilling to use its political clout to pressure Europe and Japan into faster growth. The need for allies in the War Against Terrorism makes it unlikely that it will make any effort to address this issue in the near future.

Slower U.S. growth in the near term and the eventual need to reverse the macroeconomic imbalances will also have a negative effect on Mexico and Canada, who have staked their future growth on exports to the United States. Slower U.S. growth will also compound the problems in Latin America, which is in its second recession since 1998. Indeed, the proposed Free Trade Agreement of the Americas, which would expand The North American Free Trade Agreement (NAFTA) to the rest of the hemisphere, would make Latin America even more dependent on U.S. markets.

THE POLITICS OF GLOBAL GOVERNANCE

The failure of the neo-liberal policy regime and the doubtful capacity of the U.S. economy to act as a sustained engine of growth leaves the current system of global economic governance at a dead-end. Unfortunately, the political structure of that system is at present incapable of creating a new and different path to global prosperity.

Markets do not exist in a state of nature. They are social constructs, with defined customs and regulations that are established through political struggle and compromise. The generation and distribution of income, wealth, and power is as much a political as an economic phenomenon. In the famous words of one political scientist, politics is the art of "who gets what" (Lasswell 1936). Therefore, every market has a politics.

The expanding global market system is no exception. Thus, according to a former director-general of the World Trade

Organization, the WTO represents the "constitution" of the new global economy. This may be an overstatement. But the policies of the WTO, the IMF, the World Bank, and other global regulators, represent the dominance of the investor class in the politics of the emerging global economy.

No one can deny the existence of a global investor class. Electronic technologies and modern transportation and communications system allow for extremely effective business and financial networking. Increasingly, the top echelons of transnational business are managed by multinational personnel, who have little or no loyalty to the country whose passport they happen to hold.

A global investor class implies a global working class, even though the international organization of workers is far behind that of investors. Therefore we cannot fully judge the impact of globalization without reference to the share of benefits and costs going to capital and labor. The questions of "who wins?" and "who loses?" from particular policies of the global institution cannot be answered on the basis of separate national identities alone because every country has an investor and a working class, i.e., there are rich people in poor countries and poor people in rich countries. In 1996, for example, 22% of the world's billionaires were from the developing nations.

In most cases, international agreements are negotiated by elites that have more in common with each other than with working people in the countries that they represent. As a retired U.S. State Department official put it to me bluntly a few years ago, "What you don't understand," he said, "is that when we negotiate economic agreements with these poorer countries, we are negotiating with people from the same class. That is, people whose interests are like ours - on the side of capital."

Accordingly, the fundamental purpose of the neo-liberal polices of the past 20 years has been to discipline labor in order to free capital from having to bargain with workers over the gains from rising productivity. Although labor is obviously better served when it is organized into trade unions to bargain with a unified voice, the bargaining between labor and capital goes on even if workers are unorganized. The bargaining between labor and capital is what makes up the "social contract" that is required in order to legitimize the unequal distribution of income, wealth, and power that a free market generates.

As in any bargaining, both sides are constantly maneuvering for advantage. But labor is typically at a disadvantage because it usually bargains under conditions of excess supply of unemployed workers. Moreover, the forced liberalization of finance and trade provides enormous bargaining leverage to capital, because it can now threaten to leave the economy altogether.

Moreover, unregulated globalization in one stroke puts government's domestic policies decisively on the side of capital. In an economy that is growing based on its domestic market, rising wages help everyone because they increase purchasing power and consumer demand - which is the major driver of economic growth in a modern economy. But in an economy whose growth depends on foreign markets, rising domestic wages are a problem, because they add to the burden of competing internationally.

Both the international financial institutions and the WTO have powers to enforce protection of investors' rights among nations, the former through the denial of financing, the latter through trade sanctions. But the institution charged with protecting workers' rights - the International Labor Organization (ILO) - has no enforcement power.

Until recently, the politics of the global economy has been largely viewed as "international," i.e., focussed on the questions of "which nation gets what," with the central conflict between countries that are rich and poor, developed and developing, oil haves and oil have-nots, etc. From this perspective, the institutions of international economic governance (e.g., the International Monetary Fund, the World Bank, the World Trade Organization) are presented to the global public as a sort of legislature of different geographic interests; those representing the poor countries from the South argue for redistribution and those representing rich nations from the North argue for fiscal discipline. Geographic conflicts are certainly a primary feature of global politics - as they are of national politics. But the underlying political conflicts in the global economy are not exclusively among nations. Borderless finance and production, administered by an international managerial class, has crippled the ability of most nation-states to regulate their own markets for social purposes. Increasingly, the people of any given country cannot rely on their corporations or their banks to promote their interests. The worker in Brazil, the worker in Japan, and the worker in the United States may well have more in common with each other than they have with those that manage and prosper from enterprises that are nominally Brazilian, Japanese, or American.

Although one can find a mass of data on the financial interests of the relatively tiny investor class, the mainstream media carries little systematic information on what is happening to the huge class of the world's workers as a whole. But a look at the trends within countries shows a general deterioration of the position of labor relative to capital - in both developing and developed economies.

The Global Policy Network, a new group of non-profit research organizations linked to national trade unions movements has so far posted reports on labor conditions in 27 countries on its web site (www.gpn.org). The countries examined include those among the poorest (e.g. Lesotho, Zambia), the most rapidly developing (e.g. Korea and Ireland) and the most developed (Canada, United States). The exact manifestation of labor's shrinking share of income differs from country to country but there is a common pattern in the concentration of economic growth in the "informal" sector - where workers are unorganized, contingent, and unprotected. That is, where they have little or no bargaining power with capital.

Argentina is, of course, the latest example of this relentless downward pressure on workers' living standards. No other country has embraced the neo-liberal paradigm as much as Argentina. The suicidal tying of the peso to the dollar was for years celebrated as the example of what a developing country had to do in order to gain the confidence of foreign investors. One result has been the nearly doubling of the share of the population in extreme poverty as capital relentlessly squeezed labor's income share. As a report from the Institute de Estudios y Formacion in Buenos Aires shows, labor productivity among Argentina's 500 largest firms - which dominates Argentina's international trade - rose

50% from 1993 to 1998, while real wages rose only 20%. So where did the benefits of increased efficiency go? Within those firms the share of income going to labor dropped from 35% to 28% in five years, while capital's share rose from 65% to 72% (Lozano 2001). Moreover, much of this capital found its way overseas. Many so-called "foreign" investors are in fact Argentines who have been buying high-interest Argentine bonds with accounts in banks in the United States and Europe.

Another vivid example of how neo-liberalism negatively affects workers at all levels of development is the North American Free Trade Agreement. Like most recent agreements, NAFTA protects investors at the expense of workers and the environment. Seven years after its implementation, the political protectors of capital in all three countries judge NAFTA a great success, and support the efforts to expand it to all of the Western Hemisphere through the Free Trade Agreement of the Americas.

But as a recent collaborative study by economists in Canada, Mexico, and the United States (Faux et al. 2001) shows from the perspective of the working people in all three countries, NAFTA has been a failure. All three countries saw a decline in real wages, an upward redistribution of income and a dramatic expansion of the informal sector jobs characterized by insecurity, low pay and no bargaining power.

This upward redistribution of income, wealth, and power reflects a fundamental contradiction in the global political economy:

- A global social contract must be enforced by global economic institutions
- Global economic institutions, in the absence of global democratic government, will be captured by global business interests
- Global business interests will prevent the brokering and enforcement of a global social contract.

GLOBAL CLASS POLITICS

The annual meetings in Davos (this year in New York) of the World Economic Forum are in some ways the convention of the global party of capital. We might call it the Investors' Protection

Party. Their convention in New York was paid for by the world's largest multinational corporations and was dominated by 1,000 corporate executives, along with 250 government officials, including 20 heads of state. They were accompanied by lawyers, consultants, journalists and academics who did business with each other at the receptions and dinners and in the corner of hotel lobbies, just as in any political convention.

The meeting of the World Social Forum in Porto Alegre, Brazil at the same time was in many ways a convention of a global political party in opposition, which is now searching for a common program with which to oppose the investor's agenda. The difference between these two "parties" is not, as the media would have it, the difference between globalizers and anti-globalizers. Globalization - in the sense of people exchanging goods and ideas with each other has been going on for several thousand years and will continue. Neither is it a concern with "social" as opposed to the "economic" issues. The meeting in Porto Alegre was also about economics - an economics that serves society, rather than one that is served by society. In that sense, the core contention between Davos/New York and Porto Alegre is over the rules of the global marketplace - and who will set them.

Because the Investor Protection Party dominates the global financial institutions, the party in opposition has little real access to forums, which might force those institutions to seriously consider alternatives. Demonstrators can temporarily obstruct the workings of the global institutions' managers. But as the WTO showed by moving its last meeting to Doha, international agencies have the resources and the will to circumvent street demonstrators.

As a consequence, the leaders of the NGOs, trade union, anti-poverty and religious groups in opposition find themselves drawn into largely fruitless efforts to achieve social justice by lobbying the IMF, the WTO, the World Bank, and other finance and development institutions, which have no intention of making significant change in their program. NGOs may be put on public advisory committees, but the real work goes on in private where representatives of multi-national businesses negotiate the rules.

The Party of Opposition is thus constantly forced back into a defense of national sovereignty as the only available instrument for achieving social justice. Yet sovereignty is steadily eroding under the relentless pressure of global markets. Moreover, a nationalist politics undercuts the cross-border cooperation needed to balance the cross-border political reach of business and finance. Nationalism perpetuates the myth that national identity is the only factor in determining whether one wins or loses in the global economy. It obscures the common interests of workers in all countries when faced with the alliances of investors in rich and poor nations that now dominate the global marketplace.

Still, human rights and social justice will become part of the "constitution" of the global marketplace only when enough nation-states demand it. Therefore, if the global opposition is to develop an alliance of its developing and developed country wings, it must pursue a common global program for working people of all nations that reinforces their national struggles for economic and social equity.

Such a program would support national democratic movements and leaders who understand that national social contracts cannot be maintained in a global market that lacks one of its own, and that a global social contract cannot be established in the absence of effective social democracy at the national level. The global opposition cannot demand "democracy" at the IMF and not within the nations that belong to it.

The strategy for labor must change the framework of current global political debate in which the investor class pursues its interest across borders, while the working class is constricted by those borders. The creation of a true global alternative requires a perspective through which the interests of workers in all countries are linked. In a global marketplace, workers' living standards increasingly rise and fall together. When workers in Brazil win a wage increase, it raises the bargaining power of workers in Germany. When workers in Indonesia improve their working conditions, workers in Nigeria benefit. Likewise, when the social safety net is strengthened in one country it helps those struggling for human economic and social rights in other countries as well.

So long as the struggle is seen as a struggle of nation against nation, the Party in Opposition will never be able to mount a credible alternative to the Neo-Liberal paradigm. Only when workers in all countries see that they ultimately have more in common with workers in other nations than they have with the owners of capital in their own country, will they be able to organize effectively. When investors are faced with similar demands for decent pay, healthy working conditions and human dignity at the workplace everywhere, they will be forced to have a serious debate about the economic future of the planet.

Trade Unions' Role

The definition of the global working class cannot be restricted just to unions. Nonetheless, the free trade union movement - that is, the movement of unions democratically elected by workers and accountable only to their membership - play a crucial leadership role for the world's workers. Labor unions are strategically important in part because they have the power to deny capital the human resource that is necessary for the generation of profits. The capacity to strike is the ultimate threat to the investor class.

And just as the Party in Opposition needs the support of organized labor, so labor needs the support of the NGOs and other organizations that rise in opposition to the neo-liberal program.

In recent years, trade unions and other parts of the Party in Opposition have been working closer together. The coalition of workers and environmentalists in Seattle in 1999 symbolized this effort. And in local struggles against multinational corporations around issues of privatization, pollution and injustice all over the world reflect similar partnerships. One recent example is the coalition of U.S. and Mexican union activists and university Students Against Sweatshops that forced a company producing for Nike to recognize an independent trade union whose leaders had been persecuted for protesting abominable working conditions.

Through the International Confederation of Free Trade Unions and its regional networks, unions have stepped up their efforts at global collective bargaining and joint organizing campaigns against multinational employers. The global trade union movement was crucial in the struggle against apartheid in South Africa and dictatorships in Korea and Indonesia. Today, unions all over the world are aiding in the struggle against oppression of workers' voices, from Burma to Colombia to Zimbabwe.

To move the partnership forward, the opposition will need to pay attention to areas that have sometimes divided trade unions and their allies in the developing and developed economies.

One example is the tension over labor rights and standards in international trade and investment agreements. Although virtually all trade unionists and their allies support such rights and standards, many in the Third World see the effort to enforce them with trade and financial sanctions as a vehicle for first-world protectionism.

As one Asian economist observed: "The U.S. Treasury runs the International Monetary Fund, and for years urged them to make loans to dictators who squandered the proceeds and are now dead, or retired in the South of France. Then the IMF tells us that the only way to pay their debts is to increase exports made with our cheap labor. When we do, U.S. unions complain that we are undercutting labor standards."

On the other hand, trade unionists from developed countries see their third-world brothers and sisters as being too willing to align themselves with multinational capital in opposing social protections through trade and financial agreements. They are skeptical when those in developing countries who claim to be supportive of human rights resist economic sanctions - which, in practical terms, are the only way to preserve those rights.

One strategy for overcoming this disagreement is to design a "grand bargain" that gives the working people in both developed and developing countries what they need. The bargain starts with the distinction between rights and standards.

Collective bargaining is a right that every worker is entitled to, regardless of how rich or poor is his or her society. The wages and benefits that a union settles for, however, will depend on what the particular enterprise can pay. Likewise, all workers should have a right to a minimum wage. But the level of that minimum wage will depend on the economic development level of the country or region.

Once that distinction is understood, it may be possible for labor organizations and their allies in all countries to reach agreement that would provide enforceable labor rights in exchange for guaranteed commitments of long-term development aid and debt relief. Thus, the developed world would get protection for its social standards, and the developing world would receive the flexibility and capital investment it needs for growth. Incidentally, the issue of labor rights and standards is not just an issue for developing countries but developed ones as well.

This "grand bargain" that links development with broadly increasing living standards would be connected to planning for sustainable development to create the program elements for a global social contract. Other elements would include:

- *Flexible Development*. The one-size-fits-all policies of the international financial agencies have not only failed to produce faster growth, they have allowed the leaders of recipient countries to escape responsibility for their own policies by blaming all their problems on the IMF or World Bank. Therefore, once human and political rights are ensured, countries should have the flexibility to choose their own development path, for which their leadership should be held accountable - to their citizens.
- *Winners Compensating Losers*. As long as workers who have to bear the costs of open markets expect that they will be abandoned by the society that profits at their expense, they will resist globalization. So countries need social policies that compensate those who must pay for the benefits of economic integration. Such policies would include increased public spending on health care for the uninsured, worker retraining, adequate pensions, and community redevelopment, as well as more generous unemployment compensation and wage insurance to cushion the blow of moving to lower-paying jobs.
- *Regulated Finance*. Volatile financial markets must be tamed. Since no system of global banking regulation is in sight, the simplest solution is the "Tobin Tax" - a tax on international financial transactions. The proceeds would be used for long-term investments in education and health care in poor countries. Such a tax, which has the virtue of being easily understood and can be administered with minimal bureaucratic discretion, is already supported by

many influential people around the world. Several years ago, in fact, the government of Canada proposed a discussion of the Tobin Tax for the agenda of the Group of Seven (the major economic powers) meeting in Halifax, but the U.S. Treasury quickly quashed the idea.

- *Coordinated Economic Policy.* A fully functioning global economy - like a fully functioning national economy - needs central banking and counter-cyclical public budgets in order to maintain overall growth. But there will be neither a global central bank nor a global government budget for a long time, so these functions must be performed by the governments of the three largest economies - the United States, Europe, and Japan - acting together. Having pressured the world into a system of brutal competition, the major powers have an obligation to maintain sufficient global demand with low interest rates and other macroeconomic policies. Putting pressure on their governments to act is the special responsibility of worker organizations in those countries.

REGIONALISM AND DEMOCRACY

Although international cooperation among those in the opposition is certainly growing, in a world of about 190 separate countries (most of which are desperate for investment) and more than six billion people (most of whom are poor), the development of a global political movement powerful enough to bring the investor class to the bargaining table is clearly a long way off.

Nevertheless, it is not so difficult to imagine an effective cross-border politics among limited groups of countries in subglobal geographic regions. People who live in countries in the same region tend to have more in common with one another. Language barriers are not as great. Culture is similar. And trading relations are usually the strongest. From a development perspective, regional clusters of nations can provide the economies of scale so that small third-world countries can take advantage of new technologies. From a political perspective, a path to global integration built on expanding regional markets could provide a more accommodating arena for a social-democratic alternative. Indeed, regionalism has long been a project of the mainstream left around the world. The European Union grew out of a French socialist's dream of burying Franco-German enmity. African regionalism was the vision of the late Julius Nyerere of Tanzania as a way of progressing beyond tribalism and colonialism. In Latin America, there is a history of efforts to bring together economies in the Southern Cone, in the Andes, and in Central America.

Attempts at regional integration of less-developed countries have failed more often than not, in part because ruling economic oligarchs and their foreign-investor allies are threatened by the bidding up of wages and costs that comes from a more diverse economy. Thus, the United Fruit Company-and, therefore, the U.S. State Department-was unenthusiastic about the regional integration of the Central American economies because it would have created competition for labor and weakened the politically conservative oligarchs that run those countries.

On the other hand, the European Union illustrates the greater potential for sustained economic integration when policy is focused on the development of a diverse domestic market. The extent of social protection in Europe and the rich debate over the restructuring of a continent-wide social contract reflect a comprehensive notion of economic integration as a tool for political and social development. Ironically, the European Union was inspired by U.S. economic history, which can be read as a process of regional integration supported by a federal constitution that nurtured (not without struggle) the growth of trade unions, civil rights, and a modest welfare state.

This more comprehensive approach stands in stark contrast to the North American Free Trade Agreement (NAFTA), which the U.S. government is now holding up as the model for development in all of the Western Hemisphere. In NAFTA development is narrowly defined as an expansion of the volume of goods and money that flow across the border. Accordingly, the arrangement gives extraordinary protections to investors but leaves labor, the environment, and consumers to the mercies of the deregulated markets. As a result the benefits have largely gone to capital, while labor has borne the cost of dislocation, increased insecurity, and an overwhelmed public infrastructure on both sides of the border.

Whether NAFTA was worth this cost is a subject of partisan debate in each nation. But one thing is certain: NAFTA is incomplete. Deliberately so, of course; had its promoters revealed NAFTA for what it was - the first step toward economic and political integration of the three nations - it would have been soundly rejected in each country. Be that as it may, there is no going back. Supporters of the Washington Consensus are already pushing to consolidate their agenda for the North American economy, with proposals to adopt the U.S. dollar as currency in Mexico and Canada as well as an updated version of the infamous bracero system in which the U.S. government would provide American employers with Mexican workers whose docility is guaranteed by the threat to ship them back home.

Mexico's new president, Vicente Fox, has explicitly called for the transformation of NAFTA into a wider continental agreement. He wants to open up the border to more immigration and to receive aid for schools, roads, and infrastructure from the United States and Canada similar to the "social cohesion" funds that the richer countries of western Europe provide to Spain, Portugal, Ireland, and Greece to help them grow faster.

These initiatives provide an opening for a trinational coalition of progressives to offer its own continental grand bargain that reflects the interests of working people in all three countries. In such an arrangement, the United States and Canada would agree to make capital available for sustained public investments and Mexico would agree to the enforcement of labor and environmental standards, which would rise as the country's income grows (Faux 2000).

The advantages of starting a visible and transparent political debate over North American integration could spill beyond the continent. In light of the influence of the United States, it might give hope to many people around the world who are struggling with the consequences of a mismanaged global market-a sense that even here, in the heart of the Washington Consensus, an emerging alternative vision foreshadows a globalization that works for everyone.

CONCLUSION

The failure of the neoliberal paradigm and the growing imbalances of the world's leading economy suggest that it is time for a rethinking of the politics of the global marketplace. Key to that understanding is recognition of the class dimension of the global political economy.

A major strategic task before us is the strengthening of the alliance of working people - North and South, East and West - through a common program. This should rest on a "grand bargain" in which the interests of developing and developed country workers are served. Such a grand bargain for labor would also help raise consciousness among the majority of the world's citizens of the need for international solidarity with each other.

The task is difficult. But the world's working majority has two great advantages.

One is that it is the vast majority - in every country. The second is that the world's workers are indispensable. One can imagine a world without multinational investors. It is impossible to imagine a world without workers.

10

The Failure of Utilitarian Ethics in Political Economy

INTRODUCTION

A normative argument must have a normative premise whether it is explicitly stated or not. As Gordon Clark pointed out in one of his philosophic essays, it is simply not possible to logically arrive at the conclusion that people ought to behave in some specified way simply because someone prefers it that way. The most popular ethical philosophy to employ with respect to issues of ethical behavior at the current time appears to be utilitarianism. Yet, most people use this approach almost by default and rarely, if ever, explicitly acknowledge that such a point of reference is inherent in the arguments that they make. The result is that public policy debates are often carried on without ever acknowledging the inherent flaws in the underlying ethical theory that resides behind the scene.

Indeed, the widespread confusion over this point is one of the primary reasons why western market economies have continued to drift towards the ready acceptance of socialist policies. Edmund Opitz has rightly observed that utilitarianism with its "greatest happiness principle" completely neglects the spiritual dimension of human life. Rather, it simply "asserts that men are bound together in societies solely on the basis of a rational calculation of the private advantage to be gained by social cooperation under the division of labor." But, as Opitz shows, this perspective gives rise to a serious problem. Since theft is the first labor saving device, the utilitarian principle will tend to lead to the collective use of government power so as to redistribute income in order to gain the "greatest happiness" in society. Regrettably, the rent seeking behavior that is spawned as a result of this mind set will prove detrimental to the economy. Nevertheless, this kind of action will be justified as that which is most socially expedient in order to reach the assumed ethical end. "Utilitarianism, in short, has no logical stopping place short of collectivism." If morality is ultimately had by making the individual's happiness subservient to the organic whole of society, which is what Bentham's utilitarianism asserts, then the human rights of the individual may be violated. That means property rights may be violated if it is assumed to promote the utilitarian end. However, property rights are essential in securing a free market order. As a result, utilitarianism can then be used to justify some heinous government actions. For instance, the murder of millions of human beings can be justified in the minds of reformers if it is thought to move us closer to paradise on earth. This is precisely the view that was taken by communist revolutionaries as they implemented their grand schemes of remaking society. All of this is not to say that matters of utility are unimportant in policy decisions, but merely to assert that utilitarian ethics will have the tendency of promoting collectivist policies. This will tend to hold true in most cases except when such collectivism has so thoroughly destroyed the economic enterprise as in the case of the former Soviet Union. In those cases, the very real need of material advancement will lead to reform in the other direction.

Therein lies the problem. Is the end that utilitarianism aims for truly ethical? It certainly contradicts the traditional moral philosophies. Both the older natural law philosophies as well as those founded upon religious traditions take issue with the use of force so as to gain one's material wherewithal. If it can be shown that utilitarianism suffers logically from several fatal flaws, then the rational thing that one ought to do is to reject it as a basis for making ethical judgments in policy debates in favor of a more substantive moral philosophy of life. This is the purpose of this paper. Namely, to point out the numerous shortcomings of utilitarianism. In addition, it will be worthwhile to examine a common policy issue in order to demonstrate the difference that it makes when traditional moral philosophies are employed as the foundation upon which one either approves of or disapproves of a particular government action. In this case, an examination of the debate over the delivery of public goods will prove useful.

II THE INHERENT FLAWS OF UTILITARIANISM

As is well known, Jeremy Bentham is credited as the person responsible for developing and initially promoting utilitarianism. Bentham's philosophy employs the notions of utility and hedonism in such a way as to provide a new foundation for making ethical judgments. Of course the ideas of utility and of hedonism were already present long before Bentham lived on this earth. To be sure, the concept of utility will always be fundamental to any consistent study of economics. Yet, his assertion that ethical behavior essentially culminates in the promotion of "the greatest happiness for the greatest number" of people in society was new and it departed radically from traditional ethical philosophies. As Frederick Copleston has written, "Bentham did not invent the principle of utility: what he did was to expound and apply it explicitly and universally as the basic principle of both morals and legislation." In this regard, Bentham was acting as a social reformer who sought to change the world. He vigorously attacked traditional morality and rejected notions of both the natural law and of natural human rights.

Instead of approaching ethical philosophy in its traditional way, Bentham rested his theory solely upon the concept of psychological hedonism. That is, he used the observation from utility analysis that people seek pleasure and avoid pain as the basis upon which to devise a new moral standard of behavior. In essence, Bentham sought to make evil synonymous with pain and to make virtue synonymous with pleasure. This was his main point of departure from traditional ethics. Traditional moral philosophies tend to assert that virtuous actions will ultimately result in pleasure while evil actions will ultimately result in pain. But in traditional morality these things are never paired together as if they were one and the same thing. Rather, they exist together as causal pairs. The work of Jonathan Edwards provides an excellent example of this approach. Throughout his philosophical and theological writings, Edwards argued that a person ought to set his highest affections on God alone. In fact, Edwards argued that the benevolent love of God was the only true virtue. From this position, he proceeded to argue that such affection would move the person to live a moral life in conformity to the commandments of God given in the Bible. In turn, living such a life would result in the greatest possible eternal reward and would result, therefore, in the greatest possible utility for the person. This traditional approach to moral philosophy is readily espoused throughout the Bible as well. For instance, in his discussion of Moses' faith in Christ, the writer of Hebrews says:

> By faith Moses, when he became of age, refused to be called the son of Pharaoh's daughter, choosing rather to suffer affliction with the people of God than to enjoy the passing pleasures of sin, esteeming the reproach of Christ greater riches than the treasures in Egypt; for he looked to the reward.

The point of the passage indicates that virtuous behavior is sometimes costly and painful in the short term, but exceedingly beneficial in the long term. In fact, the traditional notion of wisdom is that the wise man is the one who prudently endures some immediate pain for a greater good. The main point of this is that Jonathan Edwards and the biblical writers never confused a person's pleasure with virtuous behavior itself, but rather saw it as a by-product of a life well-lived. Nevertheless, Bentham simply asserted that they are one and the same thing, and on this basis attempted to construct a new kind of moral guide. However, his effort suffers from several underlying flaws which render it useless in serving as an ultimate compass of what people ought to do.

The Problem of Making Interpersonal Comparisons

Among the many difficulties encountered in Bentham?s approach, the first is that it is impossible to make interpersonal comparisons. It is a well-known fact that different people have different tastes. In addition, there are differences in personalities and talents that different people possess and these differences give rise to differences in their goals and ambitions. All these variations in turn give rise to a fundamental fact of human existence. Namely, that it is impossible for us to know or measure the extent of either pleasure or pain for any specific person in any particular situation. Such measures are beyond the capacity of our ability to know. While human beings can most certainly empathize with someone who is experiencing extreme hardship or enjoying great success, such efforts are only accomplished by projecting one's own inward feelings to someone else's circumstance. One person simply cannot accurately know the depth of another person's pain nor the height of his joy.

While Bentham at least recognized this problem, it did not discourage him from his ultimate pursuit. Instead, he continued to promote his new ethical philosophy and argued that it was the only way that we could go. Therefore, he pressed for a way to measure happiness. While he was never able to arrive at such a measure, he remained confident that one would soon be developed and even used the term utils as the units in which it would be measured. Economists have long since given up on the search for a cardinal measure of utility. Strangely enough however, welfare economists continue to act as if we can actually accomplish the impossible task by attempting to measure deadweight losses within the context of modern price theory. It is the rise in the prominence of welfare analysis that has given utilitarianism a standing in modern policy debates. However, such efforts cannot escape the reality that such measures cannot be made. With no adequate way to measure utility in order to make the necessary interpersonal comparisons, all such policy arguments are reduced to contests where each side claims that the rewards to be received by them would greatly outweigh whatever pain might be incurred by those who are forced to bear the costs.

An Inadequate Conception of Human Nature

Another problem with utilitarianism is that it has a very narrow conception of what it means to be a human being. Within Bentham's view, human beings are essentially understood to be passive creatures who respond to the environment in a purely mechanical fashion. As such, there are no "bad" motives, only "bad" calculations. In these terms, no person is responsible for his or her own behavior. In effect, the idea being promoted is that human action is essentially the same as that of a machine in operation. This notion reduces a human thought to nothing more than a series of bio-chemical reactions. Yet, if this is true, then there is no meaning to human thought or human action and all human reason is reduced to the point of being meaningless.

Beyond this problem, it also seems a little absurd to argue that since all human beings seek pleasure and avoid pain, that we can conclude that such a fact ought then be used as the foundation upon which an ethical theory ought to be constructed. As Opitz points out,

> Words like pleasure happiness, or satisfaction are what might be called "container words." They are words needing a content, like the word "assistant." When someone tells you he is an assistant, you are told nothing about his actual job. All you know is that he is not an executive. To make it specific, the job of being an assistant needs some entity to hook up with. Similarly, happiness or pleasure. There is no such entity as pleasure or happiness; these are mental states which may be associated with many different things.

Since this is true, pleasure cannot be the goal of human action in and of itself. It is simply the by-product of human action which is actually aimed at the attainment of some specific goal or end. To be sure, people rarely seek to refine their tastes by considering such qualitative issues until they are well fed, clothed, and housed, but that fact does not mean that such issues are unimportant. Even that great proponent of utilitarianism, J. S. Mill, came to understand this point. As a result, he too began to recognize that happiness was not something that could be had directly and tried to introduce qualitative factors into his utilitarianism.

Regrettably, Mill did not press the implication of this insight to its final conclusion. If he had, he would have abandoned his utilitarianism in favor of some other ethical philosophy. The reason why this is so is that an effort to include qualitative factors into one's ethical thinking necessarily requires an appeal to some ideal. That is, Mill must have in mind some concept or idea of what human beings ought to be, rather than what they in fact are, if he is going to include qualitative factors in his analysis. When this is done, one is forced back into the mode of the traditional ethical philosophies that existed prior to the utilitarian project. If one has an ideal of what men should be, then that ideal establishes a standard of moral behavior apart from the pursuit of pleasure itself. As Copleston comments on the matter:

Hence there must be a standard of excellence; and this is not fully worked out. The relevant point in the present context, however, is not Mill's failure to elaborate a theory of human nature. Rather is it the fact that he grafts on to Benthamism a moral theory which has little or nothing to do with balancing of pleasures and pains according to the hedonistic calculus of Bentham, and that he does not see the necessity of subjecting his original starting-point to a thorough criticism and revision.

The Fallacy of Composition

A final problem with utilitarianism that ought to be mentioned is that it is subject to being criticized because of a potential fallacy of composition. The common good is not necessarily the sum of the interests of individuals. In their book, *A History of Economic Theory and Method*, Ekelund and Hebert provide a well-conceived example to demonstrate this problem. They write:

It is presumably in the general interest of American society to have every automobile in the United States equipped with all possible safety devices. However, a majority of individual car buyers may not be willing to pay the cost of such equipment in the form of higher auto prices. In this case, the collective interest does not coincide with the sum of the individual interests. The result is a legislative and economic dilemma.

Indeed, individuals prone to political action, and held under the sway of utilitarian ethics, will likely be willing to decide in favor of the supposed collective interest over and against that of the individual. But then, what happens to individual human rights? Are they not sacrificed and set aside as unimportant? In fact, this is precisely what has happened. In democratic countries the destruction of human liberty that has taken place in the past hundred years has occurred primarily for this reason. In addition, such thinking largely served as the justification for the mass murders of millions of innocent people in communist countries where the leaders sought to establish the "workers' paradise." To put the matter simply, utilitarianism offers no cohesive way to discern between the various factions competing against one another in political debates and thus fails to provide an adequate guide for ethical human action. The failure of utilitarianism at this point is extremely important for a whole host of policy issues. Among them, the issue of the government's provision of public goods is worth our consideration.

PUBLIC GOODS AS SEEN THROUGH THE LENS OF TRADITIONAL MORALITY

It is common practice in teaching the principles of economics today to teach students that one area of market failure occurs when externalities exist. As such, the concept of externalities is presented as the notion that some human action spills over into benefits provided for, or costs imposed upon, third parties. This treatment portrays such spillovers, whether they are positive or negative, as if they were symmetric in nature. That is, a positive externality is merely the flip side of a coin in relation to a negative externality. On this basis, it is then argued that the existence of such externalities leads to an outcome that is less than optimal and that there is, therefore, grounds for government intervention. However, this judgment is fundamentally tied to utilitarianism as will be shown.

Murray Rothbard provided an excellent critique of the mainstream argument, which favors government action to extend positive externalities and provide public goods, in his book, *Man, Economy, and State.* In his critique, Rothbard points out that the notion of what is optimal in the sense argued by economists at this juncture is value laden. That is, the underlying ethical philosophy that undergirds this conception of what is optimal is utilitarianism. In fact, all welfare economics as it is currently conducted has as a basic assumption, whether it is explicitly stated or not, that the standard of ethical judgments ought to be a hedonistic calculus. In particular, with respect to the argument for government intervention in cases of positive externalities it is argued that such a situation is sub-optimal because a greater level of utility could have been had if these externalities had been extended. This is exactly the kind of hedonistic calculus that Bentham had in mind. But, as has already been shown, such an effort begs numerous questions regarding its legitimacy.

Another point that Rothbard made in his critique is that positive and negative externalities are not symmetric when viewed from a property rights perspective that embraces a more traditional view of ethics. In fact, from this perspective the two are radically different events. In the case of a negative externality, the failure that has taken place is not a failure of the market, but a failure of the governing authority to adequately protect the property rights of all the participants of the market. In this case, issues of pollution are the result of a violation of the property rights of some people by others in order to garner greater benefits. Alternatively, no such violation of property rights can be asserted in the case of positive externalities. Rather, any attempt on the part of government to extend such benefits could only be had by violating the underlying property rights of the person whose actions happen to give rise to external benefits. Nevertheless, as Rothbard pointed out, proponents of government action will invariably attempt to make their case using two lines of attack. First, those who favor government action complain that a person engaged in an activity that benefits others does too little of it. In this case, the proposition put forward is that such gifts to the community are too small.

As an illustration of the weakness of this argument, suppose on Christmas morning a child should awake and venture into the living room of his house to see what presents there might be for him. When he arrives there, he discovers numerous gifts and begins to open them. The joy of the child?s parents will naturally rise in proportion to the child's delight in receiving the gifts provided. However, if, after the last gift is opened, the child should begin complaining that the bounty he received was far too little, the parents' joy will quickly sour. Those who argue that government should extend positive externalities, might just as well argue that it also ought to intervene on the behalf of spoiled children everywhere. But this intervention would be utterly absurd. In truth, gifts are just that! They are not deserved, but are extended to others by people of goodwill. And, even if they are extended to others as a chance by-product of someone's actions, it could hardly be argued that such a gift was too little.

At this point, it might be obvious that the case for state intervention is too weak, but that has not deterred those bent on government action. "The second line of attack is to *denounce [the recipient of the external benefits] for accepting a benefit without paying [the provider of it] in return.* The recipient is denounced as an ingrate and a virtual thief for accepting the free gift." Referring back to our example of Christmas morning, it is as if the parents, after all the presents have been unwrapped, should then extend a bill to the child for payment. Or, in an alternative illustration based on the pro-government action argument, it would suggest that because my neighbors enjoy the sight of my yard being well manicured, that I should have a legitimate position on which to tax them to pay my lawn maintenance bills. While such a case is ridiculous, nevertheless, in public debate such arguments are readily offered as a reason why public funds should be expended on education, health care, and a whole host of other so called public goods.

By not realizing that positive and negative externalities are not symmetric, the entire issue of government action is skewed in favor of moving the political economy in the direction of command and control. The final result of such a movement, will tend in the direction of political totalitarianism in which any political group with enough power will seek to gain its benefits by taxing others. Alternatively, recognizing that externalities are asymmetric, will prove to be of tremendous value in sorting through all kinds of difficult cases. For example, suppose that I am the owner of ten thousand acres of land in a rural area and that ten years ago I planted trees on that land with the intention of harvesting them in twenty-five years. Suppose also that someone should buy ten acres of property directly across the road from my land and builds a house for himself on that property. Day after day, my neighbor enjoys the view of the trees on my property. However, when the logging begins, he may very well complain that I am imposing costs upon him by cutting down my trees. Is his argument correct? To be sure, my neighbor is losing something that he has come to value during the years that he has lived in his house. However, my neighbor does not have any legitimate complaint against me. My action simply means that I am no longer going to provide him with the gift of a scenic view. The fact that I had done so for fifteen years does not obligate me to continue to give this gift into perpetuity. The only way that my neighbor could have a legitimate complaint against me, is that I should actually cause damage to his own property in the process of cutting down my trees. In this case, I would need to compensate him for such costs. Whatever the case, by clarifying the issue within the framework of the more sound ethical philosophy of human rights to property, it will be far easier to sort out the underlying issues involved in such disputes. Reliance upon utilitarianism in such cases will only muddy the waters.

11

The Political Economy of Peacebuilding: A Critical Theory Perspective

How far are external agencies dictating the pattern of economic transformation in societies emerging from conflict? From current practice in a variety of situations, and from proposed reforms to peacebuilding and development, the answer seems to be: 'as far as the eye can see!' The hubris of peacebuilders keys the political economy of war-torn societies into a map captioned 'the liberal peace project' that, in its economic dimension, requires convergence towards 'market liberalisation'. This became an aggressively promoted orthodoxy, with variations, derived from the late 1990s Washington consensus on the logically correct path of development for undeveloped states. Perhaps not treated as a high priority in stabilising peace per se (the vanguard of which has been allocated to fostering security, rule of law and democratic forms), neoliberal economic policies were nevertheless barely-contested assumptions underlying external economic reconstruction assistance and management in war-torn societies.

This paper interrogates the current political economy of peacebuilding, and the proposed revisions, from a critical theory perspective in international relations concerning the power of post-industrial capitalism and globalisation ideology. Certainly, there is considerable disagreement among critical authors about the nature of so-called market democracy, the power of its non-state networks and agencies vis-à-vis states and about the pre-eminence of a fundamentalist version of neoliberalism (its passing having been identified by John Ralston Saul). From rather disparate standpoints, theorists who have grappled with the problematique of global capitalism, such as Robert Cox, Kees van der Pijl, Zygmunt Baumann, Craig Murphy, Michael Hardt and Antonio Negri, have in common, however, a concern to construct an inclusive and emancipatory concept of political economy, an approach that can also be applied to peacebuilding.

In applying a critical approach this analysis focuses on the politics of the economic projects within the liberal peace framework, first, in relation to contradictions in the 'liberal peace' project, and, second, in relation to what is here identified as a millennial revisionist agenda, represented by the work of Jeffrey Sachs, emergent at the level of international organisations during the course of 2005. This interrogation allows reflection about the objectification of war-torn societies, and on the essentialist rationale of the political economy of peacebuilding and its dysfunctional and normative/ethical contradictions. The research indicates that although the depiction of an aggressive, undifferentiated liberal peacebuilding can, and has been, refined, the millennial revisionist project ultimately fails to address these contradictions. The paper contends that an inclusive/emancipatory participation of local actors and structural diversity in political economies can be considered as alternatives to current and revisionist ideology.

THE ECONOMIC PEACEBUILDING RATIONALE

The rationale for determining rules and frameworks for the development of societies that will release them from so-called 'conflict traps' attributes economic dysfunctionalism to the objectified societies, in their pre-conflict, conflict and post-conflict stages, rather than to any dysfunctional economic precepts, structures and conditionalities generated by expressions of capitalist power and 'global governance'. A key aspect of the 'liberal peace' thus promotes a form of economic control and regulation to establish market correctives in societies that have been resistant to conventional marketisation imperatives.

Although its modern version derives from the 1999 Washington consensus, to which Kofi Annan subsequently acceded on behalf of the United Nations, the project has not been revolutionary. Its antecedents can be traced to Cobdenite teachings concerning the peaceful benefits of free trade. Of course it was not so much 'free' as imposed by the hegemon, the UK and its all-powerful navy; trade and the gun were always in symbiotic relationship. Nevertheless, the ideology survived the First World War, and only in the Second did it give way to a system of international management on Keynesian lines. Even so, poverty reduction was conceived as serving the security interests of the most powerful. Robert McNamara's 'war on poverty' at the World Bank in 1972 was driven by the notion that the poor went communist. Subsequent pressure on the US dollar in the Vietnam war and the collapse of fair trade proposals in the New International Economic Order cemented the rise of neoliberalism. In historical terms, then, one can legitimately argue that the liberal peace has been a fluid response to the logic of industrial and post-industrial capitalism.

In its most modern manifestation, the liberal project has gained enormous strength, less perhaps from the economics of profiteering and driving down costs of production, than from the rationale of globalisation. The future vision has been constructed as economics without borders. State and international regulation should survive mainly to preserve 'fair' competition and guard against fraudulence or the 'worst excesses' of environmental degradation – less to ensure that labour makes a living. The liberal peace elevates economic transformation through macro-economic stability, reduction of the role of the state, the squeezing of collective and public space, a quest for private affluence, and a reliance on privatisation and on exports and foreign investment to stimulate economic growth. The rationale appears to have worked for the wealthiest post-industrial societies, and so it must also work for the poorest and most disrupted. Indeed, the US Office of the Coordinator for Reconstruction and Stabilization has a mission to help post-conflict societies to install market economies.

However, there is plentiful evidence that choices made for war-torn societies are both inappropriate and poorly implemented. The liberal project not only ignores the socio-economic problems confronting war-torn societies, it aggravates the vulnerability of sectors of populations to poverty and does little either to alleviate people's engagement in shadow economies or to give them a say in economic reconstruction if they expect outside help. As Balakrishnan Rajagopal contends, development interventions have been divisive, with:

> social costs, through such devices as forced privatization of key national industries and increased unemployment, speculative bubbles in international finance transactions that have massive impact on real estate and housing markets, displacements of vast populations, great waves of migrations including to urban areas, elimination of subsidies for food and services and the introduction of user fees.

Market price adjustment alone cannot correct disequilibria. War results in destabilising changes in employment, production and prices. 'The ensuing collapse of market entitlements for large groups of people makes it highly dangerous to rely exclusively on the market to allocate resources, set prices and fix factor incomes.'

Together with the interim Iraq constitution perhaps the most striking example of external imposition has been in Kosovo, in spite of its status as a province of Serbia in the state of Serbia–Montenegro. Although varying in their degrees of enforcement and consensus, both Iraq and Kosovo have experienced top-down, military-backed impositions. External actors determined Kosovo's framework constitution, its international status and its official economic development. Indeed, NATO came armed with an economic vision that its most powerful members had already inserted into the Rambouillet ultimatum of 23 February 1999 before the war. This *diktat* stated that 'the economy of Kosovo shall function in accordance with free market principles', and became integral to the NATO/KLA war aim of securing the territory from Serb authority. The economic principles were only sketched out at Rambouillet, but it was assumed that they were valid and should be imposed. Security Council resolution 1244 of 10 June was less presumptuous, but supported economic development through the Balkan Stability Pact, which in turn specified free market economies throughout the region of south-east Europe. In contradiction to numerous declarations that Kosovo was to be governed in accordance with democratic principles, economic policy has been determined by the EU, the international financial institutions and national aid agencies. Under the constitutional framework, the peoples of Kosovo are entitled to protect their ethnic, cultural, religious and linguistic identities, and to be free from economic discrimination. But NATO's war aims curtailed their right to choose an economic future.

THE VIRTUAL DEATH OF THE NEOLIBERAL CONSENSUS

Critical analysis of the links between neoliberalism and unrest and the construction of lessons to be learned from the failures of economic transformation in general and in conflict areas such as Sierra Leone, Bosnia, Afghanistan and Iraq in particular, has led to reassessments of the liberal peace. Resistance to the power of neoliberalism as a framework for sustainable development and peacebuilding have also apparently been influential. These include in the present case: pressures for 'fair trade', fulfilment of the Millenium Development Goals (MDGs), debt reduction, demands for social protection for the poor and abandonment of aid conditionality. This has a historical provenance in the dialectic of system building noted by Craig Murphy, many of the ideas for moving capitalism onwards have originated with the various resistances to the impacts of global capital.

Such pressures have also affected the introduction of development policies in war-torn societies under the aegis of peacebuilding. Preliminary work by Oliver Richmond provides a nuanced typology of liberal peace that disaggregates it into several modes. At one extreme a non-consensual, hyper-conservative model attempts to maintain peace through military superiority. At the other extreme an emancipatory model combines top-down and bottom-up peacebuilding, focuses on a range of actors and emphasizes social justice. In between, conservative models have been attempted in Kosovo and East Timor respectively. In practice, in spite of the economic *diktat* of Kosovo's constitution, for example, neoliberalism was modified in Kosovo, in the light of experience in Bosnia. UNMIK learned the necessity of tackling shadow economies from experience in Bosnia and Herzegovina, where anti-crime measures and institutions had been established slowly.

UNMIK Customs was the first public body to be set up, and together with EU Customs Assistance Mission (CAM-K) reformed the collection system, tripling revenues between 1999 and 2003. The neoliberal credo of Rambouillet and the constitutional framework has been tempered in rhetoric and practice by programmes of social protection. Thus the EU's 2002 Action Programme gave priority to the delivery of public services, institution building, public administration and socially-oriented projects. The UNDP emphasized employment generation through training programmes and social justice projects for ending ethnic and gender discrimination. The World Bank provided significant sums for social and public welfare and for poverty reduction through a Trust Fund. Together with the UNDP, the Bank also supported community initiatives for infrastructure rehabilitation and attempted to strengthen the income generation capacity of vulnerable rural families. Even the IMF proposed reform to facilitate long-term planning and stressed the need for investment in education, health and social policy. In Kosovo, therefore, several partners in economic restructuring have acknowledged the importance of social justice, and have undertaken investment in poverty reduction and public services. Even here, however, in spite of slackening growth, rising unemployment and falling purchasing power in 2002–03, the IMF welcomed curbs on consumption power and advised further controls on wages, social welfare, public sector employment and compensation for workers thrown out of work by privatization. Deficit financing was not part of its lexicon, even in conditions of social distress. In the last quarter of 2001, an estimated 50 per cent of the population lived in poverty and 12 per cent in extreme poverty. In the first quarter of 2003 the unemployment rate was estimated at between 49 and 57 per cent (70 per cent among 16-24 year olds); about 25 per cent of the labour force were registered as job seekers. Not surprisingly, opinion surveys ranked unemployment and poverty among the greatest problems facing Kosovo. These were not, however, the top priorities of the external agencies.

DEVELOPMENT DEBATES

Such debates on peacebuilding have paralleled debates on development. As Murphy argues, the development project has been essential to capitalism for its promise of global stability. Weak states and weak development have not only been held up as catalysts of conflict, war has also had devastating impacts on development. War-torn societies have thus tended to be treated as particular, and sometimes acute, cases of under- or disrupted development.

The debate on development generally has evolved to the point that the Washington consensus has been declared 'dead' except as an inaccurate term of abuse. Certainly, the neoliberal agenda is now contested more seriously than in the 1990s, so that it has ceased to be an unquestioned 'common sense', ideology or doxa. This paper contends, however, that the evolving debate marks out dynamics in the liberal peace project that protect and reproduce its core assumptions. The old-style unthinking Washington consensus about development may be merely a virtual death, with a pro-poor liberal peace *redivivus* emerging from the ashes.

In many quarters, the connections between neoliberalism and the practice of human security are, as Kyle Grayson suggests, either not interrogated or have contributed to the silence that shrouds the roles of trade and finance capital in the 'conflict trap'. However, plenty of revisionists in the mainstream of international thought have recognised the chill of failure evident in neoliberalism – though without challenging the fundamentals of an ideology that, in the words of Günter Grass, 'sees mankind as nothing more than something which consumes and produces'.

A salient example was the report by an International Commission on the Balkans, chaired by former Italian Prime Minister, Giuliano Amato, and comprised almost entirely of serving and former politicians of impeccably conservative and (apparently) masculine credentials, smart suited in the group photograph and presenting an appearance of conventional authority. In spite of the huge scale and intrusive scope of international intervention in Southeast Europe, the Commission announced that the returns had been meagre and that the region was becoming a marginalised black hole. This remarkable document reiterated points made by individuals such as General Fabio Mini commander of UNMIK (who categorically announced after the ethnic cleansing of Serbs in March 1994, that the mission had failed) and of critical think tanks, such as Human Rights Watch and the International Crisis Group. According to HRW, 'The international community appears to be in absolute denial about its own failings in Kosovo. While international actors have been universally – and accurately – critical of the failures of the Kosovo Albanian leadership during and after the crisis, the dismal performance of the international community has escaped similar critical scrutiny.' But the Amato report's provenance among interested political leaders served to undermine the many scripts by international interventionist that claimed they were achieving success. The Commission on the Balkans claimed that the alternatives for the region were either integration with Europe or an even more exacting 'neo-colonialism, the two being regarded in this exercise as antithetical. The Commission argued that EU expansion to the region would solve its problems, a widely-supported solution even by critics of external intervention.

But recognition that protectorate power and weak economies in southeast Europe were marks of failure did not mean that the ideological goals, or the fundamental principles for generating *homo economicus*, were flawed. Rather, the process for getting there was all wrong. Integration with the EU and new political perspectives (Kosovo's independence, for example), were required. In effect, the Balkan Commission's report not only treated the region as a referent, and threatening, object, for which 'balkan' was the operative signifier of fragmented chaos, it relied heavily on a 'common-sense' renewal of economic neoliberalism rather than transformation.

MILLENNIAL REVISIONISM

Moreover, the linkage between post-conflict reconstruction/ development and human security has been made explicit in a series of reports that appear to be setting the framework for debates in mid-decade.

One of the most prominent, and influential, revisionist programmes has come from the Millennium Project Report to the UN Secretary-General, *Investing in Development*, released in February 2005. Indeed the Millennium Project analysis provided the nucleus of the first half of the UN Secretary-General's subsequent UN reform programme, *In Larger Freedom*. The Millennium Project was conducted by economists headed by Jeffrey D. Sachs of Columbia University. A special adviser to Kofi Annan, he had been a chief architect of structural adjustment and a proponent of the 'short sharp shock treatment' for eastern Europe and the Russian Federation that had devastating consequences for vulnerable sectors of society. Sachs, however, is merely one in a line of economists whose technical fixes for the global political economy have proved wanting in terms of human security and who have experienced a Damascene conversion. George Soros and Joseph Stiglitz have been there before.

Punctuated by such stirring phrases as 'scaling-up success', *Investing in Development* was remarkable for its commitment to pro-poor and social protection economics. Its springboard was the measurement of uneven and halting progress towards the achievement of the MDGs by the target date of 2015. To recapitulate, the MDGs include:

- reduction of extreme poverty and hunger by 50%
- universal primary education
- equal primary and secondary enrolment for girls; literacy parity for men and women; equal representation of women in parliaments
- a two-thirds reduction in mortality among the under fives
- measles immunization
- a 75% reduction in maternal mortality
- a halt to and reversal of the spread of HIV/AIDS, malaria and tuberculosis
- a 50% reduction in those without improved drinking water and sanitation
- improvement in the lives of slum dwellers
- reversal of deforestation

The Sachs review showed that by 2004 many of the goals were nowhere near being achieved, and were even further away from some benchmarks and in some regions, tuberculosis in sub-Saharan Africa having increased for example. *Investing in Development* acknowledged that the shock of market therapy would not work for Africa, and recommended a bold revision of international strategy for achieving the MDGs. The strategy had ten key components:

- Developing countries should adopt MDG-based, poverty-reduction strategies, to be in place by 2006.
- The MDG strategies should anchor the scaling up of public investment, capacity building, resource mobilization and development assistance, to strengthen governance, human rights, civil society and promote the private sector.
- The strategies should be transparent and inclusive.
- Donors should fast-track a dozen or more countries to 'scale-up' good governance.
- Partners should launch 'Quick Win' actions for economic growth (such as the distribution of anti-mosquito nets).
- Developing countries should align national strategies with regional initiatives such as NEPAD (New Partnership for Africa's Development), the Caribbean Community (CARICOM) and the EU).
- Overseas Development Aid (ODA) should increase from 0.25% of GNP in 2003 to 0.44% in 2006 and 0.7% in 2015, with improved quality of aid, and more generous debt relief.
- High-income countries should open their markets to developing country exports and raise their export competitiveness through investment.
- Scientific research should be mobilized to address the needs of the poor.
- The UN should be strengthened at various levels to support the MDGs

There seems little doubt that such a programme has considerable appeal because it is a significant step towards managing the crisis of capitalism in a way that benefits the poor and vulnerable populations of the world. Massive reduction in the number of deaths from structural violence (though the report never uses that term) can only please supporters of pro-poor causes, from debt relief to the provision of cheap, life-saving drugs to human security ideals. Nevertheless, embedded in the text of *Investing in Development* are assumptions that, taken as a whole, indicate that the liberal peace project is alive and well, even if the Washington consensus itself is moribund. The main features of what might be called Sachs 2 can be summarized as follows:

- its consumerist teleology frames the problem of development in terms of convergence and integration into the world trading system;
- entrepreneurial zeal is what drives human beings: *homo economicus* is reified without taking into account the human values discussed in the 2000 *Millennium Development Report*;
- there is a common solution: 'Whatever one's motivation for attacking the crisis of extreme poverty… the solutions are the same. All that is needed is action.'
- responsibility for failures – corruption and bad governance, for example – lie with 'them';
- the poor need to be changed – they deplete the environment, for example;
- 'sound economic policy' is a matter of rationality; rational economic management works;
- public investment should be used to establish market reforms: in other words, public funds for private enterprise;
- the MDGs can be met without dirigisme in politics and state command over the economy;
- progress can be achieved through 'Quick Win' fixes.

It is conceivable that this programme, or a variant, will forge a 'New York consensus', though the project is jeopardised by apparent US determination to undermine the MDG programme and other reforms as antithetical to US foreign policy. However, to the extent that it features strongly in the UN Secretary-General's 2005 reform programme , *In Larger Freedom*, it has already staked a claim in the UN Secretariat as the foundation for the developmental dynamic in human security, and Sachs 2 seems to be its latest manifestation. The merger of development and peacebuilding became more explicit in the High-level Panel Report, *A More Secure World: Our Responsibility* (2004) which also carried the burden, and sway, of UN's sponsorship. The UN Secretary-General's reform programme of 2005 was largely a composite of the Sachs report and the HLP Report.

Among member states, the UK's pro-poor document, *Fighting poverty to build a safer world*, produced by DFID, also merges security, development, crime, terrorism and economic growth. The UK government also supports in general terms the UN Secretary-General's reform programme and specifically encourages the IFIs to engage in security issues, so that the IMF for example incorporates conflict analysis into Emergency Post-Conflict Assistance agreements. The DFID document conforms to the Sachsian line in several respects: that crime hinders growth, foreign direct investment is the engine of growth, and problems are significantly rooted in issues of governance as well as poverty.

The HLP and the Secretary-General placed great store by the establishment of a voluntary standing fund of $250 million for peacebuilding and the creation of a Peacebuilding Commission and a UN Peacebuilding Support Office. They also recommended the involvement of economic agencies such as the World Bank at an early stage in peace processes. In principle, this could present an opportunity to institutionalise lessons learned from past experiences in the transformation of political economies from war to peace. However, the new structure will be answerable to the Security Council, where the power lies, rather than to ECOSOC and the General Assembly. Moreover, without wholesale change to the policies and programmes of the IFIs, the participation of international economic institutions in peace processes will likely reinforce aspects of the liberal peace.

PROTECTING THE LIBERAL PEACE

This analysis now draws out some of the underlying assumptions of revisionism from a critical perspective under five heads: structural violence, economics as natural law, the objectification of war-torn societies, squeezing public goods and global integration.

THE SILENCE OF STRUCTURAL VIOLENCE

First, the hubris that pervades this potential 'New York consensus' is part of a familiar critique of weak regulation, such as that in *Breaking the Conflict Trap* (2004). That critique calls for tough controls, regulation and monitoring of parties in zones of conflict and an end to 'bad governance' by corrupt, undemocratic elites in developing countries. Malfeasance, abuse, torture and even genocidal operations are certainly conducted by elites, rebels and followers against fellow inhabitants in the South. Most casualties are perpetrated by governments against citizens; and there is an ethical imperative to prevent this. But the millennial critique has also consistently maintained a silence around structural victimization and policies that have emanated from the zones of peace and probity (and the financial agencies that they dominate). The asymmetry of external pressure on state-welfare economies, protected economies, co-operative organisation and collective production denies communities economic options and can produce a politics of victimhood that stratifies and emnifies others, as occurred in Rwanda.

The North–South divide is, by definition, the precondition for having MDGs in the first place – and rendering them impossible to achieve in the second. The Collier team's agenda for international action contains one paragraph of barely ten lines recommending a re-examination of the development and trade policies of the 'North' and the removal of subsidies to 'Northern' producers. In similar vein *Investing in Development* contains a single bullet point that fires the equivalent of a blank at the way capitalist cores are themselves protected from competition and the need for reform of the WTO and IFIs. In a less brutal way, perhaps, the revisionists of this decade may be replicating suppression by the Reagan administration in the 1970s of the South's demands for a New International Economic Order that might foster alternatives to economic fundamentalism. Silence surrounds the role of interventionary core capitalism in perpetuating proverty through neoliberal policies and the structuring of the global economy.

ECONOMICS AS NATURAL LAW

Second, the revisionism still takes economics as largely independent of politics and social values. It results, as Robert Cox has suggested, in the de-politicisation of economic issues, as if a natural law or a primordial economic equivalent of the sex drive, rather than powerful interests, were guiding economic activity.

Consequently, there is only one solution to all inadequately developed societies, whether East Timor or Haiti, and it is a solution based in the economic rationalism of (capitalistic) entrepreneurship. The project is completely transparent in its notion that public monies, whether from revenues raised in developing countries or from aid derived from the public purse in the 'North' should be used to provide profit-seeking business with a leg up.

Unsurprisingly, the contradiction inherent in this so-called 'rationalism' is not addressed by the revisionists, though it is of acute concern to societies in the process of transformation from war to peace. Notoriously, aid often privileges the purchase of donor goods and expertise rather than local products and employment. Privatisation has been pursued at the expense of public goods and public space. Values other than those of economic rationalism are neglected, including the freedom to decide how markets are conducted, even though they figure in the 2000 Millennium Development document and have been espoused, among others, by John Burton and Armartya Sen. Inequalities and non-physiological needs are more significant than either absolute poverty or, beyond a survival point, physiological needs. This means that provided people are not destitute (which might be equated to the deep poverty scale of the UNDP), they may choose to live humbly in order to feel fulfilled. Such an approach recognises that the paths to modernisation may not be convergent at all, and the marginalised peoples of the world are entitled to choose the extent to which, and how, they integrate in the global economy.

OBJECTIFYING WAR-TORN SOCIETIES

Third, populations in war-torn societies are pathologised as if suffering from congenital incapacities that needs treatment through forms of therapeutic governance. In their critique of the psychosocial treatment of states as 'failed service providers run amok', Caroline Hughes and Vanessa Pupavac note that political processes divorced from the depiction of problems of conflict, oppression and poverty has opened the way for therapeutic approaches to intervention'. Archived as congenitally incapable of governance and statehood, these societies require forms of trusteeship that inevitably reflect the priorities of the trustees.

THE MANTRA OF GLOBAL ECONOMIC INTEGRATION

Fourth, the revisionists continue to regard development, at least rhetorically, as a matter of convergence and integration. Although the Sachs report does subscribe to fairer, if not fair, trade, it regards replication of an economic system, advanced in the 'North' as the goal of development. Whether this is an ideal that pervades economic representations to give hope to the undeveloped, when in practice policy makers sometimes act as though there are parallel and even divergent economic development(s), or whether the convergence/replication programme is a matter of self-delusion, is less important than its role in reinforcing a particular model of sustainable development. Similarly, the fetish for integration and participation in global trade, manifest in the Balkan Commission's Report, learns nothing from research on development by Kamal Malhotra's team for the UNDP and from critical work on the political economy of peacebuilding. Inverting the neoliberal/Sachsian mantra that integration produces trade and growth, the critical perspectives that map both historical and current transformations demonstrate that integration follows growth, which follows protectionist policies, much as the UK, United States and EU protected, and continue to protect vital economic interests while promoting freer trade. The vulnerable, it might be legitimately argued, need to be protected from the risks of integration.

SQUEEZING PUBLIC GOODS

A significant deficit in all strands of revisionism, however, concerns growth, trade and employment. Recovery generation and poverty reduction is constructed as a matter requiring physical security, state building, therapeutic governance, private (therefore largely foreign) direct investment and welfare pluralism. In the economics of social policy, for example, 'welfare pluralism' remains the order of the day. In addition to residual state supply and community/civil society provision for such basic services as health, education and water, market mechanisms and the private sector are integral to development. Indeed the *World Development Report* of 2004 'scientifically' verified the doctrine of state withdrawal and expanded market mechanisms for basic services. Economies have been opened up to liberalisation, public goods have been

poor quality and budget deficits have deprived governments of resources. Detailed analysis indicates, however, the absence of intrinsic benefits from the process:

> This welfare pluralism takes the clock back to an earlier historical era when social advances and capabilities enhancement proceeded at a much slower pace than during the decades of state-led welfare provision.... [yet] there is no reason to believe that developing countries should already embark on a path of extensive privatisation in social services, especially as large part of their populations are still not covered by the most basic education and health services.

Options

Other strands in the debate, however, construct a more substantial departure from the liberal orthodoxy. DFID, for example, denies that aid should be placed at the service of global security, and the institution is itself committed to refocusing its work on governance to include more direct support for the security of the poor. This not only entails therapeutic governance to establish accountable political systems, combating crime and promoting transparency in the management of resources and public finance. It also proposes more emphasis on the provision of basic services such as health and education, security and justice. DFID even bawls into the silence surrounding the adverse impacts of structural adjustment, citing the role of the IMF in precipitating the crisis in former Yugoslavia. Furthermore, the UK claimed to relax its aid conditionality in March 2005. Aid would continue to be linked to poverty reduction, human rights, military spending levels and misuse of aid, but would no longer be tied to global security goals. The UK would also cease demanding specific commitments from aid recipients to privatise state industries and liberalise trade, and would urge the World Bank and others to follow. Whether these declarations will carry weight in either UK politics or international political economy seems doubtful in the face of the conservatism on show at the 2005 G8 summit in Scotland. DFID itself has spent huge sums on consultancy firms to advise on privatisation in developing countries, firms whose own analytical frameworks reflect the privileging of investor interests. For example, the, pro-privatisation Adam Smith Institute (International) received over

£34 million from the UK aid budget in 1998–2003. Others have challenged some of the tenets of the liberal peace in a more fundamental way. James Boyce, for example, not only calls for substantial abandonment of conditionality, but also for reform of the aid donation system *and* for support to state economic direction. While rampant inflation can lead to social unrest, so can vicious austerity, and thus the current priorities may be ill-suited to societies emerging from conflict.

Simon Maxwell suggests that social protection should be a high priority and pro-poor growth needs to be complemented by distributive measures. Developing countries should not be suddenly exposed to liberalisation without safety netting for vulnerable sectors; and international 'governance reform' should be a precondition of more money going through the World Bank.

To soften the impact of integration pressures in southeast Europe, the Amato report advocates the development of a regional customs union, as prefigured by the economist Branko Horvat. As with the original European Payment Union and the European Community after the second world war, this would concede that mutual protection to replace national protection is a reasonable starting point, rather than aiming to engineer integration on the basis of complete free trade. A regional payments and customs union would work towards abolition of import duties between the members but maintain common tariffs, though gradually lowered, against selected imports for a period of, say, 10-15 years.

Even on their own, statist terms, proponents of the liberal peace tend to ignore plenty of examples of protectionism, and *dirigisme*, that have nursed vulnerable societies through difficult times: France, Sweden, Cuba, Asian states (including Vietnam which recovered from war quicker than Cambodia). Investment in public goods, infrastructure, social welfare systems and public employment may be necessary to help redress a situation in which a few individuals flaunt obscene affluence but public facilities are often squalid. Such dirigisme may entail controls and a degree of political authoritarianism every bit as irksome as that employed by international civil administrations in post-conflict societies. But a strong and active state role in planning and implementation, with expansionist policies to increase employment, income generation and consumption power to wean vulnerable people off illegal activity through investment in public services and social protection, may be less dysfunctional that the orthodox neoliberal model. Specifically, statist measures might include:

- Production generated by import controls and protection of critical sectors, especially agriculture;
- High taxes on luxury items and rationing or subsidies for basic foodstuffs;
- Government intervention to boost re-training, employment and public services;
- Increased purchasing power through public works;
- Deficit financing;
- Control on donor corruption and reductions in tied aid;
- Maintenance of public sector salaries.

On the other hand, at the grass-roots level, the importance of collective and cooperative production and marketing, whether part of the formal or informal economy, are often viable mechanisms for economic organisation. This is not invariably the case. Many African co-ops are not so much member-owned, as financed by, and accountable to, governments, which have used them as channels for implementing economic policy. However, independent, self-help co-operatives have been important in war-torn societies where central economic authority has been weak. They have been especially important to women (from Rwanda to Bosnia) for whom they have been vehicles of empowerment as well as economic survival. Similarly, credit unions have emancipated people from centralised banking and insurance companies. For people who have limited access to towns, who are penalised by traditional bank profiling and charges – or who need to receive remittances from diasporas abroad – credit unions serve various needs. Over £2 billion is estimated to be sent from Britain to other countries in this way, and other estimates indicate that over US$200 billion is transmitted globally through such informal channels. Credit unions number 40,000 worldwide (the largest in the United States) with an aggregate membership of over 136 million. The world coordinating body, with support from USAID, opened two unions in Afghanistan, which in the first two years attracted 2,000 members. Both co-ops and credit unions appear to have alliances and linkages with aid organisations and are given credence in the UN system, especially in the International Labour Organisation and the Food and Agriculture Organisation.

CONCLUSION

In conclusion, there have certainly been notable shifts in the development and peacebuilding debates, and potential institutional merger of the two. The liberal peace has come under sustained pressure from both critiques and failures in practice that has resulted in pragmatic shifts, to some extent towards pro-poor and emancipatory engagement with local populations.

But we are still entitled to ask the critical question: who is peacebuilding for, and what purposes does it serve? The means for achieving the good life are constructions that emerging from the discourse and policy frameworks dominated by specific capitalist interests – represented as shared, inevitable, commonsensical or the only available option when they correspond to the prevailing mode of ownership. Economic wisdom resides with the powerful. As Murphy notes, political inequality leaves many with no control over the major decisions that affect their lives. For Cox, too, 'whereas the *right* of self-assertion is celebrated, in a social and economic context the individual's capacity to exert control over the systemic factors that determine its *implementation* is removed. Consequently, just as in one-party, authoritarian regimes, politics is about depoliticizing people, by removing the economic determinants of everyday conditions from political control'. The millennial revisionism represents a significant shift. But ultimately it may perpetuate asymmetries that maintain the liberal peace, albeit in less orthodox forms. Indeed, the revisionism may intensify the grip of capitalist-dominated financial and trade institutions. The recommendations of the 2004 UN High Level Panel's report on boosting the UN's attention to peacebuilding activities includes provision for International Financial Institutions to be more actively involved in peace processes. However, without transformation of the IFIs, and the liberal agenda itself, subjugation rather than emancipation will continue to be injected into the political economy of peacebuilding.

12

The Political Economy of Migration

In December 2005, Wisconsin Congressman James Sensenbrenner convinced his Republican colleagues (and to their shame, 35 Democrats) to pass one of the most repressive immigration proposals of the last hundred years. His bill, HR 4437, would have made federal felons of all 12 million undocumented immigrants in the U.S., criminalized teachers, nurses or priests who helped them, and built a 700-mile wall on the U.S. Mexico border to keep people from crossing.

Representative Sensenbrenner is more than just a leader of Congressional xenophobes, however. His family is intimately involved in creating the conditions that cause migration, and then profits from the labor it makes available. In fact, the Sensenbrenner family connections are a microcosm of the political economy of migration itself.

James Sensenbrenner's grandfather started Kimberley Clark, one of the world's largest paper companies, and Sensenbrenner and the family trust remain important stockholders. The company's Mexican counterpart, Kimberley Clark de Mexico, is a close associate of the Mexican mining giant, Grupo Mexico. One of K-C's former executives, J. Eduardo Gonzalez, sits on its board.

Grupo Mexico was a big winner in the neoliberal economic reforms that transformed the Mexican economy over the last twenty years. In the 1990s, the corporation became the owner of two of the world's largest copper mines, in Cananea and Nacozari, which were formerly nationally-owned enterprises. The mines lie just a few dozen miles south of the Arizona border.

In 1998, Grupo Mexico provoked a strike in Cananea, over moves to reduce its workforce and labor costs. Close to a thousand miners lost their jobs. Many were blacklisted and left for "the other side."

Then last year the mining giant prevailed on the Mexican government to depose the president of the country's miners union, Napoleon Gomez Urrutia. Gomez had accused the company of industrial homicide after the terrible Pasta de Conchos disaster, when 68 men died in a coalmine explosion. Grupo Mexico also didn't like his drive to raise mining wages beyond government-set limits.

Miners in Cananea and Nacozari stopped work for months to force Gomez' reinstatement. Finally, last summer, the government gave Grupo Mexico the green light to fire all 2500 miners in Nacozari. Since there are no other jobs in tiny Sonoran mining towns the displaced families had to leave to survive. With the border just a few miles north, many sought their survival by crossing it. The profits of Grupo Mexico and its business partners went up as they destroyed unions, terminated thousands of workers, and forced their families into the migrant stream.

During those very months when workers began to go north, Sensenbrenner organized a series of rump Congressional hearings to defend his bill. He fulminated against undocumented immigrants, claiming they had no place in the United States and should leave. No one asked the Congressman about those miners from Cananea and Nacozari, however. Where did he think they would go?

Other voices in Congress criticized the Representative, arguing that the labor of migrants was needed in the U.S. economy. Not even Sensenbrenner could deny this. Some 16 million immigrants live in the U.S. with documents, and 12 million without them. If they actually did go home, whole industries would collapse. Some of the country's largest corporations, completely dependent on the work of immigrants, would go bankrupt.

One of these dependent corporations is Mr. Sensenbrenner's family business.

Every year, Kimberley Clark, a large paper company,. converts tons of wood pulp into leading brands of toilet paper. Deep in U.S. forests thousands of immigrant workers plant and tend the trees that produce that pulp..

Every year, laborers from Mexico, Central America and the Caribbean are recruited for this job. In towns like La Democracia, Guatemala, where the global fall in coffee prices has driven families to the edge of hunger, recruiters promise jobs paying more in an hour than a coffee farmer can make in a day. They offer to arrange visas to come to the U.S. as guest workers. For their services they charge thousands of dollars. Hungry families will mortgage homes and land, just to put one person on the airplane north.

In the U.S., recruiters hand the workers over to labor contractors. They, in turn, work for land management companies, who tend the forests for their owners. The landowners grow the trees, and sell them to the paper companies.

The debts of guest workers are so crushing that in 1998, 14 men drowned as the van carrying them to work careened off a bridge into the Alagash River in a Maine forest. They were speeding because it had rained the day before, keeping them from working. Carrying that load of debt, even one lost day puts a family in jeopardy.

No one gets overtime, regardless of the law. Companies charge for everything from tools to food and housing. Guest workers are routinely cheated of much of their pay. If they protest, they're put on a blacklist and won't be hired the following year. Protesting wouldn't do much good anyway. The U.S. Department of Labor sees no problem with this abuse. It almost never decertifies a guest worker contractor, no matter how many complaints are filed against it.

The paper industry depends on this system. Twenty years ago, it stopped hiring unemployed workers domestically, and began recruiting guest workers. As a result, labor costs in the forests have remained flat, while paper profits have soared. Mr. Sensenbrenner's family business didn't invent this, but the low price of labor allows landowners to sell their trees for less. Kimberley Clark certainly profits from that.

DISPLACED PEOPLE - AN INTERNATIONAL RESERVE ARMY OF LABOR

In Latin America, the neoliberal system displaces workers, from miners to coffee pickers, who join a huge flood moving north. When they arrive in the U.S., displaced workers become an indispensable part of the workforce, whether they are undocumented or laboring under work visas, in conditions of virtual servitude.

The U.S. immigration debate needs a vocabulary that describes what happens to them before they cross borders - the factors that force them into motion. In this political debate, people like the miners or pine tree planters are called job seekers, rather than political refugees. It would be more accurate to call them migrants, and the process migration.

The miner fired in Cananea or Nacozari is as much a victim of the denial of human and labor rights as he or she is a person needing to find a job in the U.S. to survive.

This year, teachers and farmers left Oaxaca, in southern Mexico, seeking a viable economic future, after they were beaten in the streets for protesting that their state's government can't and won't provide one. Oaxaca's poverty is worse than almost anywhere in Mexico, and last year teachers struck, and the capital erupted in a virtual insurrection because of it. An intransigent political elite, benefiting from the existing order, not only refused to consider any change, but tried to stop criticism with police attacks, arrests and even assassinations.

Are the fleeing Oaxacans job seekers or refugees? They're both, of course. But in the U.S. and other wealthy countries, economic rights are not considered human rights. In this official view, hunger doesn't create political refugees. In effect, the whole process that pushes people north is outside the parameters of political debate.

The key part of that process is displacement, an unmentionable word in the Washington discourse. Not one immigration proposal in Congress last year tried to come to grips with those policies that uprooted miners, teachers, tree planters and farmers, in spite of the fact that Congress' members in many cases voted for them.

Whether acknowledged or not, displacement has been indispensable to the growth of capitalism. As early as the 1700s, the English enclosure acts displaced home weavers by fencing off the commons where they raised sheep for wool. Hunger then drove weavers into the new textile mills, where they became some of the world's first wage workers. The textile mills produced the wealth of the first British capitalists. At the same time, displacement created the beginnings of the British working class.

Not long after, Karl Marx called Africa "a warren for the hunting of black skins," describing the bloody displacement of communities by the slave traders. Uprooted African farmers were then transported to the Americas, where they became an enslaved plantation workforce from Colombia and Brazil to the U.S. south. Their labor created the wealth that made the growth of capitalism possible in the U.S. and much of Latin America and the Caribbean.

Displacement and enslavement produced more than wealth. As slaveowners sought to differentiate slaves from free people, they created the first racial categories. Society was divided into those with greater and fewer rights, using skin color and origin. When Mr. Sensenbrenner called modern migrants "illegals," he used a category inherited and developed from slavery.

Today displacement and inequality are just as deeply ingrained in capitalism today as they were during the slave trade and the enclosure acts of English in the 1700s when the system was born. In the global economy, people are displaced because the economies of their countries of origin are transformed. That transformation enables corporations and elites to transfer value, or wealth, out of those countries. After World War Two, the former colonies of the U.S., Europe and Japan sought to stop that export of wealth. In countries like Iraq, Mexico and the Philippines, they embraced national economic development plans, which encouraged industries and enterprises producing for their own people. Creating stable jobs and income helped build a national market where workers and farmers could buy what was produced. Foreign investors were kept out, and important industries like oil were nationalized.

The economic reforms that followed the end of the cold war, imposed by rich countries and institutions like the World Bank and International Monetary Fund, destroyed those systems of national development. It was a very brutal and chaotic process for those at the bottom of the income scale, but for those at the top, immensely profitable. Mexico created more billionaires during the 1990s than the United States, while at the same time the government documented an official poverty rate of 40%, and an extreme poverty rate of 25%.

Mexican mines like Cananea and Nacozari, along with factories, railroads and other industrial enterprises were sold off to private investors. New owners then increased profits by attacking unions and laying off thousands of workers.

The oil industry, nationalized with the contributions of schoolchildren in the 1930s, no longer produced money for loans to small farmers or enterprises. Instead, in 1994 as the North American Free Trade Agreement went into effect, US President Bill Clinton demanded that Mexico use oil exports to pay off U.S. banks, who bailed out U.S. investors in Mexican government securities.

NAFTA rules required the Mexican government to dissolve the Conasupo stores. This government enterprise bought corn from small farmers at subsidized prices to enable them to keep farming and stay on the land. Then the stores sold tortillas made from the corn, along with milk and other farm products, to poor urban consumers at subsidized prices. NAFTA rules called this form of social welfare a barrier to the free market.

Without price supports or rural credit, hundreds of thousands of small farmers found it impossible to sell corn or other farm products, even for what it cost to produce them. When NAFTA pulled down customs barriers, large U.S. corporations (receiving U.S. subsidies) dumped agricultural products on the Mexican market at low prices. Rural families went hungry when they couldn't find buyers for their crops.

One company, Gruma, monopolized tortilla production, while the largest retailer in Mexico became Wal-Mart. In February the price of tortillas doubled. A small group of investors in both countries got even richer. But where did they expect the people displaced by this process to go?

Where Do Displaced People Go?

Displaced people become an indispensable and growing part of the workforce in this new world order. Not all cross borders. The explosive growth of export processing zones, where maquiladora factories produce for export, depends on migrant labor.

The creation of the original maquiladora program, the Border Industrial Program, on the U.S. Mexico border in 1964, was originally conceived as a way to absorb thousands of unemployed braceros, who had been laboring in the U.S. during the 22 year run of this contract labor program. In 1964, Chicano activists like Cesar Chavez, Bert Corona and Ernesto Galarza led a movement that convinced the U.S. Congress to repeal Public Law 78, which set the program up. The Mexican government then needed to find jobs for those workers, many of whom were living in burgeoning cities just south of the border.

To supply those jobs, it changed laws that had prohibited direct U.S. ownership of factories in Mexico, allowing investors to build plants taking advantage of lower Mexican wages, producing goods for the U.S. market. Over 40 years this model grew to include more than 3000 factories, employing two million people. Cities like Tijuana, Mexicali, Juarez and Matamoros mushroomed.

The maquiladora workforce was drawn from the south, from migrants displaced by the same economic changes - privatization, rural poverty, job elimination - that permitted construction of the maquiladoras themselves. A new labor regime was put in place to attract foreign investment, including the brutal repression of independent unions or challenges to the low-wage model.

Prior to the economic reforms, the U.S. Mexico border was a remote area, with a very low population, far from Mexico's industrial base and workforce. Without the simultaneous dislocation of workers from Mexican factories, and farmers from south Mexico's countryside, there would have been no labor force available to make maquiladora development possible.

This development model has since been reproduced in developing countries all over the world. In the early 1990s the U.S.

Agency for International Development not only financed the construction of industrial parks in rural El Salvador and Honduras, but then contracted with Price Waterhouse to study ways of producing workers for the factories. The recommended the incorporation of women into the maquiladora workforce at ages as young as 14, taking them from school and family farms. To keep these young women at their machines through their most productive years, USAID taught the companies to distribute birth control pills to keep them from getting pregnant.

Attention has focused on the construction of the factories and industrial parks, while the dislocation that produced the workforce has been much more hidden. Yet maquiladora workers often later become migrants traveling far beyond the nearest export processing zone. When the maquiladoras are located a stone's throw from the border, crossing it is almost inevitable.

In developed countries migrant labor is even more important.

In the U.S., industrial agriculture has always depended on it. The farm labor workforce in the U.S. southwest was formed from waves of Chinese, Japanese, Filipinos, Mexicans, and more recently, Central Americans. A growing percentage of farm workers are now indigenous people speaking languages other than Spanish, an indication that economic dislocation has reached far into the most remote parts of Mexico's countryside. On the U.S. east coast, migrants come from the Caribbean as well, joining large numbers of African Americans displaced from rural, or even urban communities.

In other industrial countries, a rising percentage of the rural workforce is now made up of migrants. Industrial agriculture based on migrant labor has expanded to developing countries also. Large corporations like Dole and Del Monte draw a workforce from displaced and impoverished rural communities, like those of AfroColombians in Colombia, or Oaxacans in Mexico.

Migrants now dominate the service industry workforce in most developed countries. As the most recent job seekers, they begin in the most marginal and contingent jobs. Day laborers on California street corners arrive from Mexico and Central America, while in Britain they come from Romania and Africa.

But migrant labor doesn't remain at the fringe of the economy. The world's oil industry is completely dependent on it. The oil kingdoms of the Gulf states - Kuwait, Qatar, Bahrain, Abu Dhabi - have many more immigrant workers than native-born ones. It was no coincidence that Halliburton Corporation brought migrants from Bangladesh and the Philippines into Iraq in the wake of the advancing U.S. invading force in 2003, intending to use them to replace Iraqi workers on the oil rigs and pipelines. Only organized action by the Iraqi oil workers forced Halliburton to retreat, and prevented the company from taking control of their industry.

Once the oil is put aboard tankers, more migrant workers guide them to their destinations. The seafaring workforce in large scale shipping today comes overwhelmingly from the Philippines and Indonesia. Migrant workers provide the world's oil and transport its goods to market.

What's in it for Employers?

Employers gain great advantages from this system, particularly lower labor costs and increased workforce flexibility. Large meatpacking companies in the U.S. Midwest, for instance, hire a workforce in which immigrants make up a majority. A steady stream of migrants crosses the border, finds its way to small meatpacking towns, and gets jobs.

Over the last 20 years, the industry's wages have steadily fallen behind the manufacturing average, a major accomplishment, from the companies' point of view. According to the Bureau of Labor Statistics, 1980 slaughtering plant wages were 1.16 times the manufacturing average. After twenty-five years, they are now .76 times that average. US manufacturing wages certainly haven't soared - in fact, they've fallen behind inflation. But meatpacking wages, in relative terms, have fallen faster.

Companies depend on this river of labor - not just on the workers in the plants themselves, but on the communities from which they come. If those communities stop producing workers, the labor supply dries up.

Seeking to keep wages low, meatpackers don't want to pay the social cost of maintaining communities that supply workers to the plants. In the tiny Mexican and Guatemalan towns that now provide workers for the plants, that cost is very low, and getting lower as economic reforms take hold. Free-market and free-trade policies have eliminated rural credit, the Conasupo system and the other subsidies.

The government budget in Guatemala's Santa Eulalia, for instance, does not provide any healthcare system for the town's residents. In public schools parents and teachers must buy the paper, pencils, books and other materials. If a road needs repair, residents can't expect a government repair crew to fix it.

The cost of all these services is now borne by workers themselves, in the form of remittance payments sent back from jobs in Nebraska slaughterhouses. Former Mexican President Vicente Fox boasted that in 2005 his country's citizens working in the U.S. sent back $18 billion. Some estimate that in 2006 that figure reached $25 billion.

The real beneficiaries of this huge flow of money are the companies that employ the labor in the U.S. Meatpackers already pay a low wage in U.S. terms. From it, workers pay not only for their own subsistence, but for that of their families thousands of miles away. Indirectly, the companies pay a much lower cost for the production of a new generation of future workers than they would if their families were living in Iowa or Nebraska. No company pays directly for a single school or clinic, nor do any pay taxes in Mexico or Guatemala that could provide those services.

At the same time, companies dependent on this immigrant stream have great flexibility in adjusting for the highs and lows of market demand. U.S. employers historically have treated immigrant labor as a convenient faucet, easily turned on and off. In the depression of the 1930s, Mexican workers were rounded up and deported by the thousands when the unemployment rate went up. When World War Two started, the U.S. government negotiated their return as braceros, when growers needed workers, but didn't want to raise wages to draw them from cities.

Guest worker and employment-based visa programs were created to acommodate the labor needs of employers. When demand is high, employers recruit workers. When demand falls, those workers not only have to leave their jobs, but the country entirely. Disabled guest workers, injured because of high line speed on the killing floor, can't stay in the community around the plant, making demands for treatment. They have to go back to hometowns where there is virtually no medical care at all. The employer doesn't have to provide compensation for those forced out of the country.

The rule of this new system, which the British government calls "managed migration," is that immigration policy and enforcement should direct immigrants to industries when their labor is needed, and remove them when it's not. As President George Bush puts it, the government should "connect willing employers with willing employees."

As guest worker programs expand, large corporations become even less responsible for the conditions of their workforce. The pine tree planters don't work directly for the paper companies, but for labor recruiters and contractors. The paper corporations control labor costs indirectly, through the price they pay for harvested trees or wood pulp. This has been the employment model in the garment and janitorial industries and in agriculture for decades, industries that depend completely on immigrants.

As these conditions are established, they expand to other industries. In the 1970s, production workers in Silicon Valley electronic plants worked directly for big manufacturers. Today women working on the line assembling printers for Hewlett Packard work for Manpower, a temporary employment agency with an office in the plant itself. Sometimes they do the same job they did when they worked for HP directly, but now without healthcare or other benefits. They get a lower wage, and can be terminated at any time. Most are women from the Philippines, Mexico and the countries of Latin America and the Asian Pacific rim.

Immigrants and Unemployment

It's no wonder that native born workers and settled immigrant communities look at the growth of this employment system with alarm. This system fosters competition among workers for jobs, and uses it to expand the section of the workforce with lower wages and fewer rights. It's not hard for people to see the system's impact on their own lives, even if they can't always identify its

One of the biggest mistakes made by immigrant advocates in the last decade was arguing that immigrants have no impact, or only a positive impact, on the wages or jobs of people in the communities around them, or that immigrants are just taking the "abandoned" jobs others won't do. This denies a reality workers can easily see for themselves. More important, advocates thus stop making clear the real causes of migration, unemployment, low wages and job competition, and no longer point to the system and corporations responsible.

The first targets of competition are other workers of color. In Los Angeles in the early 1980s, the janitor's union was driven out of the city's office buildings when contractors dumped their union workers, most of whom were African American. New janitorial contractors appeared, with no union, hiring the wave of refugees flooding into LA from repression and civil war in Central America.

Contractors and building owners thought they'd found a docile, low wage workforce, but they miscalculated. Immigrant workers used popular education and the militant union traditions of Central America, making common cause with the national organizing department of the Service Employees International Union. Together they built the first Justice for Janitors campaign in Los Angeles. Salvadoran, Guatemalan and Mexican janitors poured into the streets, confronted building owners and the LA Police Department, and eventually won new union agreements. The campaign became a model for organizing immigrant workers across the country, and rebuilt the presence of SEIU in building services. SEIU head John Sweeney became president of the AFL-CIO, using this campaign as a symbol of his commitment to organizing and revitalizing the labor movement.

But the African American community has faced a color line keeping employment very low in janitorial services in Los Angeles ever since, despite the high Black unemployment rate. In San Francisco hotels, where a similar demographic transformation took place, the percentage of African American workers is falling as industry employment grows. African Americans now make up less than 6% of the San Francisco hotel workforce, and only 6.4% of the LA hotel workforce.

In 2005 the Center for Labor Market Studies at Northeastern University found that between 2000 and 2004, jobs held by immigrants rose by 2 million. At the same time, the number of employed native-born workers fell by 958,000, and of longtime resident immigrants by 352,000. According to the report's authors, "the net growth in the nation's employed population between 2000 and 2004 takes place among new immigrants, while the number of native-born and established immigrant workers combined declines by more than 1.3 million."

Black unemployment nationally has grown at a catastrophic rate - from 10.8% to 11.8% in May of 2005 alone. Nearly half (172,000) of the 360,000 people who lost their jobs in June, 2005, were African American, although they were just 11% of the workforce. In New York City, only 51.8% of Black men from 16 to 65 had jobs in 2003, according to the Bureau of Labor Statistics. For Latinos it was 65.7%, and for whites 75.7%.

Very little of the rise in African American unemployment is a result of direct displacement by immigrants. It's caused overwhelmingly by the decline in manufacturing and cuts in public employment. In the 2001 recession 300,000 of 2,000,000 Black factory workers lost their jobs to relocation and layoffs.

But demographics in the workplace changed during a period of massive plant closings, which eliminated the jobs of hundreds of thousands of African American and Chicano workers in unionized industries. Through the postwar decades, those workers broke the color line, spent their lives in steel mills and assembly plants, and wrested a standard of living that supported stable families and communities. In the growing service and high tech industries of the 80s, those displaced workers were anathema. Employers often identified them with pro-union militancy, according to sociologist Patricia Fernandez Kelly.

In the face of this reality, the unity needed by workers today to rebuild unions and working-class political strength can't be achieved by stirring speeches. Concrete problems affect relations between immigrant and non-immigrant workers. Trying to solve these problems unites people.

Unions Struggle to Respond

The age-old question confronting the U.S. labor movement, and increasingly those of other industrial countries, is inclusion or exclusion. In the past decade, U.S. unions made real progress in organizing immigrants, and connecting migration issues to the effects of free trade and free market policies.. This was a significant change from the cold war period, in which unions supported U.S. foreign and trade policy abroad. They ignored its disastrous impact on workers of developing countries, and even assisted the destruction of the most militant sections of their labor movements.

During the cold war, unions clung to an official ideology of partnership with large corporations, maintained discriminatory policies towards women and people of color, and viewed immigrants as job competitors. In 1986 the AFL-CIO's supported the Immigration Reform and Control Act because it contained employer sanctions, which prohibit employers from hiring workers without papers. If those workers couldn't get jobs, the argument went, they'd leave.

The impact of the law was disastrous, however, especially for those unions trying to organize new members in industries like janitorial services and garment manufacturing. The new law made it a federal crime for an undocumented immigrant to hold a job, and employers used it to fire union supporters. Eventually, when organizing new workers became a higher priority, the AFL-CIO changed its position at the Los Angeles convention in 1999. It called for repeal of employer sanctions, amnesty for all undocumented people, immigration based on family reunification, and expanding the organizing rights of immigrant workers. The federation already opposed expanded guest worker programs, because of their long record of abuse and exploitation.

Unions began to see inclusion as the key to their survival. Labor support for immigrant rights was not a moral issue, but a pragmatic one. Immigrants today are the backbone of organizing drives from the Smithfield pork plant in North Carolina to Houston janitors and Cintas industrial laundry workers. The unions that are growing are mostly those that understand the willingness of many immigrants to fight and join. As a result, immigrants have gained a growing base in union leadership, and now speak out on political questions from the war in Iraq to immigration and labor law reform.

This was not an easy process. Often newly organized immigrants found themselves members of established organizations that wanted their dues and numerical strength, but not necessarily their participation in leadership. Some union leaders still see immigration itself as a threat. The 2006 national convention of the International Brotherhood of Electrical Workers invited Lou Dobbs as its keynote speaker, whose anti-immigrant tirades rival James Sensenbrenner.

On the other hand, two unions, SEIU and UNITE HERE, abandoned their support for the position they won at the 1998 AFL-CIO convention. Instead, together with national advocacy organizations like National Council of La Raza and the National Immigration Forum, they joined an alliance dominated by the country's largest employers. Employers' main purpose is convincing Congress to set up new guest worker programs.. Two farm worker unions, the United Farm Workers and the Farm Labor Organizing Committee, signed union agreements with guest worker contractors.

The meatpacking industry started lobbying for guest workers in the late 1990s, when companies organized a shadowy group, the Essential Worker Immigration Coalition (EWIC). Today it encompasses over 40 huge employer associations, including Wal-Mart, Marriott, Tyson Foods and the Associated Builders and Contractors. They recruited the Cato Institute to produce guest worker recommendations, which President Bush repeats almost word-for-word. The hard-right Manhattan Institute provides additional cover.

The corporate lobby made other inroads. John Gay, who heads the National Restaurant Association and EWIC, became board chair of the National Immigration Forum, a major Washington lobbying group. The list of corporate sponsors for the National Council of La Raza includes Wal-Mart and 14 other multinationals. They all set up umbrella groups to advocate the EWIC agenda, including the Coalition for Comprehensive Immigration Reform and the Fair Immigration Reform Movement.

While Republicans are strong guest worker supporters, the bills in Congress creating the programs have been bipartisan, with active participation from liberals like Senator Edward Kennedy and Congressman Luis Gutierrez. Their immigration proposals would have allowed corporations to bring in almost a million guest worker a year, and expanded the kind of immigration enforcement that has led to workplace raids around the country. The Bush administration proposed scrapping immigration based on family reunification (an achievement of the rights movement) for a point system favoring skills desired by large corporations. Liberals justify these proposals by arguing that employer support was necessary to gain some kind of legalization for 12 million undocumented people. Guest worker and enforcement programs were the price for that support. The Senate finally failed to approve an immigration reform bill in 2007, but it is highly likely that employers will make similar proposals after the November, 2008 elections. And after the bill failed, the administration began implementing some of the most repressive enforcement provisions by administrative order.

Meanwhile, unions have failed to formulate a bill that would unite the needs of workers across race and national lines, and campaign in Congress to pass it. Winning amnesty and greater rights for immigrants could be linked to the creation of jobs programs to reduce unemployment in those communities where it exists at crisis levels. This was the approach taken by Congresswoman Sheila Jackson Lee, who introduced a proposal to grant amnesty to undocumented immigrants and simultaneously establish job training and creation programs in communities with high unemployment.

Some unions have tried to link these issues together in bargaining. In San Francisco hotels, UNITE HERE Local 2 already has strong contract language protecting the rights of its immigrant members. In the 2006 negotiations, it added new language requiring hotels to set up a diversity committee to increase the percentage of African American workers. This could become a step toward an affirmative action program requiring hiring reflecting the diversity of San Francisco's overall workforce, benefiting immigrants and non-immigrants alike.

But unions trying to grapple with the impact of migration have to decide with whom they want to build alliances to win power. Winning affirmative action and jobs programs, linking them to amnesty and immigrant rights, would help build an alliance between workers - immigrants and native-born, Latinos,

African Americans, Asian Americans and whites. But some unions see an alliance with employers as the key, and are willing to give them new guest worker programs. This would increase job competition, put downward pressure on wages, and make affirmative action in hiring impossible. Concrete gains in jobs and wages would become much harder, and unity among workers more difficult to achieve.

ALTERNATIVES TO GROWING INEQUALITY

In all industrial countries the problem of unity between immigrants and non-immigrants is becoming much more important. The anti-immigrant riots in the UK, France and Germany are a window on what the future could be in the U.S., if unions and working communities don't make progress in resolving it. Understanding the importance of community and equality is they key to making that progress.

Migration is a complex economic and social process in which whole communities participate.. Migration creates communities, which today pose challenging questions about the nature of citizenship and equality.

Migrants are creating transnational communities all over the world. They exist at different stages of development in the flow of migrants from Algeria to France, Turkey to Germany, Pakistan to the UK, South Korea to Japan, and from developing to developed countries worldwide. According to Migrant Rights International, over 180 million people live outside the countries in which they were born - a permanent factor of life on the planet.

Today US immigration policy (and that of other industrial countries) is institutionalizing this global flow. Increasingly, the mechanisms for managing it are guest worker programs. In the Hong Kong negotiations of the World Trade Organization, corporations tabled a proposal regulating migrant labor, called Mode 4, which would establish a new, international guest worker scheme.

Conservative governments of developing countries, which have abandoned national development policies and have adopted the free market framework, see big advantages in a deal with corporations. They would gain access to workers' remittances, already the top source of foreign exchange for many, and could use them to finance services formerly financed by taxes. They could even eliminate those paid by their own elites. This would institutionalize not only inequality between migrants and non-migrants in developed countries where they work, but would divide even further the rich and poor in their countries of origin. It would create whole new forms of inequality.

Inequality is the most important product of US immigration policy, and a conscious one. Washington's current reform proposals all assume that immigrants should not be the equals of the people around them, or have the same rights. This assumption denies the reality that the migration of people is as much a product of the global economy as the migration of capital. At the same time, the philosophy these proposals reflect would reverse a 400-year history of struggle in the US to expand the rights of all people.

US immigration policy doesn't deter the flow of migrants across the border. Its basic function is defining the status of people once they're here. And a policy based on supplying labor to industry, at a price it wants to pay, has inequality built into it from the beginning.

Immigrant communities from Latin America and Asia face a hypocritical exclusion, which demands that people give up their culture, language and identity, while maintaining a color line that denies them equal social status. Chinatowns and Manilatowns owe their existence, not simply to the desire for community and group identity, but to a century of social segregation. Filipino farm workers were forbidden from marrying women of other races. Chinese immigrants were brought as debt-enslaved workers on railroads, and then prohibited from owning land. Braceros were recruited from Mexico from 1942 to 1964, on temporary work visas, contracted to western growers. The objective was the same in every case - the creation of a mobile, rootless low-wage labor force. The roots of this inequality lie in slavery. The current concept of the "illegal" person has its roots in the Black Codes, used to define who could be enslaved and who couldn't. It reinterprets the idea that a slave counted as only three-fifths of a person.

Calling someone an "illegal" doesn't refer to an illegal act or the violation of a law. It is the existence, the status of the person that is illegal, or illegitimate. This justifies exclusion from the rights and social benefits accorded people in the surrounding community. Braceros called themselves illegal, even though they had temporary visas, because they used the word in this sense of exclusion.

Illegality is a social category. Workers forced into it receive a smaller share of the value they produce, an additional exploitation. The value they produce, but don't receive, is a source of additional profit for companies dependent on that labor. Inequality is profitable.

An immigration policy that denies community inevitably produces rootless people, vulnerable to exploitation. It undermines workplace and community rights, affecting non-immigrants as well. It inhibits the development of families and culture.

The alternative is a policy that recognizes and values communities, and sees their creation and support as desirable. It reinforces indigenous culture and language, protects the rights of everyone, and seeks to integrate immigrants into the broader society. The UN's International Convention on the Protection of the Rights of All Migrant Workers and Members of Their Families proposes this kind of framework, establishing equality of treatment with citizens of the host country. Both sending and receiving countries are responsible for protecting migrants, and retain the right to determine who is admitted to their territories, and who has the right to work.

Predictably, the countries that have ratified it are the sending countries. Those countries most interested in guest worker schemes, like the U.S., have not. In the global migration of labor, the countries sending migrants have little influence over the conditions facing their citizens in the places they go to work, or the rules under which migration is possible.

In evaluating the various proposals for immigration reform in Congress and elsewhere, labor and immigrant rights activists need clear criteria to decide which promote equality and community, and which don't. Some ideas for criteria include:

- A long-term perspective. Some proposals help to prepare for longer-range efforts to change a system that produces insecurity and inequality. Others, like guest worker programs or increased enforcement of employer sanctions, create a playing field on which progressive movement becomes even more difficult.

- Greater equality, which itself is the prerequisite for unity among workers across race and national lines. Proposals to deny people rights or benefits because of immigration status move away from equality. Equal status itself is a common ground, a goal uniting many diverse communities.
- Immigration status must not be linked to employment. That link is one main characteristic of guest worker programs, and the common thread running through exploitative schemes going back a century. Workers can't be free if they have to leave the country if they lose their jobs. Healthy immigrant communities need employed workers, but they also need students, old and young people, caregivers, disabled and those who don't have traditional jobs.
- More protection for the right to organize. To raise the low price of immigrant labor, immigrant workers have to be able to organize. Given half a chance, immigrant workers and their communities will organize for better jobs and wages, schools and healthcare. When they gain political power for themselves, other working class communities around them benefit. Measures like permanent legal status make it easier to organize. Employer sanctions, enforcement and raids, even as a price for legalization, make organizing much more difficult.
- Linking trade and migration. Modern migration is a "problem" because so much of it caused by forcible dislocation. Changing corporate trade policy and stopping neoliberal reforms is as central to immigration reform as gaining legal status for undocumented immigrants.
- Greater solidarity between workers and unions. U.S. workers have been forced into a global labor market. They have a direct interest in helping workers abroad to organize and raise living standards, fighting privatization and the plunder of developing countries, and stopping U.S. wars

and military intervention. They need not minor protections in trade agreements, but unity with workers globally to scrap those agreements, and to change the economic and political structure of which they're a part.

- Protecting the right to move. Freedom of movement is a human right. Even in a more just world, migration will continue. Families and communities are now connected over thousands of miles and many borders. Links between people will grow - they are part of the human potential. Immigration policy should make movement easier, without selling workers to employers as a price for it.
- Creating common ground between immigrants and other workers. It's not possible to win major changes in immigration policy without making it part of a struggle for other goals. To end job competition, workers need the Humphrey-Hawkins Full Employment Act. To gain organizing rights for immigrants, all workers need the Employee Free Choice Act.
- Congress isn't deciding "what can stop immigration?" With over 180 million people in the world living outside their countries of origin, nothing can. The real question Congress is deciding is the status of people here. Outside the Washington beltway, community coalitions, labor and immigrant rights groups are advocating alternatives that would give immigrants far more rights and equality than employment-based visas. Congress could, for instance,
- Give permanent residence visas, or green cards, to people already here. Those visas don't require people to stay, but give them the chance to come and go - to work, study, or take care of family in the U.S. or their home country. Green card holders can't be deported if they lose a job.
- Expand the number of green cards available for new migrants, opening the door to legal immigration far enough to accommodate those now coming illegally. Most immigrants already come through family networks. Eliminating the years-long backlog in processing family reunification visas would help them, and strengthen communities.

- Allow people to apply for green cards, in the future, after they've been here a few years. The U.S. wouldn't develop the huge undocumented population it has today.
- Stop the enforcement program that has led to thousands of deportations and firings, and a border so heavily militarized that migrants cross, and die, in the most dangerous areas.
- Prohibit companies from recruiting outside the U.S. - formerly a traditional part of US immigration policy. At Ellis Island, having a pre-arranged job was grounds for being sent back. Companies can always hire immigrants with green cards (or anyone else) living here, and green card holders are in a much better position to demand rights and higher wages.

It's not likely that many corporations will support such a program. That's why those who claim to represent the interests of immigrants in Washington must choose whose side they're on.

Today working people of all countries are asked to accept continuing globalization, in which capital is free to go wherever it can earn the highest profits. By that same token migrants must have the same freedom, with rights and status equal to those of anyone else. People in Mexico, Guatemala, China, the US and every other country need the same things. Secure jobs at a living wage. Rights in our workplaces and communities. The freedom to travel and seek a future for our families. The borders between our countries should be common ground to unite us, not lines to divide us.

13

Political Economy in the Age of Financial Globalization

INTRODUCTION

The recent phase of neo-liberal restructuring in Turkey following the crisis of February 2001 represents a real rupture in the history of the Turkish economy. Our central argument in this paper is that Turkey has benefited significantly from the presence of a double external anchor, with both the IMF and the EU playing significant and complementary roles in the recent transformation process. Especially, the EU has been an important catalyst for change in the political and economic realms. The significance of the EU's influence has increased considerably following the EU's Helsinki Summit of December 1999 whereby Turkey has been given a formal candidate country status. As a result of the Helsinki decision, the key political and economic actors involved faced a more powerful set of incentives for change and the implementation of deep-seated institutional reforms.

There is already a large literature on the importance of the EU anchor for Turkey. The present paper, however, goes beyond the existing literature by providing a discussion of the EU anchor the EU anchor is discussed here as part of a package that involves the role of the IMF, the impact of the crises and the role of key domestic actors. Hence, it provides a rather nuanced analysis of how the 'anchor' actually operates in a specific national context.

The economic crisis of February 2001 was a major setback for the Turkish economy. A major collapse of output was accompanied by a dramatic increase in unemployment. The crisis differed from the earlier crises that the Turkish economy had encountered in the sense that the burden of the crisis fell not only on unskilled labor or wage earners. All sections of society rich and poor, educated and uneducated have been affected by the crises in varying degrees. In spite of these negative ramifications, a positive side-effect of the crisis has been to help to break down resistance to reform and to improve the hand of key external actors such as the IMF and the EU in accelerating the momentum of the reform process.

The experience of Turkey is important in illustrating the importance of two general propositions. First proposition is that for "emerging markets", which are exposed to the forces of financial globalization, the regional context within which they find themselves is a crucial variable in terms of their ability to deal with global forces effectively. Second, state capacity is also a critical variable that influences the ability of countries to benefit from a globalizing world economy. These two processes are, to a certain extent, interdependent.

Powerful external anchors play an important role in the process of reform implementation and the development of state capacity. External anchors, such as the IMF or the EU can help domestic policy-makers to override strong resistance on the part of domestic interest groups. A good example would be the resistance of domestic banking lobbies against reform involving tighter regulation of the banking and the financial system. External anchors can generate greater *commitment* on the part of key economic agents. They make the reforms more *credible* by *tying the hands* of governments through conditional agreements. By rendering the reform process more credible, external anchors can also contribute to the development of strong *constituencies* or public support for the reform process. The impact of external anchors is not confined to reform implementation in the short-run. They can have a significant impact on the process of long-term improvements in the *institutional capacities* of the state. The critical point, however, is that actors themselves need to display a high degree of *commitment* to assist the reform process. For example, if IMF financial assistance is weak and EU conditionality is not accompanied by the prospect of full-membership, this will be interpreted as a sign of weak commitment on the part of key external anchors. This, in turn, will significantly reduce both the *incentives* to undertake reform and the *credibility* of the reform process itself.

State capacity is about the degree to which ultimate decision-making power is concentrated in the hands of relatively small number of officials and degree to which these officials act autonomously. Partial centralization in bureaucracy and its administrative core, along with increased autonomy of some of this bureaucracy, contribute to strengthening of state capacity in economic and financial realms. In the Turkish context, the EU, IMF and World Bank have been external actors pushing forward for the institutional reforms that would contribute the strengthening of regulatory capacity in economic governance (e.g., establishment of Competition Authority, Banking Regulation and Supervision Authority, the Central Bankreform of 2001). However, there are limits to relying mainly on external actors. First, there is a need for convergence of political and bureaucratic will as well as a high degree of domestic societal mobilization for institutional reforms in the direction of strengthening state capacity in Turkey. Second, state's long-term *developmental* and *redistributive* roles are insufficiently emphasized in the institutional reforms pressed by the external anchors. The primary emphasis remains on developing the *regulatory* capacity of the state.

TURKEY AND THE EU IN THE CONTEXT OF FINANCIAL GLOBALIZATION

The opening up of the Turkish economy is not a new process. The process effectively started in 1980, following the major crisis of the previous model of import-substituting industrialization in the late 1970s. The first phase of Turkish neo-liberalism constituted the "de-regulation phase" that involved an attempt to reduce the weight of the state in economic affairs and elimination of controls over key relative prices. This phase involved key multilateral actors such as the IMF, the World Bank and the OECD. It has been, on the whole, more successful than the second phase of Turkish neo-liberalism during the 1990s which would be classified as the "rhetorical transition and the institutional crisis" phase (Table 1). "Rhetorical transition" refers to the fact that regulatory institutions have been set up during this period. However, the emergence of such institutions as legal entities failed to be translated into effective implementation. As a consequence, the Turkish state faced an "institutional crisis" in which the opening up of the economy was not complemented with a parallel development in the institutional capacities of the state to undertake effective regulation.

The critical turning point in Turkish neo-liberalism was the decision taken in August 1989 to open up the capital accounts completely. The decision to move to full convertibility in 1989 meant that the Turkish economy was fully exposed to the forces of financial globalization. What became obvious during the context of the 1990s, however, was that the Turkish economy was ill-equipped to deal with the forces of financial globalization for two basic reasons. Firstly, the macro-economy was inherently unstable; the Turkish economy was characterized by a combination of large fiscal deficits and chronically high rates of inflation. Secondly, the financial system was not properly regulated. The decision to liberalize the capital accounts fully in the summer of 1989 was a premature decision.

The consequence of this decision, in the midst of high degree of domestic economic and political instability, was that the Turkish economy's performance became heavily dependent on highly volatile short-term capital flows with costly ramifications. Given its domestic weaknesses, the Turkish economy has failed to capitalize during this period on the growing volume of foreign direct investment directed towards emerging markets. The 1990s as a decade also illustrates how the interplay of politics and economics has a crucial influence on the performance of the Turkish economy. In striking contrast to the experience of the 1980s, the Turkish political system during the 1990s has been characterized by successive weak coalition governments which lacked the political will and the capacity to impose fiscal discipline and create an environment conducive to sustained economic growth. The fact that the country has been going through a costly war against terrorism in the South-East also exercised a negative impact on investment as well as constituting a drain on fiscal resources.

Furthermore, leader-dominated political parties whose primary objective was to distribute patronage resources to their clients as opposed to developing coherent social and economic policies constituted one of Turkey's primary "democratic deficits" during the period. Yet another major element of the democratic deficit involved the politicization and weakening of the bureaucratic apparatus. These democratic deficits, in turn, had a significant spill-over on the economy resulting in a kind of economic structure characterized by pervasive rent-seeking and corruption.

One positive development of the period was the reactivation of the Customs Union (CU) agreement with the EU which became effective at the end of 1995. Turkey, during the premiership of Turgut Özal, had applied for full-membership of the European Community in 1987. However, the outcome of the application was negative. Instead, a decision was taken to reactive the CU agreement as the natural corollary of the long-standing Ankara agreement of 1963. For Turkish policy-makers, the CU signified a natural intermediate step towards EU membership in the long-run; but there was certainly no serious political support for eventual Turkish membership in the EU circles (EU Commission, 1999). The CU agreement was important in accelerating and basically completing the process of trade liberalization which had already started in the early 1980s. Consequently, Turkish firms have been strongly exposed to external competition. This helped to engineer a transformative impact on the Turkish industry with previously inward-oriented sectors such as the manufacture of cars emerging as important export industries in recent years. However, this transformation has been limited: during the period between 1990 and 2004, the share of agriculture in Gross National Product decreased to 11.3 per cent from 17.3 per cent, that of industry remained constant at 25 per cent, whereas the share of services increased from 38.2 per cent to 45.5 per cent. This partial transformation had also manifested itself in terms of trade. Turkey runs trade surplus only in "labor intensive, capital-based" sectors.

The CU agreement has also been instrumental in the process of accomplishing some key regulatory reforms. Important regulatory institutions such as the Competition Authority have been set up as a response to meet the basic conditions of the CU agreement. Although the primary emphasis was on the economic realm, the CU also included political conditionality relating to the improvement of human rights practices in Turkey. Nevertheless, the CU *per se,* without the prospect of full EU membership, failed to exercise a sufficiently powerful transformative influence on the Turkish economy or democracy. Turkey was clearly in a disadvantageous position vis-à-vis its Eastern European counterparts. These countries had already lined up for full membership. Having started the negotiation process in the mid-1990s, they have been receiving significant EU assistance in the process under the auspices of the PHARE program (European Commission, 1999). In contrast, Turkey failed to receive any financial assistance as part of the CU agreement due to the Greek veto. There was certainly a credibility and commitment problem on both sides. Turkish policy makers were not sufficiently committed to reform, because the incentives provided by the EU appeared to lack strength and credibility. Similarly, from the EU perspective, Turkey did not seem to exhibit the kind of commitment necessary to satisfy the conditions for full membership even in the long-run.

By the end of the decade, in spite of the CU, the Turkish economy was characterized by considerable instability. A lop-sided pattern of growth had developed which was heavily dependent on the accumulation of domestic and external debt and inflows of short-term speculative capital. This pattern of development, in turn, helped to generate a strong rentier class, whose fortunes became increasingly dependent on lending to the government at high rates of interest. Not surprisingly, the profitability of large industrial establishments became progressively dependent on their financial rather than manufacturing activities.

In the kind of environment described, Turkey encountered its first crisis of the neo-liberal era in 1994. The crisis of 1994 was an important setback to the Turkish economy. Nevertheless, the fact that crisis was short-lived followed by a rapid recovery meant that the behavior of policy makers and, hence, the underlying imbalances in the Turkish economy could not be reversed. Indeed, by the end of the 1990s, with chronic fiscal deficits and high rates of inflation, there was growing awareness that the Turkish economy was on an unsustainable course. This led to the signing of a stand-by agreement with the IMF in December 1999 which involved a combination of measures aimed at fiscal adjustment and medium-term structural reforms. The agreement was unique in the history of the Turkish economy in that an agreement with the IMF was signed without actually experiencing a financial or balance of payments crisis. What was ironic, however, is that the presence of an IMF program failed to provide sufficient protection. The Turkish economy remained highly vulnerable given the broad extent of adjustment and the weak commitment on the part of the coalition government to some of the key components of the program such as privatization and the regulation of the banking system. Therefore, it was not surprising that the Turkish economy experienced what is popularly referred to as the "twin crises" in November 2000 and February 2001. The IMF was exposed to criticism for these crises due to failures in program design involving insufficient focus on the problems of the banking sector and the adoption of a controlled exchange rate system as well as the provision of inadequate financial assistance.

Crises became far more frequent in the era of financial globalization with costly consequences. Although, the Turkish economy managed to grow at high rates in certain years, the frequency and the depth of the crises helped to pull down the average growth rate. This in turn limited the economy's ability to converge to the standards of high income economies within a reasonable time span.

THE 2001 CRISIS AS A TURNING POINT: THE SIGNIFICANCE OF THE TURKEY-IMF-EU TRIANGLE

The crisis of February 2001 was particularly costly in terms of its economic consequences. From a longer-term perspective, however, the very depth of the crisis constituted an advantage in the sense that it helped to change the balance of power in Turkey's political economy quite radically in favor of the "pro-reform coalition". This shift in the balance of power was particularly evident in the IMF's relations with the on-going coalition government, which up to the point of the crisis, had been a reluctant partner in the reform process. The coalition government whose two dominant members were the left of center, the Democratic Left Party (the DSP) under the leadership of the Prime Minister Bülent Ecevit, and the right of center, the Nationalist Action Party (the MHP) under the leadership of Devlet Bahçeli, was quite nationalistic in outlook. Given that their base of electoral support was primarily derived from poorer segments of society, they were reluctant to endorse key elements of the IMF-inspired reform package, the massive cuts in agricultural subsidies being a good example. Following the crisis of February 2001, the resistance of the coalition government to key components of the reform package was effectively broken and the IMF gained the upper hand. This shift in the underlying balance of power in the policy-making process was also, in part, a consequence of the fact that the IMF was willing to allocate substantial financial resources to help Turkey's recovery process. Clearly, geo-political considerations came to the picture in the sense that Turkey was a key ally of the United States in the Middle East which is a region of critical interest from a US foreign policy perspective. Argentina which experienced a similar crisis in the same year of Turkey, for example, was not equally fortunate in eliciting similar magnitudes of IMF support.

The increase in the power of the IMF to push the reform process was evident in a number of different areas and notably in the banking sector. A new agency, The Bank Regulatory and Supervisory Agency, the BRSA, had been established in June 1999 following the ratification of the IMF sponsored Banking Act. It took responsibility for banking supervision and regulation from the Treasury and the Central Bank and became operational in September 2000. BRSA also incorporated Sworn Bank Auditors and Savings Deposit Insurance Fund (SDIF) in 2001. Further, the regulation and supervision of non-bank financial institutions have been transferred from the Treasury to the BRSA in 2005. However, in the pre-crisis period, there was no natural constituency pressuring for the establishment of an agency like the BRSA and there was lack of political and bureaucratic will as well as fierce resistance from powerful banking lobbies.

As a result, the BRSA was unable to perform a proper regulatory role in such a way as to prevent the twin crises which essentially stemmed from the malfunctioning and under-regulation of both the private and the public components of the banking system. Following the February crisis, however, the BRSA was able to obtain, with IMF support in the background, the partial autonomy from politicians and interest groups involved to press ahead with tough regulatory measures with some domestic support. The BRSA example is a good illustration of a major characteristic of the new era which we label as the "re-regulation" phase. Re-regulation refers to the development of regulatory capacities of the state which involves not only the setting up of new institutions but also a significant increase in their powers of implementation. There is no doubt that effective measures have been taken in the direction of stronger financial regulation in Turkey after the 2001 crisis. Turkey is on the way to establishing a regulatory state. However, "a regulatory state, which can adopt a proactive approach in the financial services industry by steering and coordinating policy community still does not exist" in Turkey. For that reason, significant progress needs to be made in terms of strengthening regulatory institutions as well as developing a strong state capacity.

Another interesting aspect of the economic governance in the post-crisis period involved the appointment of Kemal Dervi° as the Minister responsible for the Treasury in the coalition government. Dervi°, with a distinguished career at the World Bank, was brought into government by Prime Minister Ecevit to help the process of Turkey's economic recovery through the implementation of "The Strong Economy Program". What is interesting in the context is that, although Dervi° was formally a member of the coalition government with strong affinities to Ecevit's DSP, he was an above politics figure at the same time. His role was a kind of technocrat who was brought into office not as an elected politician or a party member. He was appointed as part of a top-down process of restructuring because he benefiting from being a member of transnational policy community. Thus, the changing balance of power involved not only a shift in the powers of the IMF with respect to the incumbent government, but also a shift in the powers and autonomy of the team of technocrats assembled around the personality of Dervi° working in close co-operation with the IMF and the World Bank.

The strong credentials of Dervi° arguably provided a kind of legitimacy to the program which would otherwise have been missing if the program was portrayed simply as an externally imposed set of disciplines. He was an influential actor with joint memberships of the domestic and transnational policy communities. He performed the function of "mediator" to effectively administer the government's relations with the twin organizations (The IMF and the WB). Similarly, the twin organizations also needed him not only because he effectively translated policy ideas and policy paradigms into domestic policy but also he facilitated *policy formulation* and *implementation.* This, in turn, prevented both a debtor moral hazard and a road accident similar to one that happened in the previous program. Arguably, without such a "policy entrepreneur" Turkey could not have developed a kind of trust on the part of external anchors which was necessary to attain large scale financial assistance. Needless to say, the IMF was interested in the economic transformation of Turkey for its own sake but to ensure that Turkey would not default on its debt. Nevertheless, without such assistance, it would have been very difficult to generate a successful restructuring process.

Following the Helsinki decision of 1999, the EU became a far more powerful actor in the Turkish setting in facilitating the process of fundamental economic and political reforms. Nevertheless, the early focus of the EU was much more on the political side of the reform process; specifically in the realm of civil and human rights. Economic reforms which are integral component of the Copenhagen criteria were not the immediate concern of the EU. The fact that there was an-ongoing IMF program implicitly entailed a certain division of responsibility with the IMF taking care of the economic side and the EU more actively involved on the political side.

This pattern, however, changed quite radically, in the post-crisis era with the EU emerging as a critical element of the pro-reform coalition in the economic sphere. The material hardships associated with the 2001 crisis have rendered the potential economic benefits of EU membership all the more attractive. The opinion polls taken in 2002 suggested that there was a strong broad-based support for EU membership with 74 per cent of Turkish public supporting full-membership. What was also crucial was that economic actors, both domestic and foreign, recognized the importance of the EU as a kind of long-term and permanent external anchor. The IMF, by its very nature, could not fulfill this role due to its temporary role whose responsibility is confined to the completion of the recovery process. In other words, the redefinition of Turkey's relations with the EU after December 1999 was instrumental in implementing the difficult economic reform process and helped the IMF in breaking the resistance of anti-reform forces. This has been the powerful new element of a double external anchor.

The context within which Turkey has found itself after 2001 helped to generate a kind of virtuous cycle whereby economic and democratization reforms could go hand in hand. Market participants which were the principal actors promoting economic reform also became strong supporters of EU conditionality, primarily for its economic benefits. As a consequence, the coalition government in power was not able to resist the kind of far-reaching democratization reforms implemented during the summer of 2002. This was due to the fact that the failure to implement such reforms would mean a loss of trust on the part of the market participants in the government's ability to maintain the momentum of the economic recovery process. Markets, in a way, became an instrument of political reform. Political reforms, in turn, helped to generate greater confidence in Turkey's ability to create a favorable climate for domestic and foreign investment. Indeed, it is interesting to refer the reports of transnational private financial actors such as rating agencies and transnational banks who monitored the EU related political reforms quite closely in their assessments concerning the future performance of the Turkish economy. These transnational financial actors were not interested in political reforms such as democratization, human rights or the resolution of Cyprus issue *per se*. However, they conceived the accomplishments of these political reforms as a necessary step for stabilizing the economy and consolidation of economic reforms.

The process of reform implementation has taken a new and positive shape following the victory of the Justice and Development Party (the AKP) in the elections of November 2002. Capitalizing on its broad-based political support, the new government was able to accelerate the pace of economic and political reforms, with mutually reinforcing consequences. As a result, a more favorable environment conducive to economic reforms was created as Turkey came progressively close to the EU. The key steps in this process were the Copenhagen Summit of 2002, the historic decision of the EU Council in December 2004 to initiate accession negotiations and finally October 2005 decision confirming the initiation of the negotiation process. Hence a combination of powerful external pressures and the display of political leadership and will at home helped to produce an economic environment which by the late 2005 sharply differed from the situation that Turkey had found itself in February 2001.

Has Sustainable Growth been Consolidated in the 2001-2005 Era? A Critical Evaluation

The 'Strong Economy Program', which was put into practice in the aftermath of the 2001 crisis, has continued to be implemented in an uninterrupted fashion during the early years of the AKP government. The outcome judged by the principal macroeconomic indicators has been rather impressive. Turkey has been able to accomplish tight fiscal discipline. Inflation, for the first time over a period of three decades, has been stabilized at single digit levels. The dramatic fall in inflation rates has been accompanied by a strong surge in economic growth. Indeed, Turkey has managed to achieve a record growth rate in real GNP of 9.9 per cent in 2004. The combination of falling inflation and high rates of economic growth suggests that the prospects of achieving sustained growth as opposed to temporary spurts are higher than at any time in the course of the post-1980 neo-liberal era.

Moreover, a cause of concern is the lop-sided pattern in Turkey's recent recovery process. Certainly, the better-off regions or the wealthier and more educated sections of society have been the principal gainers of this process whereas the rural poor, in particular, has been feeling the negative effects of the massive cuts in agricultural subsidies. Although employment has been expanding in the Turkish economy in the post-crisis period, the unemployment rates tend to be high. If growth does not sufficiently translate into employment creating, this could be a serious economic and political problem given disproportionately young population. Youth unemployment, which is likely to be concentrated in poorer regions of the country, could be a source of electoral support for nationalist parties that could lead to Euro-skepticism and rising threat to Turkey's EU aspirations and the continuity of the economic program. Turkey's current tax system, which involves a heavy burden on employers, discourages formal employment and encourages the use of informal labor in the economy where the underground or the informal component reaches serious magnitudes. This brings us to the point that the reform process is incomplete in key areas such as the tax system and the social security structure. Finally, one should also be aware of the fact that the increase in FDI outflows has been increasing parallel to the increase in the inflows of FDI, as many Turkish firms themselves become international. This might not be a problem as long as FDI inflows reach significant magnitudes and FDI outflows create important trade and investment links with neighboring countries. If, however, inflows insufficient to match outflows this could exert a detrimental effect on the future performance of the Turkish economy.

The favorable investment climate has also been accompanied by a noticeable increase in inflows of foreign direct investment. In 2003, the amount of FDI inflows amounted to 745 million dollars. This figure was fairly representative of weak FDI performance in the neo-liberal era. In 2005, however, FDI inflows amounted to 8,427 million dollars, representing a phenomenal increase. The EU-25 constituted 38 per cent of total FDI inflows in 2005. Banking and telecommunications sectors were the leading sectors for FDI inflows. In addition to the overall improvement in the political and macroeconomic environment, the AKP government has made a serious effort during the course of 2003 to improve the investment climate by eliminating legal, institutional and bureaucratic obstacles to FDI through new legislation. The dramatic increase in FDI inflows was closely associated with large-scale privatization. What is also striking is that the recent recovery process has been based primarily on improvements in productivity. This might again be interpreted as a sign of a major departure from the preceding patterns of the Turkish economy. Total factor productivity growth accounted for 3.3 per cent of overall growth in the 1990-2000 period. In sharp contrast, the contribution of total factor productivity increased to 51.3 per cent in the 2002-2004 period.

Several factors have been collectively responsible for this quite striking upturn in economic performance. The commitment of the AKP government to the success of the economic program is important, although one should be careful not to exaggerate the contribution of the present government considering the important steps that had already been taken by the economic team led by Kemal Dervi° under the previous coalition government. Turkey has benefited from the presence of a government which had a comfortable majority in Parliament and from the displayed firm commitment to the basic ingredients of the program. The fact that Turkey had two powerful external anchors also constituted a considerable advantage in improving the investment climate. One may underline the ability of the coalition government, if somewhat reluctantly, and then of the AKP government, perhaps more willingly, to accomplish the politically difficult set of democratization reforms. Bringing Turkey closer to the EU in the process, these political reforms had favorable repercussions on the perceptions and expectations of economic actors. Similarly, the AKP government's foreign policy initiatives involving the promotion of a peaceful settlement to the Cyprus dispute along the lines of the Annan Plan and the development of friendly relations with all neighboring countries had positive spin-off effects in the economic sphere.

Important institutional reforms such as the Central Bank Law of 2001 were also important in creating an environment for legally independent Central Bank which was among crucial steps in bringing inflation rates to single digit figures.

Without the political commitment of government in power and without broad based public support in favor of stabilization, institutional reforms in themselves might have failed to generate the desired outcome. The very depth of the crisis itself was an important factor in shaping public opinion and helping to generate broad-based support, thereby limiting potential resistance to tight fiscal discipline and longer-term structural reforms. Turkey has also benefited from the buoyancy of global liquidity.

A three or four year period is too early to judge whether a process of sustained growth has been fully consolidated. Inevitably, growth accelerates in the early stages as countries tend to bounce back from the crisis. A similar process of recovery was also evident in Argentina; where the domestic and external environment was less conducive to economic recovery. Although inflows of FDI have been increasing at the moment in Turkey, the real challenge for the Turkish economy will be whether these flows will accelerate on a sustained basis over time. A cause for concern in the recent recovery process concerns the co-existence of a large current account deficit and large inflows of short-term capital. In the past, the co-existence of such forces tended to undermine investor confidence, precipitating speculative attacks and financial crises. In the current context such an outcome is less likely, given a much more tightly regulated banking system and a broadly favorable set of expectations on the part of key market actors. The fact that a flexible exchange rate regime is being implemented in the post-crisis period is also a source of protection for any possible speculative attack. Nevertheless, over-optimism could be costly if policy-makers fail to take action in line with these possible danger signals.

Bibliography

Ashok, Vasant: *Indian Economy in the World Setting, Bombay, Himalaya, 1988.*

Balchin, P., & Kieve, L.: *Urban Land Economics, London, MacMillan Press, 1977.*

Barro, Robert J., : *Economic Growth. McGraw-Hill, 1995.*

Behari, Madhuri: *Indian Economy since Independence: Chronology of Events, Delhi, D.K. Publications, 1983.*

Bhuleshkar, Vasant: *Indian Economy in the World Setting, Bombay, Himalaya, 1988.*

Campbell, J.Y., Lo, A.W.: *The Econometrics of Financial Markets, Princeton University Press, 1996.*

Chaudhuri, Pramit: *The Indian Economy: Poverty and Development, New York, St. Martin's Press, 1979.*

Clark, D. D.: *Internet Economics, Massachusetts, MIT Press, 1997.*

Dhingra, C.: *The Indian Economy: Resources, Planning, Development, and Problems, Delhi, Sultan Chand, 1983.*

Ehrenberg, Ronald: *Modern Labor Economics, Harper Collins, 1994.*

Goyal, S.K.: *Agricultural Prices and Its Impact on the Indian Economy: A Case Study of Haryana, New Delhi, Classical, 1992.*

Huang, Chi-fu: *Foundations of Financial Economics, Prentice-Hall, 1988.*

Kelly, F. P.: *Charging and Accounting for Bursty Connections, Massachusetts, MIT Press, 1997.*

Little, I.M.D.: *India: Macroeconomics and Political Economy, 1964-1991, Washington, World Bank, 1994.*

MacKinley, A.C.: *The Econometrics of Financial Markets, Princeton University Press, 1996.*

Pranab, K.: *The Political Economy of Development in India, Delhi, Oxford University Press, 1984.*

Robert H. Litzenberger: *Foundations of Financial Economics, Prentice-Hall, 1988.*

Index